Studia Fennica
Historica 2

The Finnish Literature Society (SKS) was founded in 1831 and has, from the very beginning, engaged in publishing operations. It nowadays publishes literature in the fields of ethnology and folkloristics, linguistics, literary research and cultural history.

The first volume of the Studia Fennica series appeared in 1933. Since 1992, the series has been divided into three thematic subseries: Ethnologica, Folkloristica and Linguistica. Two additional subseries were formed in 2002, Historica and Litteraria. The subseries Anthropologica was formed in 2007.

In addition to its publishing activities, the Finnish Literature Society maintains research activities and infrastructures, an archive containing folklore and literary collections, a research library and promotes Finnish literature abroad.

Studia fennica editorial board
Anna-Leena Siikala
Rauno Endén
Teppo Korhonen
Pentti Leino
Auli Viikari
Kristiina Näyhö

oa.finlit.fi

Editorial Office
SKS
P.O. Box 259
FI-00171 Helsinki
www.finlit.fi

Jussi Hanska

Strategies of Sanity and Survival

Religious Responses to
Natural Disasters in the Middle Ages

Finnish Literature Society · Helsinki

Studia Fennica Historica 2

The publication has undergone a peer review.

The open access publication of this volume has received part funding via a Jane and Aatos Erkko Foundation grant.

© 2002 Jussi Hanska and SKS
License CC-BY-NC-ND 4.0. International

A digital edition of a printed book first published in 2002 by the Finnish Literature Society.
Cover Design: Timo Numminen
EPUB: eLibris Media Oy

ISBN 978-951-746-357-7 (Print)
ISBN 978-952-222-818-5 (PDF)
ISBN 978-952-222-819-2 (EPUB)

ISSN 0085-6835 (Studia Fennica)
ISSN 0355-8924 (Studia Fennica Historica)

DOI: https://doi.org/10.21435/sfh.2

This work is licensed under a Creative Commons CC-BY-NC-ND 4.0. International License.
To view a copy of the license, please visit http://creativecommons.org/licenses/by-nc-nd/4.0/

A free open access version of the book is available at https://doi.org/10.21435/sf or by scanning this QR code with your mobile device.

Contents

ACKNOWLEDGEMENTS 7

INTRODUCTION 9

1 THE BACKGROUND 15
    Disastrous Times 15
    In the Shadow of *the Black Death* 18
    Sources and Problems 24
    The Predecessors 29

2 SEEKING DIVINE PROTECTION 32
    Religion vs. Magic 33
    Heavenly Helpers 42
    Medieval Rationalism 45

3 AT THE MOMENT OF PERIL 48
    Collective reactions 48
        Processions 49
        Sermons 64
            Actual Catastrophe sermons 65
            Rogation Day Sermons 68
            The Setting of Catastrophe Sermons 78
        Votive Masses and Collective Prayers 81
    Individual Reactions 87

4 THE AFTERMATH – EXPLAINING AND SURVIVING NATURAL DISASTERS 101
    Scapegoats and Political Explanations 102
    Scientific Explanations 105
    Apocalyptic Explanations 112
    Divine Intervention 116
        God's Punishment 116
        Demons on the Loose 126
        Causality of Punishment 128
        Purgatory in this World 132
    Pastoral Care and Spiritual Healing 143

5 EPILOGUE: THE EXTENDED MIDDLE AGES   150
            Post-Tridentine Catholicism   153
            Protestant Revolution?   160
                Popular resistance   161
                Moderate Reformers   163
            The Waning of the Traditional Religion   164

CONCLUSIONS   169

APPENDIX 1   179

APPENDIX 2   189

BIBLIOGRAPHY   202

INDEX NOMINUM ET LOCORUM   211

INDEX RERUM   217

Acknowledgements

I started writing this book as a side project roughly six years ago while I was working with the Finnish Academy project on the history of Mendicant orders. That project was successfully concluded and new ones were inaugurated. All along, The '*disaster book*' travelled with these research projects as a free rider (if one is allowed to use a term familiar in economic science). Therefore the first expression of gratitude is due to the Finnish Academy for financing this book without ever knowing that they did. I would, nevertheless, like to excuse myself pointing out that the actual work I was supposed to do was always carried out despite the fact that occasionally this side project felt more interesting.

I would also like to thank the Kone foundation for giving me a research grant for two years for writing this book. Sadly, I was only able to benefit from three months of that grant. Then I started a new Finnish Academy project on the *Penitenzieria Apostolica*. These three months at the beginning of 1998 was the only period when I have been able to concentrate on writing this book as a full time project. Consequently, it was also the most fruitful period in the long process of making this book, and as such its meaning for the eventual outcome was most crucial.

During all these years I have received steady support from the department of history at the University of Tampere. I would like to thank my home department for providing me with an office and administrative services. For this I would like to thank professors Marjatta Hietala and Pertti Haapala. The department of history is not only an institution, it is also a community. In the case of our department this means: a collection of sympathetic people with whom I have had a pleasure to spend countless hours discussing my work and other issues of even more burning importance, such as ice hockey and football. Out of my collegues in the history department I would especially like to mention doctors Christian Krötzl and Kirsi Salonen with whom I worked in the *Penitenzieria Apostolica* project.

There are numerous persons who have contributed to this book with their time, advice, and encouragement. Before thanking them individually, I would like to thank them all collegially and apologise to those whose name is not mentioned. It is not because of a lack of good will, but because of the huge number of people who have contributed.

Perhaps the person who has contributed most to the process of making this book has been Doctor Bert Roest. He read the first manuscript and made several useful comments and suggestions, not to mention his encouragement. I would also like to thank other people who have read the manuscript and made their suggestions. They are Doctor Antti Ruotsala, Doctor Tuomas M.S. Lehtonen, and the anonymous referee of the Finnish Historical Society. Their remarks have been most useful, although in some cases I have stubbornly chosen to keep my ground. Their contribution has without doubt made the final version better than it would have been. Needless to say, they are not to be blamed for any remaining mistakes or faults.

Numerous scholars have kindly contributed to this book by giving their advice on individual issues, suggesting books, articles, and manuscripts to be read, sometimes even sending me their own copies. For these reasons I would like to thank: Father Louis-Jacques Bataillon OP, Father Athanasius Sulavik OP, Professor David d'Avray, Professor Gary Dickson, Doctor Stephan Borgehammar, Doctor Michele Bassi, Doctor Alexis Charansonnet, Doctor Veronica O'Mara, and M.A. Suzanne Paul.

I would also like to express my gratitude to the numerous libraries that have helped me in getting together all the material needed in writing this book: Biblioteca Apostolica Vaticana, the library of the École Français in Rome, Uppsala universitetsbibliotek, The British Library, Biblioteca Laurenziana in Florence, Helsinki and Tampere university libraries, and lastly but not least, *Studium Catholicum* in Helsinki and its former librarian, the late Father Martti Voutilainen OP.

The Finnish Literature Society was kind enough to accept this *libellus* to be published in their series. I am deeply grateful and honoured. Especially, I wish to thank Rauno Endén and Johanna Ilmakunnas with whom it has been, once again, a great pleasure to work with. I would also like to thank M.A. Daniel Blackie for his brave effort in trying to make this book closely resemble the English language. Finally, I thank my wife Terhi and my sons Patrick and Julius for not allowing me to be totally and irretrievably lost in the dusty world of archives, libraries and manuscripts.

Tampere, March 2002
Jussi Hanska

Introduction

Today we live in times of unforeseen technological and scientific change, yet we are still unable to predict and control nature. Every now and then we find ourselves dealing with the unexpected, be it a hurricane, an earthquake or a flood. We have all the advantages of modern society, such as central governments committed to the welfare of their citizens, international aid organisations, good infrastructures, and scientific knowledge that allows us to forecast possible catastrophes and minimise their effects on the population. Despite all these, natural disasters cause unforeseen damage and social problems. This was even more so during the Middle Ages and the early modern period.

I do not use the word medieval in a precise manner; it is simply a general term used here to describe the feelings and attitudes of people living during a considerably long time period. It is, by necessity, an oversimplification. The ideas presented here regarding 'medieval man' were certainly not accepted by everyone in all the parts of Europe, or during all the centuries covered in this book. Nevertheless, it is my firm belief that most of the ideas were shared by a reasonably large majority of the population.

Medieval ideas of nature were very ambivalent. Nature was a benevolent provider of human needs and as such it was an absolute prerequisite for life itself. At the same time, it was also seen as an erratic and irrational element, which could bring sudden destruction and wreak havoc among society.[1] In a situation like that, one needed strategies of survival. In the first place, it was important to try to protect oneself and the whole community against the wrath of nature, that is, to survive biologically. When all possible precautions had been taken and the catastrophe still struck, it was equally important to find some explanation for it, to process it and get on with life, that is, to survive mentally.

Élisabeth Carpentier has asked in her classic study *Une ville devant la peste* whether it is possible to use the methods of psychoanalysis in studying the *Black Death*. She claims that concrete religious manifestations, such as

---

1. Donald Weinstein and Rudolph M. Bell, *Saints & Society. Christendom, 1000–1700* (Chicago, 1982), pp. 145–146.

flagellant movements, would provide the materials on which such a study could perhaps be based. She also argues that there might be some evidence in less spectacular manifestations of the religious battle against the plague epidemics, which could be equally useful when properly used. She therefore proposed that the influence of religion on the fight against the *Black Death* deserved thorough research.[2]

This book attempts to find out how medieval people used religion as a means to fight, survive and explain natural disasters, not only plague epidemics, but all kinds of natural disasters; floods, droughts, earthquakes and so on. It might be a good moment to point out that the very word natural disaster is a modern construct. It was not known in the medieval period.[3] If one would look for a medieval concept that would cover all the phenomena we like to call natural disasters, it would be *tribulatio*. If we considered what kinds of things were presented as *tribulationes*, we see that it was much wider concept than natural disaster is today. *Tribulatio* includes wars and other catastrophes, which today would be known as *manmade disasters*.

The oldest appearance of a concept that comes close to the modern term natural disaster, is found in a German encyclopaedia printed in Leipzig in 1740. It has an entry called *Natur Ubel*. This word is used to designate all those problems caused by man's imperfections resulting the Fall. These included unhealthy air, pestilence, normal as well as epidemic diseases, natural accidents, damage caused by bad weather, bad harvests, famines, wars, fires, water damages and so on. The encyclopaedia also points out that not only sinners suffer these tribulations, but also the just.[4] Thus we see that an idea of natural disasters as a common category, even though it was still strictly connected to theology and morals, had started to develop by the middle of the eighteenth century. With the passing of time this idea developed into the concept of natural disasters, as it is understood today.

But how are natural disasters understood today? Strangely enough I have been able to find only one definition for natural disaster in encyclopaedias and dictionaries. Whether this means that the concept of natural disaster is so obvious that it needs no clarification, or that it has been considered to be one of those concepts that are not important enough to have their own entry,

---

2. Élisabeth Carpentier, *Une village devant la peste. Orvieto et la peste noire de 1348* (Bruxelles, 1993; deuxième édition revue), p. 25.
3. Jacques Berlioz, 'Les recits exemplaires, sources imprevues de l'histoire des catastrophes naturelles au Moyen-Age', in *Sources travaux historiques* no. 33 (1933). Histoire des catastrophes naturelles. Paysages-environment, p. 8.
4. *Grosses Universallexicon aller Wissenschaften und Künste*. Vol. N-Net (Leipzig und Halle, 1740), f. Hhhh3r. 'Natur Ubel, Ubel der Natur, Naturliche Ubel, Mala naturae, Mala naturalia, sind die jenigen Unvollkommenheiten, die in dem Lauffe der Natur zugleich mit eingepflohten sind, nachdem der erste Mensch gefallen, da sie vor dem nicht gewesen, und auch niemals gekommen seyn würden. Dahin gehören zum exempel ungesunde Lufft, Pest, gewöhnliche Krankheiten allerley Art, graszirende ansteckende Kranckheiten, natürliche Ungklücksfälle, Wetter-Schaden, Witterungs-Unannehmlichkeiten, unfruchtbare Jahre, theure Zeit, Krieges-Feuers- und Wassers-Noth etc. Diese Ubel sind allen Menschen gemein, und betreffen den Frommen sowol als den Gottlosen.'

is an open question. Nevertheless, the German dictionary that bothered to include it defines the concept *Naturkatastrophen* as follows: '*disastrous natural phenomenon, for example big vulcanic eruption, serious earthquake, a wide reaching flood, a long lasting drought.*'[5]

This is not a definition in the strict sense of the word. It is more like a random catalogue of things that can be called natural disasters. The same thing can also be said of the few definitions I have been able to find in research literature concerning natural disasters. A good example is the definition given by B. G. McGaughey, Kenneth J. Hoffman and Craig H. Lewellyn: '*Disasters are often classified as either natural or manmade based on their perceived cause. Natural disasters include earthquakes, floods, hurricanes, etc.*'[6]

In the absence of a proper definition, it is important to define just what is the subject of this book: how do we intend to define the concept of natural disaster. Let us for the moment forget the word natural and look into the concept disaster, which luckily has been treated in different dictionaries. *The Oxford English Dictionary* explains the word *disaster* as follows: '*Anything that befalls of ruinous or distressing nature; a sudden or great misfortune, mishap, or misadventure; a calamity.*' Webster's Encyclopaedic Dictionary gives almost the same explanation. According to Webster's, a disaster is '*a calamitous event, especially one occurring suddenly and causing a great damage or hardship.*'

Thus natural disaster could be defined as a calamitous event caused by nature, as opposed to those disasters caused by man. One problem remains, however. According to the English or American understanding of the word disaster, it is something that supposedly occurs suddenly. As we have seen above, that is not how it was perceived in the eighteenth-century German dictionary. This also included more long lasting disasters.

There are, indeed, some major disasters, which do not occur suddenly but during the course of a considerably long periods of time. Such disasters are, for example, long lasting heavy rains or long lasting droughts. In medieval society, the effects of such disasters were truly terrible, as they are in underdeveloped societies today. Furthermore, as will be shown, the responses of medieval society to these long-term disasters were equal to the more traditional types of natural disasters. It is not reasonable to exclude them from a book that is dealing with medieval men and natural disasters. Therefore I have decided to adopt the wider understanding of the word natural disaster.

---

5. *Meyers Enzyklopädisches Lexikon*. Band 16 Mei-Nat (Mannheim, 1976), p. 813. 'Naturkatastrophen = folgenschwere Naturerreignisse, z.B. große Vulkanaisbrüche, schwere Erdbeben, weiträumige Überschwemmungen, langanhaltende Dürre-perioden.'
6. B. G. McGaughey, Kenneth J. Hoffman and Craig H. Lewellyn, 'The Human experience of earthquakes', in *Individual and community responses to Trauma and Disaster. The structure of human chaos*. Edited by Robert J. Ursano, Brian G. McGaughey and Carol S. Fullerton (Cambridge, 1995), p. 137.

It has become customary to separate man-made disasters from natural disasters. This was not the case during the Middle Ages. All tribulations were regarded as equal and caused by similar reasons. Both were ultimately originating from either God or, with His allowance, from the devil and his army of demons. Many medieval sources treat wars in the same context as floods, earthquakes and other natural disasters. They were explained and understood as very much similar processes.

Here, however, I have preferred to define the subject of this book according to the modern understanding of the word natural disasters. Man-made disasters, such as wars, have been excluded, despite the fact that such exclusion is more or less artificial. This, I feel is a necessary concession to the modern understanding of the concept of natural disaster. One might say that this book is concerned with natural disasters in the widest possible sense of the word, that is, all the disasters which nature causes according to our modern understanding.

The key problem of this book, coping with natural disasters, can be divided into three important questions. Firstly, how did people try to protect themselves against such phenomena? The emphasis is on the spiritual means of protecting oneself. Scientific means of foreseeing disasters and preparing oneself against them are discussed only briefly. Partly this is because it is the spiritual life of medieval man that interests the writer of this book; partly it is because in the middle ages spiritual or religious means of seeking protection were considered to be more important than scientific and technological ones.

The role of the Christian religion in medieval Europe has often been overestimated. Nevertheless, there are few seriously deny the dominant position of religion and magic compared to technology and sciences in medieval society. These forms of religious 'disaster management', religion and magic, or as seen by Keith Thomas, magical religion, occupy the central position in this book.[7]

The second question is how did medieval men respond to imminent danger? The idea is to sketch an impressionistic picture of what happened in a medieval community when disaster struck. How did people react to the situation and what concrete measures were taken?

The third and most difficult problem is: how did people pull themselves together when the acute crisis was over, and more importantly, how did they overcome the situation to get on with their lives? This problem deals with the psychology of an individual person. What were the effects of natural disasters on him? How did he try to deal with the situation at a mental level?

This book shares the tripartite division of Élisabeth Carpentier's study: *avant*, *pendant* and *aprés*. However, it operates on a slightly different level. Carpentier concentrates on the community of Orvieto before, during and after the *Black Death*, that is, on what the process actually did to the city of Orvieto and its inhabitants. This book, on the contrary, is not interested in

---

7. Keith Thomas, *Religion & the Decline of Magic* (New York, 1971), p. 50.

demographic trends or economic changes. The attention is focused on the mental state of common people, that is, the victims of disasters and, more importantly, the survivors.

These three key problems concerning religion and natural disasters are approached from two different perspectives. The first is the collective one. This book seeks to present the collective reactions and feelings to natural cataclysms. The second, far more problematic perspective of this study concerns individual man. What were the reactions of individual persons in the case of a natural disaster? Did they overlap with the reactions and publicly stated opinions of communities, or did there exist an individual way of perceiving natural disasters that was different from the publicly spoken and well documented official, or as it also could be called, ecclesiastical perception? Were individual responses compatible with the official theological views of the causes of cataclysms and the means of protecting oneself against them?

The disposition of the book is built around a certain chronology, a chronology of a disaster. The first main chapter deals with the background information that the reader needs to appreciate the points made in later chapters. How big a problem were natural disasters in reality? To what extent have natural disasters been studied by historians? What are the sources used in this book and what kind of problems do they pose? This chapter points out the problems caused by the overemphasis of existing studies on the plague epidemic we often call the *Black Death*.

The second chapter deals with anticipating disasters and preparing oneself against them. What were the means of gaining protection against disasters? This chapter deals with the historical process of disaster prevention, and its slow metamorphosis from pagan magical rites to the religious ceremonies performed by the Church. It also evaluates the cult of protective saints. Furthermore, this chapter discusses the rationality of medieval means of disaster management.

The third chapter deals with the short and hectic moments when the disaster actually occurred. What were the feelings and reactions of the people? These are looked at on the collective as well as on the individual level. The latter was particularly important in cases where there simply was no time to organise collective liturgical ceremonies. This chapter includes a rather long section on medieval catastrophe sermons and their meaning for the reactions and activities of the congregation.

The fourth chapter deals with the aftermath of disasters. It analyses the different contemporary explanations for the disasters. The most important means of explaining natural disasters that were available for medieval man were scientific, or from the point of view of modern natural sciences, pseudo-scientific explanations, and religious explanations. It is shown that both of these explanations were divided into different sub-categories. Finally, this chapter deals with the means available to the church to help the survivors of natural disasters to understand what happened.

The fifth and final chapter is a sort of epilogue for this book. It takes the story to the early modern period and examines how medieval means of coping with natural disasters survived reformation and renaissance to slowly wither away with the dawn of modern scientific thinking. This chapter emphasises the continuity of medieval mentality, that is the phenomenon called *long Moyen Âge* by the eminent French historian Jacques Le Goff. The development of post-Tridentine Catholicism is compared to the various forms of Protestantism that came into being in the course of the sixteenth century. As the title suggests, this chapter is merely an epilogue to the actual substance of the book, and hence it is not based on an examination of primary sources, but is rather a general over view based on existing historical work. Nevertheless, one feels that it is important to establish the strong continuity between the medieval and early modern period in respect of dealing with natural disasters.

1 The Background

Disastrous Times

Before we embark on an analysis of disasters and the means used to protect oneself against them, and to survive and explain them, it is important to establish just how frequently natural disasters occurred, and how important they were from the point of view of everyday life. This is even more important, since the global nature of modern day information and news services causes us to overlook a good deal of such catastrophes when they are only of a local importance. We are informed about natural disasters when they kill enough people, when they happen in our own backyard, or when they endanger some cultural treasures that are considered to be of universal importance. Good examples of such media disasters are the floods in Florence in 1968, and the earthquake that damaged the Basilica of Saint Francis in Assisi while this book was written.

If an earthquake only destroys some property or kills an 'insignificant number of people' we do not get to read about it in our daily newspaper. All these things make modern people perceive natural disasters as something huge and terrifying, which, luckily enough, happens only rarely, and only in certain geographic areas. The fact is however, that natural disasters, especially when the word is understood in the broader sense used in this book, happen every day and cause huge amounts of economic damage and significant loss of human lives.

This also holds true for the Middle Ages. Here it is impossible to provide a thorough list of all known natural disasters during the Middle Ages, nor is it necessary. The idea is to look into the period of the thirteenth and fourteenth centuries using secondary sources to give the reader an impression of how frequently these disasters occurred and what conditions influenced their severity.

Why choose these two centuries? The thirteenth century has traditionally been seen as a time of wealth, growth and prosperity. Even though the image of the thirteenth century as a golden age has been questioned by modern historical research, the fact remains that the climatic conditions were reasonably good from the point of view of agriculture, which, of course, was the single most important issue for the essentially agricultural medieval society. It was a time of relative well being when compared to the centuries immediately preceding or following it.[8] The thirteenth century saw no epidemics comparable to the *Black Death*. Thus it could be labelled as a model century, in which everything was as good as it could be during the Middle Ages.

The Fourteenth century, of course, was completely the opposite. Barbara Tuchman rightly calls it '*the calamitous fourteenth century*' in her popular book, *Distant Mirror*. The climatic conditions were much worse than during the preceding century and there was also the *Black Death* and other outbreaks of the plague. All these problems were aggravated by constant warfare and the problems caused by the great schism.

Looking at the conditions of these two centuries from the view point of natural disasters, one can obtain an idea about what was the scale of these disasters between the good times and bad times. Some natural disasters, such as earthquakes, are of course totally independent from general climatic conditions, but they generated others, such as floods and droughts. It is also worth pointing out, as self-evident or banal it may sound, that the ferocity and damage caused by some disasters was very much dependent on general climatic conditions. People weakened by consecutive crop failures were rather vulnerable to outbreaks of epidemics.

In fact, even during the prosperous thirteenth century, a large share of the European population did not have enough resources to be in the best possible physical condition to tolerate the hardships brought on by natural disasters. Many families were living in a state of perpetual malnutrition, which made them more susceptible to epidemics.[9]

Robert Fossier has compiled a summary of climatic problems and crop failures in England between the late tenth century and the year 1325. From this catalogue, we can identify one year of total catastrophe during the thirteenth century, that is, the year 1250. Furthermore there were several years with exceptional rains and floods: 1246, 1248 and 1285. In addition, there were outbreaks of epidemic disease during the years 1277 and 1299.[10]

When we come to fourteenth century England the first thing that needs to be mentioned is the great famine of 1315–1317, which in some regions even lasted until 1322. According to Robert Fossier and H. Neveaux, the famine was caused mainly by several bad harvests. The year 1314 had been average whereas the years 1315 and 1316 were bad. The yield ratio of 1317 was an average one, so that the scarcity ended only with the good harvests of 1318. One average year followed by two years of continuous rains and crop failures

---

8. See for instance M. Bourin-Derruau, *Temps d'equilibres, temps de ruptures XIIIe siècle*. Nouvelle histoire de la France Médiévale 4 (Paris, 1990), p. 7; Carlo Cipolla, Before the Industrial Revolution. European Society and Economy, 1000–1700 (London, 1980), pp. 204–207; Jussi Hanska, *"And the Rich Man also died; and He was buried in Hell". The Social Ethod in Mendicant Sermons*. Bibliotheca Historica 28 (Helsinki, 1997), pp. 17–20.
9. Robert Fossier, 'Le temps de la faim', in *Les Malheures des temps. Histoire des fléaux et des calamités en France*. Sous la direction de Jean Delumeau et Yves Lequin (Larousse, 1987), p. 135; Jussi Hanska, *"And the Rich Man also died; and He was buried in Hell"*, p. 19.
10. Robert Fossier, 'Le temps de la faim', pp. 137–140.

was a murderous combination. This was the worst recorded famine during the Middle Ages because of its long duration and wide geographical area. It covered the whole of Germany, Northern France, The British Isles (with the exception of Northern Scotland), and the Southern parts of Scandinavia.[11]

It has been proposed that this famine was the beginning of the demographic crisis of the fourteenth century. Some historians, however, have claimed that it did not have any long lasting effects on the population. Be that as it may, the fact remains that a considerably large part of the population perished during the famine. Some starved to death, while others died of epidemic diseases. According to Ian Kershaw, the death toll in the countryside was roughly ten percent and in the towns it was probably even more.[12] Zvi Razi has calculated that roughly fifteen percent of the tenants of the Halesowen manor perished during the famine.[13] It is not clear whether these figures can be generalised to other countries and areas that suffered from the famine, but it is clear that the mortality was very high indeed.

Northern Europe had hardly survived the famine years when it was struck by an even more terrible disaster; the *Black Death* (1347–1349). Here it is not necessary to go in to the details concerning the havoc caused by this epidemic. Suffice to say that it was not the last outbreak of the plague in the fourteenth century; others were to follow all through the century and beyond.[14]

The history of these times of massive mortality is well known, but let us now turn our attention to some less well-known disasters, which, nevertheless, were often very important on a local level. Especially so if one takes into account the fact that local catastrophes, say for instance crop failures, were terrible regional killers. There was no strong central government to distribute food to the most needy, and even in the cases where there might have been the will to help, the infrastructure was so undeveloped, and the means of transportation so limited, that the level of assistance was poor at best. Even if there were good enough roads and means of transportation, there was often many 'custom barriers' and dangers on route that seriously hindered the chance of help arriving on time.[15]

---

11. William Chester Jordan, *The Great Famine: Northern Europe in the Early Fourteenth Century*. Princeton N.J, 1996), pp. 7–21; Robert Fossier & H. Neveaux, 'La Fin d'une embellie', in *Les Malheures des temps. Histoire des fléaux et des calamités en France*, p. 150; Ian Kershaw, 'The Great Famine and Agrarian Crisis in England 1315–1322', *Past and Present* 59 (1973), pp. 3–13.
12. Ian Kershaw, 'The Great Famine and Agrarian Crisis in England 1315–1322', p. 11.
13. Zvi Razi, *Life, Marriage and Death in a Medieval Parish. Economy. Society and Demography in Halesowen 1270–1400* (Cambridge, 1980), p. 40.
14. There were very few years when there would not have been an outbreak of epidemics somewhere in Europe. Jean-Noël Biraben, *Les hommes et la peste en France et dans les payes européens et méditerranéens.* Tome I (Paris, 1975), pp. 363–364.
15. See for example Jacques Le Goff, *Medieval Civilization 400–1500* (Oxford, 1988), p. 233.

If we take a quick look at the sources of the thirteenth and fourteenth centuries we cannot avoid noticing that such local disasters were very common indeed. Jacques Chiffoleau who has studied the region around Avignon from 1320 to 1480 gives examples of local disasters, which caused serious problems. If we limit ourselves to the fourteenth century alone we find the following disasters. The rivers Rhône and Durance flooded in 1342, 1353, 1359, 1376 and 1398 causing damage to bridges, houses, fields and even people. Extremely cold winter (*'hyems aspera'*, *'grande fregor'*) is mentioned on the years 1308–1309, 1311, 1353, 1362, 1364, and 1382. It is very likely that these winters caused at least some damage to agriculture. Furthermore, there were problems with drought in 1355 and 1377. All this leads to the conclusion that in the Avignon region there was a famine every fifth year.[16]

Jacques Toussaert has studied the religious sentiment of maritime Flanders. In doing so he has put together a list of local catastrophes in the fourteenth century. The coast was seriously damaged by storms in 1317, 1321, 1334, 1356, 1367, 1372 and 1391. These storms caused much more than just a little bit of damage and some fallen trees. For example, in the storms of 1317 whole villages were destroyed. In addition there were serious floods in 1375 and 1399 (not including floods caused by human action during wars). There were also heavy rains, which had serious consequences for the crop yields in 1346, 1360 and 1382. At last, there is some evidence on the local outbreaks of epidemic diseases that caused high mortality to individual villages and areas.[17]

Many more examples of natural disasters on the local level could be produced by analysing studies concerning local history or extracting the information from medieval chronicles. This, however, is hardly necessary to prove the point. Local natural disasters, even if they did not produce a similar lasting outcry as the *Black Death*, were nevertheless, often problems of equal magnitude on the local level. To make it worse, they were very common indeed. One may safely assume that every generation had to face at least one serious natural disaster. Therefore there was an unquestionable need for protective measures and means of disaster management.

In the Shadow of the Black Death

Despite the frequency and importance of various natural disasters there has been a tendency in historical research and writing to overlook them. The notable exception to this trend is the *Black Death* to which has been devoted

---

16. Jacques Chiffoleau, *La comptabilité de l'au-delà. Les hommes, la mort et la religion dans la région d'Avignon à la fin du Moyen Age (vers 1320-vers 1480)*. Collection de l'Ecole Française de Rome 47 (Roma, 1980), pp. 101–102.
17. Jacques Toussaert, *Le sentiment religieux, la vie et la pratique religieuse des laïcs en Flandre Maritime et au "West-Hoeck" de langue flamande aux XIVe, Xve et debut du XVIe siécle* (Paris, 1963), pp. 503–509.

an ever increasing number of books and articles.[18] While it is completely rational and reasonable that a disaster, which, as proved beyond any doubt, had a huge impact on European history, should be studied vigorously, it nevertheless has produced some side effects, which tend to give us an unbalanced view of the history of medieval Europe. In fact it leads us to two historical misconceptions. First of all, we tend to assume that the *Black Death* was a unique disaster, unmatched by anything before or after it. This tendency is noted and criticised by Carlo Cipolla in his classic *Before the Industrial Revolution*.[19] Second problem is related to the first one. Once historians have accepted the idea of the uniqueness of the *Black Death*, they often, though not always, assume that the reactions of medieval men to it were unique as well.

Let us first look more carefully into the assumption that the *Black Death* was a unique catastrophe. On a macro level this assumption is definitely correct. The mortality rate was without precedent. In fact, reading the latest books by demographically oriented historians, one gets the impression that the death toll of one third once put forward in school books seems to be an under rather than overestimation.

Carlo Cipolla has estimated that the plague killed about 25 million people out of a total European population of round 80 million. This means that a little more than 31 per cent of the total population perished.[20] Jean-Noël Biraben quite rightly states that the loss of life during the *Black Death* can be measured with reasonable accuracy only in few cases. The cases he then presents (the parishes of Givry-en-Bourgogne and Saint-Nizier-de-Lyon in France) fit the one-third theory very well. He estimates that the mortality rate in Givry would have been between 27 and 30 per cent, and in Saint Nizier roughly between 25 and 30 per cent.[21]

If we look at the situation in England, by far the best-documented area of Europe thanks to the reasonably well-preserved manorial records, we see that estimations of the overall mortality caused by the plague have varied between 20 and 50 per cent. Higher figures come from those historians who

---

18. Here it is simply impossible to present even a selective look into the most important contributions for the history of the epidemic. Any such bibliography would demand a book of its own, and still be outdated by the time it comes out of the print. However, see Patrizia Salvadori, 'La peste e la lebbra in Medioevo Latino. Un prospetto bibliogeografico', in *The Regulation of Evil. Social and Cultural Attitudes to Epidemics in the Late Middle Ages*. Edited by Agostino Paravicini Bagliani and Francesco Santi. Micrologus' Library 2 (Firenze, 1998). Concerning England, see the bibliography in Colin Platt, *King Death. The Black Death and its aftermath in late-Medieval England* (London, 1996), pp. 231–251. For the general history of the Plague the most comprehensive book seems to be Jean-Noël Biraben, *Les hommes et la peste en France et dans les pays européens et méditerranées*. 2 Volumes (Paris, 1975–1976).
19. Carlo Cipolla, *Before the Industrial Revolution*, p. 130. 'Historians always mention *Black Death* but generally leave readers with the impression that no serious epidemics hit Europe before 1348 or afterwards.'
20. Carlo Cipolla, *Before the Industrial Revolution*, p. 131.
21. Jean-Noël Biraben, *Les hommes et la peste en France et dans les pays européens et méditerranées*. Tome I, pp. 156–171.

have concentrated on a reasonably small and well-documented population (normally tenants of some manor) to count mortality, and generalised their results to the whole of land. Smaller figures are partly based on demographic and partly on indirect evidence. J.C. Russel, for instance, has calculated the level of mortality among landlords in 1348–1349 and generalised these results to the population as a whole.[22]

Zvi Razi has studied the manor of Halesowen west of Birmingham in Worcestershire. He uses manorial records, which have been reasonably well preserved, and studies them with very sound methods. According to Razi's estimation the death toll in Halesowen was at least 40 per cent of the tenants of the manor.[23] Considering the fact that a great majority of the inhabitants of fourteenth-century England lived in villages, one is tempted to assume that the overall rate of mortality in England was in reality higher than the 'classical estimation of one third'. The newest study concerning the *Black Death* in England strongly supports this conclusion. In it Colin Platt puts forward figures presented in recent demographical studies on small communities. These figures vary from one community to another, but none of them are below 40 per cent and some rise even over 70 per cent.[24]

To have some geographical variation we may look at the situation in Scandinavia. It has been estimated that the population of Norway was roughly 350 000 around the year 1300. By 1450–1500 it had dropped to around 125 000. Much of this loss was due to the *Black Death* and the following outbreaks of plague.[25] Not to venture too long with the estimations of mortality caused by the *Black Death* we must remember that it really does not matter whether the actual mortality rate was 20 per cent, 70 per cent or something in between. It was devastating enough to be viewed as the greatest catastrophe in European history.

In addition to its severity the *Black Death* was also exceptional for its pan-European effect. The doctor of Pope Clement VI, Guy de Chauliac, wrote that this epidemic did not resemble earlier ones in any respect. They affected only one region while this one was universal. They could be cured, but for this one there was no cure whatsoever.[26]

All this seems to corroborate the assumption of many historians that the *Black Death* was a catastrophe of unparalleled magnitude. Why then did I state above that such an opinion is a historical misconception? The answer lies in the adopted perspective. *The Black Death* is unique from the point of view of historical demography, economic consequences, or from any

---

22. For a synopsis of theories concerning the mortality rates in England see Zvi Razi, *Life, Marriage and Death in a Medieval Parish*, pp. 99–100.
23. Zvi Razi, Life, *Marriage and Death in a Medieval Parish*, p. 106.
24. Colin Platt, *King Death. The Black Death and its aftermath in late-medieval England*, pp. 9–10.
25. Ole Jorgen Benedictow, *Plague in the Late Medieval Nordic Countries. Epidemiological Studies* (Oslo, 1992), p. 104.
26. Jean-Noël Biraben, 'Temps de l'Apocalypse', in *Les Malheurs des temps. Histoire des fléaux et des calamités en France*, p. 180.

other universal point of view, but if we descend to the level of the everyday experience of medieval villagers or inhabitants of a small medieval town, we get a slightly modified picture.

It is true that most contemporary chronicles describe the *Black Death* as the worst catastrophe ever, but it is equally true that if we read these same chronicles a few decades later or before the *Black Death*, we find a few more 'worst disasters ever'. It is important to remember that medieval man's sense of reality was geographically and historically constricted. Collective memory rarely stretched beyond a couple of generations and 'ancient rights' were often but a few decades old. The phrase '*the worst catastrophe ever*' therefore did not necessarily mean the same as it means to us, more likely it simply meant the worst catastrophe within the scope of the memory of the writer, or at most, within the memory of the oldest surviving member of the community.

This becomes apparent if we take a medieval chronicle, for example the chronicle of the Benedictine monastery of Bury St Edmunds. As has been shown, there was a strong tradition of writing history in Bury. Three monks wrote the chronicle. The first one compiled the chronicle from the Creation to 1265, and others continued his work until the year 1301.[27] Yet if one looks carefully, the writers of this chronicle never compared contemporary events to earlier ones recorded by themselves or by their predecessors. When some phenomenon needed to be categorised, they invariably trusted either in their own judgement or in the opinions of the oldest living members of the community.

An interesting example is the description of a storm that occurred in January 1295:

> '*On 19 January and all that night and the next day a hurricane blew accompanied by heavy, continuous downpour; the storm was so terrible that the centenarians who saw it could remember nothing similar. All the winter seed both in Holland and in the Marshland was almost totally destroyed by the rain.*'[28]

Instead of searching parallel cases from the very chronicle he was writing, the chronicler chose to ask the opinion of the centenarians ('*centenarii*'). Had he read a few folios back in his own manuscript, he would have found several examples of similar storms meticulously described in older annals. Yet he chose to interview the centenarians to be able to put this storm in perspective. This and numerous other cases in medieval chronicles clearly prove that the medieval conception of history was different from our's. It was in many respects limited to the individual's or his contemporaries' own lifetime.

This means that while the *Black Death* was the ultimate disaster for the generation, living through it, it may very well not have been the ultimate

---

27. *The Chronicle of Bury St Edmunds 1212–1301*. Edited with an Introduction, Notes and Translation by Antonia Gransden (London, 1964), pp. xv–xvii.
28. *The Chronicle of Bury St Edmunds*, p. 126.

disaster for the next generation. This is arguable when it comes to clerics and other literate men who could read about the horrors of the *Black Death*, but it certainly is true in the case of the large illiterate masses who were living from one crop to another, trying to make ends meet. For them the ultimate disaster was not a distant epidemic they might or might not have heard about. For them the ultimate disaster was the worst disaster that struck their community during their own lifetime.

František Graus, who has studied mostly the conditions in Germany during the fourteenth century, came to the same conclusion. According to him, the occurrence of new plague epidemics reduced the interest to the *Black Death* at most to a level of antiquarian curiosity. It was a catastrophe, and a terrible one too, but nevertheless, only one in a long chain of catastrophes.[29] Even for the learned people who were experiencing consecutive outbreaks of the plague, the *Black Death* was merely a vague memory of the past, something they did not have the time to think about, for there were enough problems in the face of the present plague, or some other natural disaster.

Let us take another, much later example. R.J. Morris writes on the cholera epidemics that '*the approach and arrival of these epidemics, especially that of 1832, created a crisis atmosphere in the country quite unlike that produced by any other threat apart from foreign invasion. The normally calm Quarterly Review viewed the approach of 'one of the most terrible pestilences which have ever desolated the earth' with considerable horror.*'[30] Admittedly, cholera was not perceived as the most terrible pestilence, but it certainly caused a public horror comparable to the earlier outbreaks of the plague, which from the demographic point of view were on a totally different scale. For historians of mentalities it is not important how severe the catastrophe actually was, but how it was interpreted and what kinds of reactions it caused.

It can even be speculated that for some contemporaries the *Black Death* was not the ultimate disaster. They may have lived in an area less affected or even in one of those places which the plague simply passed by. For those people the ultimate catastrophe may very well have been the famine years 1315–1317 or the almost equally catastrophic crop failures of 1332, 1345 and 1348.

It is also debatable how the *Black Death* was interpreted in more remote and agrarian parts of Europe. Was the majority of the rural population really aware that it was an universal catastrophe instead of something affecting their province or area only? On the other hand, we know that the mobility of people and information was reasonably high in the Middle Ages, much higher than once proposed by those who liked to present the Middle Ages as a thousand years of stability.

Thus, we must take into account that the plague was something totally new and that the information, that is, the horror stories concerning its effect, probably spread also to those areas, which did not suffer as much. It may be

---

29. František Graus, *Pest-Geißler-Judenmorde. Das 14. Jahrhundert als Krisenzeit*. Veröffentlichungen des Max-Planck-Instituts für Geschichte 86 (Göttingen, 1988; zweite durchgesehene Auflage), p. 35.
30. R.J. Morris, *Cholera 1832. The Social Response to an Epidemic* (London, 1976), p. 14.

that the very novelty; and not necessarily the death toll of *the Black Death* was the fact that made it a disaster larger than life. We see that in Orvieto this epidemic caused a mental shock for the completely unprepared residents. When the plague returned in 1363 the reactions were not so violent, and the later outbursts produced even more mollified comments in sources.[31] The conclusion seems to be that the *Black Death* was very probably the ultimate disaster for the generation that lived through it, but not necessarily for the generations following it. A cynic might add that it most certainly meant nothing for the numerous medieval generations that had lived before the *Black Death*.

This apparently self-evident fact brings us back to the second main problem caused by the 'overemphasis' of historians on the *Black Death*. The fact that the *Black Death* and the sources concerning it are much better known to historians than the sources concerning smaller scale everyday natural disasters poses another serious problem for the history of medieval men in confronting natural disasters. It is a popular misconception that many things that happened and ideas that were presented in connection with the *Black Death* were somehow unique, or at least were developed or invented during it. While in practise the spiritual responses to the plague were in most cases hundreds of years old. They had been invented for and used against other 'greatest disasters ever'.

The specific position of the *Black Death* in historical writing is natural, and there are plenty of completely understandable reasons why it should have been studied more than other natural disasters, which have remained practically untouched by historians. The most important reason is of course the universal nature of the cataclysm. It is undeniable that an unforeseen number of people died because of it. Yet, even this extremely high mortality should be seen in its proper context, and not through modern eyes. There had been several cataclysms that were unforeseen and killed great numbers of people before the *Black Death*, and they were reported in sources with an equal horror. Epidemics, droughts and floods that killed major parts of the population in some areas were equally terrible for the inhabitants of the area affected than the *Black Death* was in an European context.

The problem with the sources is to avoid the easy way out, that is, using mostly the printed and readily available sources concerning the *Black Death*. The sources concerning other natural disasters, which were perhaps not equally destructive and universal, but nevertheless equally fascinating, have not been collected into accessible anthologies. In many cases they remain unprinted, hidden in manuscript libraries and archives. It is vital to use these sources, for only by incorporating them can we obtain the *longue durée* history of medieval men and natural disasters. Only then can we see what was particular for the *Black Death* and what was standard practise under any threat of natural disaster.

---

31. Élisabeth Carpentier, *Une ville devant la peste*, p. 225.

Sources and Problems

Studying the *longue durée* of medieval men in front of natural disasters within the limits of a single book is bound to cause some difficulties. Some of these difficulties concern the sources, especially the problem of selecting the sources to be studied and those to be left out or used only sporadically. Other difficulties pertain to method.

The most interesting methodological problem in this book is the dilemma of collective vs. individual attitudes and mentalities. What can we really know about the worldview of an individual medieval man? In a recent book about the origins of European individualism, the eminent Russian historian Aaron Gurevich writes about the use of psychology in history, or one might say on the history of mentalities:

> '*Historians of ideas have uncovered diverse aspects of the picture of the world on which people based their thinking in a particular society, and in this way, they put together hypothetical reconstructions of the sets of values within which that thinking operated. Yet what they were dealing with was mainly collective psychology, the extra personal aspects of individual consciousness, the general attitudes that are shared by members of large and small social groups, while the unique constellation made up of elements of a world picture in the mind of a given, specific individual escapes our attention in the vast majority of cases.*'[32]

Individual views and beliefs about natural disasters would be very interesting, but reaching them seems to be nearly impossible due the fact that medieval people rarely left behind any material describing their inner feelings or their true beliefs. This lack of sources has often been assumed to prove that personal feelings and opinions were utterly unimportant to medieval men. The importance of a collective perception of the world and its phenomena has been emphasised.

Perhaps medieval men were in reality much more individualistic than the surviving sources reveal. One has to remember that writing was not a hobby of every individual. Putting thoughts onto parchment was always an end product of a long process of thinking, planning, and making preliminary notes on fly leafs or wax tablets. To write a book one needed to have a considerable amount of parchment. Writing even a modest and short *libellus* was a fairly expensive thing to do. It would be naive to think that economic considerations were overlooked when producing books. Because of the expenses involved, it was customary to write books only for a very good reason. The texts that were eventually put on parchment had gone through serious consideration and they were in most cases stripped bare of anything not relevant for the book's function.

Telling stories about one's own life, not to mention one's inner feelings, was not normally considered to be a good enough reason to waste expensive

---

32. Aaron Gurevich, *The Origins of European Individualism* (Oxford, 1995), p. 2.

parchment. Even if someone could afford to write such things it was highly unlikely that others would be willing to invest their money in copying them. A good example is the highly personal chronicle of an Italian Franciscan brother, Salimbene de Adam. It is an autobiography disguised in the form of a chronicle. Salimbene tells his readers endless numbers of anecdotes about himself, about his travels, and other material of 'human interest'. Salimbene's chronicle was not exclusively or even consciously a biography; it was meant to be an historical work including material suitable for preaching and moral education.[33] However, it turned out to be much more personal than was customary in the thirteenth century.

It is probably no co-incidence that his chronicle has only survived in one single medieval manuscript and all his other works have completely vanished. As a general rule one can say that interesting details about the history and feelings of individuals were only recorded when they were interesting from the point of view of general didactic purposes. One could say that the majority of medieval literature was in some sense didactic.[34]

This explains the sad fact that, while there is a good deal of source material concerning the public opinions and reactions to disasters, there are only a few sources that describe personal feelings, opinions and reactions of individual persons. If we forget the writings of the clergy, they are nearly non-existent. Even the rare material that exists is often very difficult to isolate from the endless sea of data contained in the sources. In most cases the few sources that allow us a glimpse on the real world of individual man amount to few odd lines in the pages of a chronicle. If this is not bad enough, there remains the problem of interpreting such fragments correctly. It is not only a question of reading the sources and reproducing the obvious evidence, but of trying to recreate popular and individual responses to catastrophes by reading between the lines and using circumstantial evidence.

To clarify what I mean here it might be useful to take an example. Suppose that we have a chronicle describing a serious natural disaster, say long lasting heavy rains, which threaten to destroy the crops. Let us again suppose that the writer of this chronicle says that a procession was organised with relics of such and such saint, and that all the inhabitants of the town participated barefooted and singing penitential psalms. How are we to know whether all the inhabitants actually took part in the procession, and even if we assume that they did, what was their motivation in doing so? Did they actually believe that the procession was going to stop to the rains, or did they simply participate because it would have been socially or politically unacceptable behaviour not to do so?

Perhaps some people did not want to risk being criticised or being treated harshly because of failing to conform by staying at home? Was going

---

33. Bert Roest, *Reading the Book of History. Intellectual Contexts and Educational Functions of Franciscan Historiography 1226–ca. 1350* (Groningen, 1996), pp. 47–49, 224.
34. On the case of chronicles, see Carla Casagrande and Silvana Vecchio, 'Cronache, morale, predicazione: Salimbene da Parma e Jacopo da Varagine', *Studi Medievali*, ser. 3, t. 30 (1989).

barefooted a sign of true contrition and penance, or simply an age-old custom followed when processioning. These problems are nearly impossible to answer. Therefore it is gratifying to find sources that seem to give us a more reliable description of the general feeling and moods of the public.

Sometimes, however, the reportator of the events indulges himself in describing the feelings of the people affected. Such is the case in some chronicles and, for example, in some *reportationes* of the sermons of Bernardino da Siena. Even in these cases we have to judge whether the descriptions are reliable and how much rhetorical exaggeration is involved. However, there is, and indeed there must be, a limit to a scepticism. It is difficult to see why the sources should completely dream up reactions of the people in front of disasters.

One way of trying to find out the responses of individual people to natural disasters is to compare modern psychological knowledge of the symptoms and actions of catastrophe victims to stories and descriptions emerging from medieval sources. There are, of course, countless methodological problems connected with using such theories on people living in an essentially different society from ours, and of whom we know only through secondary, and sometimes even misleading sources. These problems are dealt with in detail in the appropriate chapters.

What then are the sources that should be used in studying natural disasters during the Middle Ages? It was fairly common for chroniclers to note all the exceptional meteorological happenings and their effects on people. Famines, floods, storms, earthquakes, heavy rains, droughts and so on were in many cases meticulously recorded in monastic or urban chronicles. The problem with these chronicles is, however, that in many cases they tend to leave us with a rather sketchy description of what had happened. Only rarely do they indulge in telling their readers about the measures taken to overcome the disaster, or the opinions, feelings and attitudes of the victims. Let us present an example. The chronicle of Westminster Abbey describes the drought of 1384 as follows:

> '*During this summer there was so great a drought that streams and springs which normally gushed from the ground in ceaseless flow, and indeed, as seemed yet more remarkable, even the deepest wells, all dried up. The drought lasted until the Nativity of the Virgin (8 September)...*'[35]

A drought lasting for the whole of the summer, even drying the deepest wells, would have caused unforeseen suffering among the rural population. In fact, the chronicle does tell us later that in the course of the summer great numbers of cattle died through the shortage of water. This would have caused economic difficulties for the peasants and, most likely, famine and starvation. Nevertheless, the chronicle chooses to remain silent about what happened beyond the fact that there was terrible drought and the death of the

---

35. *The Westminster Chronicle 1381–1394*. Edited and translated by L.C. Hector and Barbara F. Harvey (Oxford, 1982), p. 89.

cattle. We do not hear the reactions of the peasants, how they felt, or what according to them was the reason for such a disaster. Neither do we know whether they, or someone else, tried to do something to limit the damage and improve their situation.

Too often we end up in such a situation. The sources tell us enough to know that something had happened, but they do not allow us to form a complete picture of the situation. Luckily there are some exceptions to this rule – the only problem is that they are few and far between. This study takes a wide geographical and temporal perspective in order to find sufficient sources to allow us to put them all together, to obtain an overall picture of individual and collective reactions to natural disasters.

What then are these sources? We have already mentioned the chronicles that are the most important descriptive source. The great number of existing medieval chronicles makes it impossible to analyse them all in a book written by a single historian within a reasonable period of time. Thus chronicles are used in the present study in a selective way. In practise this means that such chronicles that have been readily available have been used. No thorough searches have been made to isolate chronicle material.

Two particular chronicles, however, deserve a special mention here: those of Matthew Paris and Salimbene de Adam. These two chronicles I have studied systematically because they are not typical medieval chronicles. Both of these thirteenth-century writers had a wider scope of interest than the average chronicler, and therefore they often describe attitudes and opinions of men in greater detail than most of their contemporaries. This anomalism makes them especially interesting sources for a study of mentalities.

Another important group of sources is formed by the catastrophe sermons. These sermons were delivered in connection with some natural disaster and later on written down to serve as model sermons to be used in equal circumstances. In some cases we get to know the exact time and location of the original sermon. In others we only know the type of catastrophe the sermon was intended to be used in. Sometimes they were, no doubt, written only to be used as models without any real historical context.

Catastrophe sermons are an extremely important group of sources for many reasons. They allow us to know the message communicated by the Church to the faithful in times of crisis. They reflect the doctrine as it was taught to the people, not in the overtly sophisticated form of university theology. These sermons, no doubt, were a major factor forming the ideas and views of the European population over the meaning of natural disasters. They also informed people how the Church expected them to behave under such circumstances. Despite their importance as a means of communication, catastrophe sermons are a genre of sources never used when studying natural disasters, not even in connection with the *Black Death*.

Another important factor is that catastrophe sermons, despite the fact that sermon studies has been one of the fastest growing areas of medieval studies over the past decade or so, have been a very much-neglected group of sources. Herve Martin mentions them in his thorough book on the preachers in Northern France in the Late Middle Ages.[36] Save for two articles I have published in the process of writing this book, catastrophe sermons have not been studied by anyone.[37] Therefore a special emphasis is put on homiletic sources even though this is by no means exclusively a study of medieval catastrophe sermons. Every book has to have its *raison d'étre* – so it is said. In this case it is the sermons. They considerably broaden the overall view of medieval natural disasters.

The third main group of sources concerning natural disasters are the liturgical sources. There are a reasonably high number of specific prayers, invocations and Masses for catastrophic circumstances. They tell us a great deal about the ceremonies connected with preventing natural disasters and relieving communities from them. Furthermore, there are masses of hagiographical evidence of the battle against natural disasters. Many saints were considered to be specific protectors against these calamities and their miracles include stories of such cases.

In addition to chronicles, sermons and liturgical sources there are other potential genres of sources. Elisabeth Carpentier notes that in Orvieto the government of the city took some positive action to improve the moral standards of its inhabitants even before the *Black Death* moved in. She supposes that these measures were taken because of the famines of 1346 and 1347. The city officials were willing to avoid further punishment by removing those phenomena that had caused the wrath of God in the first place.[38] It is tempting to assume that equal action was taken also in other places in the face of an immediate catastrophe. We can learn more about natural disasters and what kind of action was taken because of them by studying the sources concerning the government of medieval towns. This, however, is done here only when the sources have been readily available, for it would be impossible to search all the regional archives for such material.

In addition to these three source genres, I have used numerous other categories of sources to consolidate the picture drawn from the main sources. The problem, and I realise it painfully well, is that in most cases it is only possible to go through a small proportion of all the relevant material. Nevertheless, it is my firm belief that even with a limited corpus of sources a reasonably clear and homogenous picture of medieval man and natural disaster can be produced.

It is important that the readers should appreciate that it is virtually impossible to master all the genres of the sources used here. Those readers who are specialists of, say liturgy, hagiography or art history, will without

---

36. Herve Martin, *Le métier de prédicateur à la fin du Moyen Age 1350–1520* (Paris, 1988), pp. 549–551.
37. Jussi Hanska, 'Cessante causa cessat et effectus. Sin and Natural Disasters in Medieval Sermons', in *Roma, magistra mundi. Itineraria culturae medievalis. Mélanges offerts au Père L.E. Boyle à l'occasion de son 75e anniversaire* (Louvain-La-Neuve, 1998), pp. 141–153; Jussi Hanska, 'Late Medieval Catastrophe Sermons: Vanishing Tradition or Common Custom?', *Medieval Sermon Studies* 45 (2001), pp. 58–74.
38. Elisabeth Carpentier, *Une ville devant la peste*, p. 111.

doubt find gaps in the evidence pertaining to their particular branch of *eruditas*. Not all the relevant books have been read, or even the most important single sources used. Nevertheless, it was more important to write a book on the whole phenomenon of medieval man and natural disasters rather than to write a study of catastrophe sermons only, which would have been easier for me, as my previous studies have concentrated nearly exclusively on medieval sermon literature. This book is meant to raise questions and make suggestions. It is the job of the specialists of different branches of erudition to seek the final answers to these questions and verify or falsify these suggestions with more specific and accurate studies.

The Predecessors

The problem caused by vast amounts and different genres of sources is difficult indeed and it would certainly be impossible if one would have to start from the beginning. Luckily there are plenty of high quality studies that deal with the sources and problems of the present study. In fact, such studies are sufficiently numerous that one has to break the well-established custom of introducing and analysing the most important earlier studies on which this book is built. Instead of numbering a few books or articles I shall try to give a general impression of the state of current historical research on natural disasters. The footnotes will show my debt to individual works and historians.

Serge Briffaud has noticed that, even though natural disasters have always been present somewhere on the horizons of research, they have rarely been the subjects of historical study on their own right.[39] By this he means that historical works of earlier generations are full of occasional references to natural disasters, and even some speculation as to their meaning to the relevant issues of the time.

There are, however, a few important exceptions to this rule, The *Black Death* has for long been studied in its own right. Some attention has also been paid to certain other individual disasters or genres of natural disasters. One of the most thoroughly studied disasters is the great famine of the early fourteenth century.[40] Another case of regionally studied natural disasters is the earthquakes in Italy. The motive of these Italian studies has, quite understandably, from the beginning been the vulnerability of the area to earthquakes.[41] Yet, even in Italy the study of earthquakes has

---

39. Serge Briffaud, 'Introduction. Vers une nouvelle histoire des catastrophes', in *Sources travaux historiques* no. 33 (1933). Histoire des catastrophes naturelles. Paysages-environment, p. 3.
40. See the bibliography in William Chester Jordan, *The Great Famine. Northern Europe in the Early Fourteenth Century* (Princeton, New Jersey 1996).
41. A good example of the imminent connection of historical studies and actual realities is the still valuable study of Marcello Bonito. It was written in the aftermath of the earthquake of 5 June 1666 which turned Naples into pile of ruins; Marcello Bonito, *Terra tremante, overo continuatione de terremoti della creatione del Mondo fino al tempo presente* (Napoli, 1691).

been marginalized into specific studies concerning them. One seeks in vain earthquakes from the national histories of Italy. The same has been true about the histories of provinces and cities until lately.[42]

Serge Briffaud continues his analysis of the state of research by stating that whereas natural disasters were once seen to be a way of measuring the level of development of the society in question, now, after the arrival of the (inevitable) *nouvelle histoire*, they are seen more and more as sources of social and mental functions of society.[43] František Graus holds more or less the same opinion. According to him, historians have long concentrated on describing and analysing the damage and death toll of single natural disasters, and failed to study disasters as social phenomena. Only recently have some historians, especially Arno Borst, taken a more holistic attitude, which he calls '*Katastrophenforschung*'.[44] Graus is referring to Arno Borst's groundbreaking article *Das Erdbeben von 1348*, which despite its name and concentration on one single natural disaster makes a valuable contribution to understanding such phenomena in general.[45]

Finally, some interesting studies on natural disasters and their effects in the urban context have been produced in the ever-growing field of urban history. A good example of such activities was the five year long project *Destruction and Reconstruction of Towns* by the *Internationale Kommission für Städtegeschichte*. The project produced several publications, the most important one from the point of view of our theme being a collection of essays concerning the destruction of cities through earthquakes, fire and water.[46]

In practise, this means that the focus of studies during the last few years has transferred from historical demography, and from the history of institutions and economics to the history of mentalities. The statistical counting of the death toll has given way to questions such as how did the society or community deal with natural disasters, and what were their effects on individual persons.

Despite the rising interest of historians in natural disasters, a lot remains to be done. For instance, there still does not exist a general study of natural disasters and their impact on medieval society. In fact, there are only two books that come close to such a synthesis.

One is the *Histoire des Fléaux et des calamités en France* edited by Jean Delumeau and Yves Lequin.[47] Despite the fact that it only discusses the

---

42. Emanuela Guidoboni, 'Les conséquences des tremblements de terre sur les villes en Italie', in *Stadtzerstörung und Wiederaufbau. Zerstörungen durch Erdbeben, Feuer und Wasser*. Hrsg. Martin Körner (Bern – Stuttgart – Wien, 1999), p. 45.
43. Serge Briffaud, 'Introduction. Vers une nouvelle histoire des catastrophes', p. 3.
44. František Graus, *Pest-Geißler-Judenmorde. Das 14. Jahrhundert als Krisenzeit*, pp. 13–14.
45. Arno Borst, 'Das Erdbeben von 1348. Ein historischer Beitrag zur Katastrophenforschung', *Historische Zeitschrift* 3/1981, pp. 529–569.
46. *Stadtzerstörung und Wiederaufbau*. Band 1. *Zerstörung durch Erdbeben, Feuer und Wasser*. Hrsg. Martin Körner (Bern – Stuttgart – Wien, 1999).
47. *Histoire des Fleaux et des calamités en France*. Sous la direction de Jean Delumeau et Yves Lequin (Larousse, 1987).

situation in France, many of the points made by the authors are significant and can be generalized to other parts of Europe as well. However, since the book is meant for a wider audience, it is not adequately documented, though it is obvious to reader that vast amounts of source material have been used. It is equally obvious that the lack of visible documentation does not in this case mean a lack of academic competence.

The other one is the recent book by Jacques Berlioz on Natural catastrophes and calamities in the Middle Ages.[48] Alas, despite its name this book is not a general history of natural disasters in the Middle Ages. It is a collection of articles that were published earlier in different journals. Most of these articles are based on *exemplum* stories dealing with some kind of natural disasters. The collection of Étienne de Bourbon is particularly well represented. However, the volume contains one previously unpublished article. It is titled *Catastrophes naturelles et calamités au Moyen Age*.

It is a general view of natural disasters in medieval history. Covering roughly twenty pages it is not very long, but it certainly makes interesting reading. It covers many, although not all, of the topics considered in this book. On the whole one might say that Berlioz's book is a cousin of this one. It is a general history of natural disasters seen through one particular source genre, namely *exemplum* collections, whereas this book is a general history of natural disasters seen (mostly) through medieval sermons.

---

48. Jacques Berlioz, *Catastrophes naturelles et calamités au Moyen Age* (Firenze, 1998).

2 Seeking Divine Protection

This book is not primarily concerned with the scientific or technological means of avoiding natural disasters, but a few words must be said about them. This is important because we need to emphasise the fact that even though medieval men generally attributed natural disasters to supernatural powers, they nevertheless were no more fatalistic in confrontation with them than we are.

Modern anthropologists generally agree, and it fits well with common sense, that premodern men as well as members of primitive cultures have always been bound to use all the technological and scientific knowledge available to them to protect themselves and understand the reasons and logic of cataclysms. On the part of primitive cultures this common sense rule has been observed and verified already by Bronislaw Malinowski.[49] This is equally true for medieval man. If there were means of preventing disaster or limiting its damage, they were most rigorously used. One did not leave it to God alone to provide for water if it was possible to construct an irrigation system. One must not overestimate the technical abilities of medieval people, but it is equally dangerous to presume that they were ignorant in the field of technology and natural sciences.

According to the widely accepted theological opinion, nature was always friendly and submissive to man in those days when man still lived in the Paradise of Eden. Nature took care of his needs and obeyed him willingly. After the Fall, man had to face a new kind of nature, hostile and dangerous. Augustine writes in his *De genesi* that harmful plants exist only as a consequence of human sinfulness, not because of a perverse act of creation on God's part. By committing the original sin, man had lost his control over nature.[50]

---

49. See for instance Bronislaw Malinowski, 'Magic Science and Religion', in B. Malinowski, *Magic Science and Religion and Other Essays* (Westport, Connecticut, 1984; first published in 1948), pp. 28–29.
50. George Ovitt, Jr., *The Restoration of the Perfection. Labor and Technology in Medieval Culture* (New Brunswick and London, 1987), p. 78.

Augustine only speaks directly about the control over animals and plants, but his words can be applied *mutatis mutandis* to the whole of nature. Thus, according to this theological view, natural disasters entered the stage when man lost his control over nature. The ideal of man's superiority over nature remained alive in Christian theology. The progeny of Adam was to restore that early perfection by hard labour and through the reshaping of his moral character.[51]

In this ideal, gaining control over natural phenomena through science and technology was a completely acceptable practice as long as it worked. If it failed it was a sign of man's fallen state rather than a sign of his lacking technological knowledge. Thus it was completely acceptable to try to control nature. Success in doing so was perceived as an evident sign of inner virtuousness.

However, in practise there was not much one could do to prevent natural disasters. Effective means of protection against epidemics, for example, were extremely scarce. They were virtually non-existent before the Late Middle Ages, and even then they were mostly concerned with the plague. The first temporary health boards were set up in Italian towns during the *Black Death*. They normally were dissolved after the acute crisis situation was over. Only in 1486 was the first permanent health board, which was also concerned with preventive measures, founded in Venice. The rest of Europe was even less advanced in these matters.[52]

We may conclude that there certainly were scientific and technological measures taken to prevent natural disasters. Some of them might even have been limitedly useful. Nevertheless, throughout the whole of the Middle Ages the emphasis was on the spiritual or supernatural means of self protection.

Religion vs. Magic

As we have seen, the possibilities for avoiding disasters or even helping the victims to survive were rather limited. When human means of protecting the community from the hostile forces of nature were found to be inadequate, the divine element entered. Supernatural assistance seemed to be the only alternative. Like so many other so-called primitive societies, pre-Christian Europeans tried to control nature by magical means. By magical, we mean practices, which disregarded natural causality, and anticipated positive results from man's participation in the universe. Some of these practices survived the christianisation of Europe, for we find traces of them in medieval sources.

Aaron Gurevich has analysed these practices as they appear in early medieval penitentials. Magic rites were performed for numerous reasons:

---

51. George Ovitt, Jr., *The Restoration of the Perfection*, p. 85.
52. Carlo M. Cipolla, *Miasmas and Disease. Public Health and the Environment in the Pre-Industrial Age* (New Haven and London, 1992; first published in italian 1989), pp. 1–2.

Gregory the Great's procession during the plague of 589.

healing, love, and fertility of different sorts. The rites that are particularly interesting for us here are those performed at the Calends of January to secure good harvest for the coming year.[53] The pagan rites and celebrations, which were meant to secure good harvest, had assimilated with the Christian practises.

It is known that special processions in the time of natural disasters were organised as early as in the fourth century. Saint John Chrysostom mentions litanies held in April 399, when heavy rains were endangering the harvest. Similarly, Mamertus, bishop of Vienne, organised processions about the year

---

53. Aron Gurevich, *Medieval Popular Culture. Problems of Belief and Perception* (Cambridge, 1990), pp. 80–82.

470 after an earthquake and lightning.[54] The most famous early procession, however, was organised by Pope Pelagius II in November 589. The overflow of the Tiber had caused flooding in Rome. In turn, or so the contemporaries thought, this caused an outbreak of plague epidemic. Pelagius II ordered a general fast and procession. It turned out to be his last papal act, for he and seventy other people died of the plague in the middle of the procession. These processions were continued until the end of the epidemic by Gregory the Great, Pelagius' successor on Saint Peter's see.

According to medieval sources, it was Gregory the Great who ordered such processions to be organised throughout western Christendom, and thus they came to be known as *Litania romana* or *Litania Gregoriana*.[55] The litanies of Gregory the Great were also known as greater litanies to distinguish them from earlier litanies instituted by the above-mentioned bishop Mamertus of Vienne. Gregory's litanies were called major, because he was a pope, and they were first performed in the city of Rome, Mamertus' litanies were called minor litanies, because he was merely a bishop and because they were first performed in the less important Christian centre of Vienne.

Major litanies were normally performed on the feast of Saint Mark's Day (25th April) whereas the minor litanies were held on Monday, Tuesday, and Wednesday before Ascension Day. Rogation Day ceremonies retained their original penitential nature. Penance was supposed to make God look more favourably upon the supplications of his people. The specific liturgical form used on that day was the greater litany, a public penitential procession from one church to another, during which a litany of saints was sung.

On 25 April the pagan Romans used to hold a procession to honour the goddess Robigo. Prayers were offered to obtain her protection for the crops. The Christian Romans simply followed the old custom, only the forms of the rites and prayers were christianised or baptised as the scholars of late antiquity often say. The Church simply replaced old Roman ceremonies with the newly invented Christian processions. These took place in connection with saint Mark's Day, but the function and the form of these processions had nothing to do with the apostle. They were essentially borrowed from the *robigalia* feast.[56]

---

54. Terence Bailey, *The Processions of Sarum and the Western Church*. Pontifical Intitute of Medieval Studies. Studies and Texts 21 (Toronto, 1971), pp. 95–96.
55 . On the medieval tradition of litanies, see André Vauchez, 'Liturgy and Folk Culture in the Golden Legend', in André Vauchez, *The Laity in the Middle Ages. Religious Beliefs and Devotional Practices* (Notre Dame, 1993), pp. 129–139.
56. There are numerous medieval sources that reproduce histories of Gregory and Mamertus. See for instance: Iohannes Beleth, *Summa de ecclesiasticis officiis*. Edita ab Heriberto Douteil. CCCM 41A (Turnhout, 1975), p. 232–235; Sicardus Cremonensis, *Mitrale sive de officiis ecclesiasticis summa*. PL 213, col. 367; Guillaume Durand, *Rationale divinorum officiorum* (Roma, 1477), ff. 235r–v. See also Terence Bailey, *The Processions of Sarum and the Western Church*, p. 94; Adolph Franz, *Die kirchlichen Benediktionen im Mittelalter*. Zweite Band (Freiburg im Breslau, 1909), pp. 2–7; Andrew Hughes, *Medieval Manuscripts of Mass and Office. A Guide to their Organization and Terminology* (Toronto, 1995; first published in 1982), p. 13; John Harper, *The Forms and Orders of Western Liturgy from the Tenth to the Eighteenth Century. A Historical Introduction and Guide for*

Some later medieval writers thought that Gregory the Great instituted the Greater Litany during the great pestilence in Rome. Honorius Augustodunensis writes in his *Gemma ecclesiae* that the *Greater Litany* is read in Church once a year in order to ask God to protect the people and domestic animals from pestilence.[57] Modern historians know from the writings of Gregory himself that in his time this practise was already well established.[58] Nevertheless, during the Middle Ages and immediately after, the common idea was that Gregory invented the Greater Litany.[59]

This attribution gave the *litania majora* higher authority. In the course of the centuries the movement toward a uniform liturgical practise imposed *litania majora* processions on the whole of the West. The minor litanies invented by Mamertus, originally celebrated only in the Gallican church, were eventually accepted in the whole of western Christendom as well. They were adopted in Rome by order of Pope Leo III around the year 800. The ninth century also saw them adopted in Germany.[60]

The essential nature of Rogation processions is obvious even with a cursory look into surviving liturgical sources. They were a sort of bargain in which the community traded penitential activities and bowed before God for Divine protection and hope of a good year to come. André Vauchez has expressed doubts about the survival of the Greater Litany processions in urban surroundings. He proposed that Litanies were mostly celebrated in the countryside to obtain protection for crops, and even there the feast could sometimes have been confused with the feast of the Invention of the Holy Cross (May 3). It is known that in the post-medieval period masses were celebrated on that day to ward off storms and preserve the fruits of the earth.[61]

Students and Musicians (Oxford, 1993; first published in 1991), p. 137; Philippe Rouillard, 'Procession', in *Catholisme hier, aujourd'hui, demain*. Vol. 53 Primauté-propres (Paris, 1988), col. 1112. André Vauchez does not seem to be entirely convinced on the hypothesis of Greater Litany replacing robigalia feast; 'Liturgy and Folk Culture', p. 132.

57. Pierre-André Segal, *L'homme et le miracle dans la France médiévale (XIe–XIIe siècle)* (Paris, 1985), 157–158; Honorius Augustodunensis, *Gemma animae*. PL 172, col. 680–681.
58. Gregory the Great, *Epistolae Gregorii Magni, appendix ad sancti Gregorii epistolas III, charta quae relicta est de litania majore, in basilica sanctae Mariae*. PL 77, col. 1329. 'Solemnitas annuae devotionis nos, filii dilectissimi, admonet, ut litaniam quae major ab omnibus appellatur sollicitis ac devotionis debeamus, auxiliante Domino, mentibus celebrare, per quam a nostris excessibus, ejus misericordiae supplicantes purgari aliquatenus mereamur.'; Terence Bailey, *The Processions of Sarum and the Western Church*, p. 94.
59. That was, for instance the belief of bishop Carlo Borromeo of Milan when he used Gregory's Litany as an example of the utility of processions against plague; Heinrich Dormeier, 'Il culto dei santi a Milano in balia della peste (1576–1577)', in *Modelli di santità e modelli di comportamento*. A cura di Giulia Barone, Marina Caffiero, Francesco Scorza Barcellona (Torino, 1994), p. 235.
60. Terence Bailey, *The Processions of Sarum and the Western Church*, pp. 97–98; Adolph Franz, *Die kirchlichen Benediktionen im Mittelalter*, pp. 7–8.
61. André Vauchez, 'Liturgy and Folk Culture', p. 133.

Irrespective of whether Vauchez's hypothesis is valid or not, it remains clear that processions, masses and other protective liturgical ceremonies were celebrated in spring time to secure crops.

The pagan Roman rites of securing a good harvest, which were substituted by Rogation Days, were not of course followed in the whole Western Europe. Nevertheless, there was no lack of similar pagan rites that could be replaced. Different sorts of magic were also performed to avert storms and change the climate. The penitential of Burchard of Worms describes one such event. During a long lasting drought the women of German villages used to inspect a great number of young girls, strip one naked, and place her at the head of a procession walking out of the village. Once outside the girl would dig up a root of a certain herb, put it on her left foot, and return to the village walking backwards like a crab. Gurevich cites many other examples from Burchard's penitential and concludes that *'medieval villagers were not too far removed from such animistic people'*.[62]

The Rogation Day processions and the case outlined by Burchard of Worms do not constitute the only existing examples of such superstitious or pagan survivals in medieval or even early modern Europe. Sometimes these old pagan beliefs were mixed with newer Christian doctrines to produce totally new ways of protecting communities and assuring good crops.[63] It was the strategy of the early Church to absorb old pagan rites as much as possible into the new Christian religion. Gregory the Great emphasised that it was essential to be very cautious when destroying the remains of pagan cults. Sometimes it might be a good idea to burn idols, but in other cases better results could be achieved by reinforcing the old cults with a new Christian meaning.[64]

The eclectic nature of early medieval Christianity has raised the question: How Christian was Europe? This problem is relevant to this study because the central hypothesis of this book is that the Church had a central role in medieval 'disaster management'. If one is to argue that the role of the Christian church was most important in helping people survive and understand natural disasters, one needs to be sure of the predominant role of the Church in shaping people's mentalities.

Indeed, the significance of Christianity during the Middle Ages has been one of the crucial questions of medieval historiography. Some eminent French historians, most notably Jacques Le Goff and Jean-Claude Schmitt, have argued mostly on the basis of *exempla* material that there were two distinct medieval cultures; clerical and bookish Christian culture and a popular

---

62. Aron Gurevich, *Medieval Popular Culture*, p. 82.
63. See for example Carlo Ginzburg, *The Night Battles. Witchcraft and Agrarian Cults in the Sixteenth and Seventeeth Centuries* (Baltimore, 1992; originally published in Italy 1966), pp. 4–10. Ginzburg is describing a folkloristic fertility cult which was obviously influenced by the Christian demonology.
64. Franco Cardini, *Minima medievalia* (Firenze, 1987), p. 305; Jean-Claude Schmitt, 'Religione e guarigione nell'Occidente medievale', in J.-C. Schmitt, Religione, folklore e società nell'Occidente medievale (Bari, 1988), p. 289.

culture, subscribed to by the great majority of the people, which remained essentially pagan.[65]

These ethnologically oriented historians take the view that new Christian rituals and cults established on the old pagan sites were not really Christian. They were merely the same old pagan customs re-created with new names. The Catholic historian Jean Delumeau does not accept this idea. He states that historians ought to make a methodological distinction between direct relationships and similarities. It was not a question of old cults and beliefs with new names, but of new cults and beliefs with some familiar details and often-familiar geographical locations.

The American historian John van Engen argues that Le Goff's and Schmitt's idea of a semi-pagan medieval Europe filled with remnants of 'Indo-European folklore' is rather dogmatic and ahistorical. He concludes that:

> 'Recent study of popular religious culture has forced historians to focus on its distinctive and sometimes non-Christian character and function. But any approach that denies the reality of Christianisation as crucial to the formation and flowering of medieval religious culture will miss wholly its inner dynamic.'[66]

Aside from the views and theories of French historians, there have been less controversial critics of the traditional concept of the Christian Middle Ages. According to František Graus, early medievalists took their model of medieval religiosity from the baroque, and thus committed a fundamental mistake. They were projecting their romantic notions of a lost golden age of Christianity on the past. In reality, Christian Europe was never as homogenous and religious as has been thought. Graus, however, does not even try to deny the importance of the Christian religion.[67]

We may conclude that by the end of the twelfth century medieval Europe was thoroughly christianised, save perhaps some remote areas in Scandinavia and Eastern Europe. When we speak of christianised Europe, we must, however, take into account that the Christianity of the common medieval peasant was very different from today's Christianity, which emphasises personal religious experience.[68]

---

65. See for example, Jacques Le Goff, 'Culture cléricale et traditions folkloriques dans la civilization mérovingienne', in J. Le Goff, Pour un autre Moyen Age (Paris, 1977), pp.
66. John Van Engen, 'The Christian Middle Ages as an Historiographical Problem', *AHR* 3/1986. The quotation is from the page 552. Later on Jean-Claude Schmitt and M. Lauwers have emphasised that Van Engen's had not correctly interpreted the writings of French historical antropology school; Jean-Claude Schmitt, *Religione, folklore e società nell'Occidente medievale* (Roma-Bari, 1988), pp. 13–20; M. Lauwers, '«Religion populaire», culture folklorique, mentalités. Notes pour une anthropologie culturelle du moyen âge', *Revue d'histoire ecclesiastique* 82/2 (1987), pp. 255–256.
67. František Graus, *Pest-Geißler-Judenmorde. Das 14. Jahrhundert als Krisenzeit*, p. 65.
68. For a short and sound description of the medieval lay christianity see André Vauchez, 'Lay Belief around 1200: Religious Mentalities of the Feodal World', in André Vauchez, *The Laity in the Middle Ages. Religious Beliefs and Devotional Practices*. Edited and introduced by Daniel E. Bornstein (Notre Dame, Indiana, 1993), pp. 85–93.

At the heart of medieval Christianity were rituals performed on a parochial level. They demanded attention, not necessarily personal belief. As Keith Thomas points out, these rituals could be interpreted not as symbolical acts, but as magical ones. He proposes that the concepts of magic (a kind of manipulation) and prayer (a form of supplication) were often confused in the minds of ordinary Christians. Thomas concludes that the line between magic and religion is difficult to recognise in medieval England.[69] His views might be expanded to cover the whole of medieval Western Europe.

Franco Cardini presents an example of a ritual to protect fields against bad harvests and evil magic. It involves all kinds of Christian elements, such as use of holy water and *Pater noster* prayers; yet, the ritual itself is not that of liturgical blessing, but rather magical. It does not ask fertility from God, leaving the eventual outcome to His decision. The ritual is based on the assumption that prayers and holy water will produce the desired results on their charismatic power alone. It is not a question of supplication but of manipulation.[70] There are numerous comparable examples in sources throughout Europe.

In Germany, the peasants used to erect big crosses near their fields. Their function was to protect the crops against bad weather and storms. Sometimes these '*Wetterkreuze*' were given a more official status by the local clergy who consecrated them and sprinkled them with holy water. An extant manuscript from the eleventh century gives a ready-made liturgy for such an occasion. Once the cross was made, it was brought before the church door on Friday. Then the mass on the Holy Cross was sung, and hereafter the priest came to the cross with blessed grain and holy water. Psalm 66 *Deus misereatur* and the litany against hailstorms were sung followed by the actual blessing of the cross. Holy water was sprinkled, thurible was waived, and symbols of the four evangelists were carved on the cross. The incipits of the four gospels were generally considered to be a powerful protective amulet against storms.

Finally the priest said:

> '*Let this holy cross be sanctified in the name of the Father, and Son and the Holy Ghost, so that it can protect Christian people against aerial powers and spiritual enemies, who have been given the power to harm the soil...*'

From this point on the text is lost and we do not know how the cross was eventually put in to it's proper position. Traces of similar ceremonies have been found from the thirteenth and the fourteenth centuries.[71] In the beginning of fifteenth century, Johannes von Werden wrote that the crucifix was an effective means of protection against demons that are afraid of it. Therefore,

---

69. Keith Thomas, *Religion and Decline of Magic*, pp. 41–50.
70. Franco Cardini, *Minima medievalia*, p. 305. For the actual description of the rite see Franco Cardini, *Magia, stregoneria, superstizioni nell'Occidente medievale* (Firenze, 1979), pp. 229–231.
71. Adolph Franz, *Die kirchlichen Benediktionen im Mittelalter*, pp. 13.

he continues, in some parishes the crucifix is taken out from the church and placed outside against the storm so that the demons can see the sign of the eternal ruler and flee in front of it.[72]

Similar examples can be found all over medieval Christendom. Étienne de Bourbon says that in Savoy the inhabitants of mountain regions were in the habit of erecting crosses on the mountaintops to expel demons.[73] Vincent Ferrier advised people to toll the church bells and bring out the crosses for protection against storms.[74] The phrasing of Vincent is not totally clear, but he seems to imply that specific crosses such as German '*Wetterkreuze*', or it is also possible that the normal ritual crucifixes in churches were brought out to prevent storms. It seems that the use of crosses against bad weather was not only a German custom, but also known all throughout Christian Europe.

There were numerous ways of mixing religion and magic when people were seeking protection from disasters and epidemics. Some people had specific prayers written on pieces of parchment, which they carried them with them as lucky charms. Others wore different religious medallions and protective amulets. Especially popular was the *Agnus Dei* symbol. Others had holy water sprinkled on them as a protection against the contagion of diseases.[75]

The Observant Franciscan preacher Bernardino Tomitano da Feltre told his audiences that once his more famous namesake Bernardino da Siena had shown to the people of Padua and Bologna the sign of Christ, that is, the letters IHS. Many people made amulets with these letters on circumcision day and, he emphasised, no one of those who did so died of the plague. He also tells that the plague never struck Siena since this sign was put in the middle of the Palladio (where it still is).[76]

---

72. Johannes von Werden, *Dormi secure de sanctis* (Strasbourg, 1493). De rogationibus. Sermo 22, f. G3r. 'Secundo crux defertur quia est signum summi regis quod demones ualde timent. Unde dicit Chrysostomus: "Signum dominicem ubicumque demones uiderint fugiunt timentes baculum quo plagam receperunt." Exemplum huius require inuentionis crucis. Unde hoc est ratio in quibusdam ecclesiis crux de ecclesia trahitur tempore tempestatis et opponitur tempestate ut scilicet demones uideant signum eterni regis et territe fugiunt.'
73. Jacques Berlioz, 'Les recits exemplaires, sources imprevues de l'histoire des catastrophes naturelles en Moyen-Age', p. 13.
74. Vincent Ferrier, *Sermones aestivales*. Feria secunda rogationum, sermo secundus (Nürnberg, 1492), p. 176. 'Ideo quando apparent malae nubes et tornitrua, pulsantur campanae et cruces extrahuntur...'
75. Jean-Claude Schmitt, 'Religione e guarigione nell'Occidente medievale', p. 294.
76. Sermoni del beato Bernardino Tomitano da Feltre. A cura di P. Carlo Varischi da Milano. Tomo II (Milano, 1964). Sermo in feria quinta post secundam dominicam post pasca in die Sancti Marci. De peste, p. 273. Bernardino's claim that Siena had not been struck by the plague after making the IHS sign is mistaken. There in fact had been an outbreak of epidemics in 1433. Perhaps he did not know it, perhaps he was more after rhetoric efficiency than truth; Jean-Noël Biraben, *Les hommes et la peste*, Tome I, p. 395.

When the christianisation of Europe advanced from the twelfth century onwards, the Church adopted more uncompromising attitude towards what it called superstition, be it remnants of ancient pagan cults or superstitious applications of Christian liturgy and symbols. In his *Summa* Thomas Aquinas presents superstition as a vice contrary to the real religion. That was the general idea; superstitions were seen as useless tricks and rituals, which in the Late Middle Ages were more and more frequently connected with the worship of demons.[77]

In the thirteenth century and before, however, superstitious practices were in most cases condemned as vain and futile nonsense rather than as diabolical. They did not deserve the harsh treatment, that was reserved for heretics.[78] The relative leniency of inquisitors towards different superstitious practises does not mean that these practises were considered to be harmless and were thus overlooked. There is plenty of evidence showing that this was not the case. If one looks at the important pastoral handbooks of the thirteenth century one finds that superstition is ever present in them.[79]

However, one should not jump to conclusions concerning the character of medieval Christianity on the basis of its love of rituals. Medieval religion consisted by no means of only magical rites baptised by giving them Christian names and functions. While there is no lack of examples of magical use of Christian rites and religious artefacts, there are equally plenty of examples of true and personal Christian devotion even among the lowest strata of medieval society. A case in point is the various revivalist movements. And furthermore, how are we to know that most or even many parishioners interpreted, say a religious procession, as some kind of magic ceremony intended to secure good harvest? Occasional cases where popular healers and other such persons used Christian lore as a magic means do not prove conclusively that this was a general way of perceiving the rites of the Church.

Medieval Christianity was neither similar to the modern, personal faith nor identical to magic disguised as religion. The truth lies somewhere between the traditional cliché of the Christian Middle Ages, and the more or less artificial construction of a dominant Indo-European folk culture. Paradoxically, the magic features of catholic Christianity caused it to be blamed as superstitious by the Enlightenment philosophers. They were accusing the Church of the very same things it had been accusing simple countrymen for centuries. For the philosophers *Rogationes*, relics, and miracles were all superstitious beliefs.[80] Religion and magic both began to be seen as enemies of rational scientific worldview.

---

77. Franco Cardini, *Minima medievalia*, pp. 303–304.
78. See for instance Jean-Claude Schmitt, *Le saint Lévrier. Guinefort guérisseur d'enfants depuis le XIIIe siècle* (Paris, 1979), p. 55.
79. Johannes von Freiburg, *Confessionale*. British Library MS Add. 19581, f. 187v. 'Deinde circa finem querere poteris de sortilegiis et superstitionibus si aliqua talia fecit uel fieri procurauit...' For further examples see Jean-Claude Schmitt, *Medioevo «superstizioso»* (Bari, 1992), pp. 114–117 and 124–131.
80. Franco Cardini, *Minima medievalia*, p. 313.

Heavenly Helpers

All things considered, there was logical continuity from pre-Christian times to medieval times in the practises and means of controlling nature. The only thing that changed was, that, with the christianisation of Europe, the task of controlling nature was removed from the animistic religion and pagan deities and given to God, Christ, the Virgin Mary, and to the numerous saints.

The role of the Holy Virgin as a heavenly helper in several of the dangers medieval man could encounter has been thoroughly studied. The Virgin's most essential role was that of *Mater misericordiae*. She was interpreted as a gentle mother figure whose role was to protect people and try to placate the wrath of God. Christ was not generally represented as the merciful figure he has turned out to be in modern Christian thinking, but as a vengeful judge who will come to judge mankind come the day of judgement. Although there was a change in this during the later middle ages when Christ lost some of his early medieval severity.[81]

One of the essential roles of the saints was to control and overcome the adverse forces of nature: they defeated disease, calmed stormy seas, saved harvests from locusts, and so on. According to Carlo Cipolla the dream of a common man, harnessing nature, was reflected in the saints. Mastery of nature was a recurrent theme in medieval hagiographical writings. Several saints were reputed to be able to control the natural and animal world. One might even say that one of the essential attributes of saintliness was the power to control nature.[82]

Asking for the protection of saints against different natural disasters was by no means an arbitrous activity. There were good reasons for turning to a particular saint in a particular situation. In his essay on the plague in Milan, Heinrich Dormeier presented an interesting categorisation of plague saints. It can be used even more generally to describe the rules according which the different saints were chosen to protect under different threats. Dormeier distinguished three categories of plague saints:

1. Traditional plague saints

2. Regional plague saints, that is, saints whose intervention has been found effective in a localised area on previous occasions.

---

81 On the role of Holy Virgin see for example Jean Delumeau, *Rassurer et proteger: le sentiment de sécurité dans l'Occident d'autrefois* (Paris, 1989), pp. 261–289 and Raoul Manselli, *Il sopranaturale e la religione popolare del medioevo* (Roma, 1986), pp. 43–44.
82 André Vauchez, *La sainteté en Occident aux derniers siècles du Moyen Age: d'apres les procès de canonisation et les documents hagiographiques* (Rome, 1988), p. 543; Michael E. Goodich, *Violence and Miracle in the Fourteenth Century. Private Grief and Public Salvation* (Chicago, 1995), pp. 106; Carlo Cipolla, *Before the Industrial Revolution*, pp. 183–184; Aron Gurevich, *Medieval Popular Culture*, p. 45; Donald Weinstein and Rudolph M. Bell, *Saints & Society*, p. 143–144.

Typical iconographic presentation of the Madonna della misericordia. *The holy virgin protects the faithfull with her mantel. Andrea della Robbia (c. 1500), Santa Maria in Gradi, Arezzo. (Photo: Volker Rödel).*

3. Patron saints of a diocese, a community or of individual persons, and those saints whose feast happens to be in the time of the disaster.[83]

In the cases of natural disasters other than the plague, saints belonging to categories two and three were normally evoked. Some saints, for example, were regarded as specialised protectors against earthquakes. However, such attributions were often local. It is, for example, difficult to imagine that saint Agatha would have been revered as protector against earthquakes outside Sicily and Southern Italy even though these were not the only earthquake regions of the medieval Europe.[84] Such local roles were not important for

---

83. Heinrich Dormeier, 'Il culto dei santi a Milano in balia della peste (1576–1577)', pp. 236–237.
84. Sara Cabibbo, *Il paradiso del Magnifico Regno. Agiografi, santi e culti nella Sicilia spagnola* (Roma, 1996), p. 93.

the image and function of that particular saint on the universal level. Here it is not important to catalogue all the saints with specific patronage to protect people against natural disasters. Suffice it to say that there were numerous such protective cults.[85]

It is tempting to assume that, when it comes to preventive protection against natural disasters, the role of local patron saints was the most important one. After all, they were supposed to ensure the fertility of fields and animals, and save the community from disease, storm and flood. The community confirmed the protection of the patron saint by celebrating solemnly his festival with different rites and ceremonies. In processions his relics would be carried between significant points of village territory. The banquets were organised for his/her glory and attended by all the inhabitants of community.[86]

A good example is the relationship between the city of Pisa and its patron, saint Peter the apostle. Federico Pisano Visconti says in a sermon that the station church chosen for the second Rogation Day was San Piero a Grado. According to the Pisan tradition it was built on the place where saint Peter first set his foot on Italian soil. Peter had personally built the first little chapel and altar. Later on the still existing church was built on the place of Peter's chapel. It was used as a station church because saint Peter was the city's patron saint, and because he had, as a Prince of Apostles, the power over all other saints and thus could persuade them to work on behalf of the Pisans. The sermon ends with following exhortation to prayer:

> '*When Emperor Nero held the city of Pisa and had the whole body* [of saint Peter] *decapitated, his head remained here in the church of saint Russorio ad gradus Arnensis, which is a great sign of the fact that blessed Peter loves us, and we should love and honour him equally. We all should turn to him without fear, so that he would pray to God on behalf of us, so that God will guard our city, our souls, and bodies, and liberate us from pestilence, hunger, and sword or war, and that He would direct the ships of our merchants to harbours safely, and that He would concede us the fruits of the earth in time.*'[87]

---

85. See for instance Jean Delumeau, *Rassurer et protéger*, p. 218. Further examples can be found from Butler's, *Oxford Dictionary of Saints*, or any of the numerous handbooks of medieval saints.
86. Stephen Wilson, '*Introduction*', in Saints and their Cults. Studies in Religious Sociology, Folklore and History. Edited by Stephen Wilson (Cambridge, 1983), p. 24.
87. Federico Pisano Visconti, *Sermones*. Secunda die rogationum in ecclesia sancti Petri ad gradus. Firenze Biblioteca Medicea Laurenziana MS Plut. 33.sin.1, f. 48v. '...et tunc uolens uenire circa mare in Ytaliam. Primo applicuit ad locum istum qui dicebatur gradus Arnenses, et ideo uocatur ista ecclesia sanctus Petrus ad gradus, et manibus suis fecit hic altare et ecclesiam paruam. Quando Nero imperator tenebat ciuitatem Pisanam qui et beatum torpetem fecit decollari, hic ad gradus Arnenses cuius caput requiescit in ecclesia beati Russorii. Propter quod magnum signum est quod nos dilexerit beatus Petrus et nos eodem modo debemus eum diligere et honorare et ad ipsum secure recurrere ut pro nobis Deum roget quod custodiat et ciuitatem nostram, animas et corpora nostra, et liberet nos a pestilentia, fame et gladio siue guerra, et reducat mercatores nostros ad portum salutis et concedat nobis fructus terre in tempore suo.'

Thus saint Peter's specific love of the Pisans was manifested in his willingness to stay in the city. Therefore the Pisans were able to trust in his continuous protection. There is no reason to wonder why the well being of Pisan merchants and their ships is especially mentioned in this prayer; the well being of the whole city was very much dependent on the fortunes of its merchants.

It is tempting to assume that other saints were only summoned to intervene when an actual catastrophe was at hand. Then the specific problem was known, and which specific saints had the qualities needed to solve it, either through their expertise or because of the fact that their feast was conveniently at hand. However, if we look into the preventive measures against possible yet unforeseen dangers, the role of patron saints was more important than that of other saints. It was he who had the duty to look after the interests of his clients.

Medieval Rationalism

An interesting question is to what extent people believed that these measures really had any effect on their safety? Living in a modern western society, we take it for granted that magical tricks are unable to produce any real effects. Magic is strongly opposed to our rational worldview. It seems absurd to many of us to assume that ceremonies such as *rogationes* could have been honestly believed to secure good harvests.

Indeed, we do not know what the proportion of the population was that actually believed in the effectiveness of processions, prayers, amulets or the protection of the saints. We have some documented information about the heretics who refused to believe in the teachings of the church. In addition to the heretics, it is also reasonable to assume that there were others who simply did not believe at all. Equally we have a good deal of information about people who took the protective religion most seriously, for example the thousands of written testimonies on the intervention of saints in surviving *inquisitiones in partibus* hearings during the canonization processes.[88] However, it is impossible to know what was the ratio of believers and agnostics at any given time. Nevertheless, one must not underestimate the role of protective rites and cults from the point of view of modern ideas of what is rational and what is not.

The superiority of a rational worldview is embedded in the western tradition of thinking. We tend to believe that the western rational thought system provides us with an explicit and coherent view of the world, where everything falls in to place and operates according to a rational logic of cause and effect. At the same time, the magical view of the world is considered to be incoherent. It is merely a collection of practices, beliefs,

---

88. This source genre is thoroughly analysed in Andre Vauchez' ground-breaking book *La sainteté en Occident aux derniers siècles du Moyen Age: d'apres les procès de canonisation et les documents hagiographiques* (Rome, 1988).

gests and ritual techniques without any real base in observation and logic.[89]

Relying on magic or at best on religion seems to be a sure sign of the deficient intellectual and logical capacities of medieval man. Such a view, however, is very ahistorical, and unfair. In fact, given the context, medieval people behaved very rationally. A person may act rationally, believe rationally, or both. If a person acts rationally on the basis of his beliefs, it can be called rationality in weak sense. If he is acting rationally on the basis of rationally held beliefs we are dealing with a strong form of rationality.[90] In this context acting rationally according to one's magical or religious beliefs is rationality in a weak sense of the word.

In order to decide whether or not medieval man was lacking in intelligence and logic, we should ask, whether he actually had a chance of acting rationally in the strong sense of the word. In fact, there is nothing to indicate that medieval man was not willing to do anything within his knowledge and ability that was rational in the strong sense of the word. On the contrary, numerous sources describe completely rational activities, under taken on the basis of contemporary scientific understanding and observation to prevent disasters or alleviate their effects.

The only exception to this rule seems to be the processions at the times of plague epidemics. It was well known that the disease spread through contagion, many municipal authorities therefore had explicitly forbidden any public meetings during the epidemics. Despite this, people were willing take the risk and to organise religious processions, for they believed more in the power of divine intervention than they feared contagion.[91] This is of course irrational and dangerous behaviour for anyone who knows how contagious diseases spread. Yet, for people who believe that God has ultimate control over nature, it is absolutely rational to throw oneself at His mercy.

The problem is that medieval man simply lacked the scientific knowledge available today, which would have enabled him to protect himself with measures we label rational, that is, rational in the strong sense of the word. We should not forget that the traditional religious worldview was very much self-supporting. Everything could be explained in religious terms. C. Jarvie and Joseph Agassi have noted this in the context of magic. They write, '*The strength of the magical world-view is that it is a complete world-view, one that explains anything and everything in terms of magic, failed magic, or magical conspiracies. It combines very smoothly with even a sophisticated technology, because it explains its success.*'[92] This can be applied to the medieval religious world-view as well. If natural disasters cease or do not occur at all, God has obviously heard the prayers of his people. In the case

---

89. Franco Cardini, *Minima medievalia*, p. 303.
90. C. Jarvie and Joseph Agassi, 'The Problem of Rationality and Magic', in *Rationality*. Edited by Bryan R. Wilson (Oxford, 1977), p. 173.
91. Jean-Noël Biraben, *Les hommes et la peste en France et dans les pays européens et méditerranées*, Tome I. p. 66.
92. C. Jarvie and Joseph Agassi, 'The Problem of Rationality and Magic', p. 192.

of an opposite outcome, the explanation is that people have sinned, that their prayers were not earnest, or that God in his wisdom simply saw it fit to punish the community, perhaps as a trial before greater rewards.

The religious world-view was not only all-explaining, it was also presented as the only possible way of explaining the world. People were not encouraged to seek alternative solutions. Robin Horton writes about traditional culture in a modern African context. He concludes that *'in traditional cultures there is no developed awareness of alternatives to the established body of theoretical tenets; whereas in scientifically oriented cultures, such an awareness is highly developed.'*[93] Those who are involved in scientific research know that Horton's view of science is some what idealised; nevertheless, compared to traditional cultures it is valid.

In practise this lack of a developed awareness of alternatives meant that people were brought up within a system that was well thought-out and did not encourage questioning or experimental methods. In short, they were living in a coherent world explained by concepts and mechanisms that were taken for granted.

This becomes very clear if we consider how, in the end, the scientific monopoly of Christian Church was broken. Modern natural science was started by medieval university men, not because they wanted to question the truths presented by the Church, but because they wanted to confirm them. Alas, these most pious enquiries brought results that were not always expected. For centuries, for example, Christian scientists were looking for the traces of Noah's flood. What they found was hard proof that the world was not created six thousand years ago, as the Church thought, but that it in fact was (as they thought) several millions of years older. It is fascinating to note that it took centuries for natural scientists to accept that the Church had got it wrong. As long as possible, they were willing to find means of explaining the evidence in such manner that it would not go against accepted doctrines.[94] So one may conclude that within the historical context medieval man believed and behaved in a very rational manner.

---

93. Robin Horton, 'African Thought and Western Science', in *Rationality*. Edited by Bryan R. Wilson (Oxford, 1977), p. 153.
94. On the history of Noah's flood see Norman Cohn, *Noah's flood: the Genesis Story in Western Thought* (New Haven, 1996).

3 At the Moment of Peril

Collective reactions

Despite all the spiritual and practical precautions taken, disasters could still not be avoided. What, then was done in the midst of disaster; how did people try to cope with the situation? More important still, how did they try to stop it? Studying human reactions and behaviour during catastrophes is difficult, not in the least because of the hectic nature of the phenomena. Some catastrophes, such as earthquakes, happened so quickly that there was hardly time to do anything, at least anything planned and rational. In the case of long-term disasters such as droughts, it is difficult to decide whether we are actually dealing with post-disaster activities or with measures taken during the catastrophe. The best results are achieved with the sources that discuss longer lasting disasters, such as famines and floods. In the evaluation of these sources it is important to distinguish between individual and community responses to disasters.

It has been emphasised that common expressions of penance were the most important spiritual means of fighting natural disasters. Individual penance was simply not enough, some collective and common forms were called on to impress and placate God with the continuity of the prayers and chants and the numbers of participants. Jean Delumeau has rightly labelled catastrophe liturgy as quantitative religion.[95] If we take a look into these collective religious responses in front of natural disasters, we find that there were basically three important spiritual means of dealing with the catastrophes: sermons, processions, and votive Masses.

With these instruments the community turned towards God and the saints to seek protection in the moment of danger. Sometimes it is difficult to distinguish between these measures, since processions were actually part of some Masses, and sermons usually took place after Mass, and occasionally also in connection with processions. There are numerous examples of sermons held at some stage of a procession. Hence, bishop Federico Pisano Visconti addressed his fellow citizens in his second Rogation Day sermon as follows:

---

95. Jean Delumeau, *La peur en Occident XIVe–XVIIIe siècles* (Paris, 1978), pp. 138–140.

> *'Yesterday we preached on the first loaf, that is, the faith. Today we have to speak shortly of the second, that is hope. The reason for this is that we are somewhat tired having walked the long way to be here at St. Peter the Apostle ad Gradum. Nevertheless, let us pray to blessed Peter to whom God gave specific grace of preaching, so that he might intercede on behalf of us with our Lord Jesus Christ.'*[96]

From this passage it is obvious that Federico was preaching in a station church where the procession ended. Similar passages can be found in other sermons. Thus we have established that sermons, masses and processions were all part of the liturgical setting of a catastrophe situation. They were all parts of a greater whole that could be called catastrophe liturgy. Nevertheless, for the sake of clarity all these measures are treated in separate chapters.

Processions

Processions are among the most fascinating phenomena in medieval history, for they provide us with a glimpse of medieval popular religion as it really was. Masses and sermons were essentially clerical matters, although they are interesting and can be informative about public opinions and practices. Processions, though led by the clergy, were open to anyone. In fact, the presence of the public was required. Without participation of the populace there could not have been a procession. Thus, ordinary Christians were encouraged to express their religious feelings, and to actively participate in a religious ceremony. In sermons and masses their function was to participate only passively.

In the previous chapter we have seen that processions were organised on a yearly basis to obtain protection from God and, most of all, to secure the growing of crops. In addition to Rogation Days, processions and litanies were performed in cases of natural disasters in line with the examples set by Mamertus and Gregory the Great.[97]

Let us now look at some of the other early descriptions of these *processiones causa necessitatis*. In his book about miracles in medieval France, Pierre-André Segal has included a description of an early twelfth-century

---

96. Federico Pisano Visconti. *Sermones*. In letaniis, sermo secundus. Firenze Medicea Laurenziana MS Plut.33.Sin.1, f. 48v. 'Heri diximus de primo pane, scilicet, fidei. Hodie dicere credimus breuiter de secundo, scilicet, spei, quia propter longam uiam quam fecimus ueniendo pedes huc ad beatum Petrum apostolum ad gradum, sumus aliquantulum fatigati, tamen rogemus beatum Petrum cui Deus magnam dedit gratiam predicandi ut ipse pro nobis intercedat ad Dominum Ihesum Christum.' Federico did use the *thema Amice accomoda mihi tres panes* on all of his three Rogation Day sermons. These loaves were compared to three theological virtues, hence the word *loaf* in quotation.
97. Terence Bailey, *The Processions of Sarum and the Western Church*, p. 26; John Harper, *The Forms and Orders of Western Liturgy from the Tenth to the Eighteenth Century*, p. 137.

procession. Sometime in the 1120's an epidemic ravished the area of Soissons. Seeing that the epidemic was taking a very nasty turn, and remembering how Gregory the Great had managed to save the inhabitants of Rome from the plague, the bishop of Soissons decided to organise a procession. He sent messengers to the nearby abbey of Saint-Médard, where the relics of saint Gregory were stored.

These and other relics from the nearby churches were brought to the cathedral, which served as a starting place of the procession. People were exhorted to do penance through fasting, praying and almsgiving. Then the bishop celebrated mass and held a sermon, after which the procession was ready to get started. The participants were required to walk barefooted. The procession circulated the town, forming a sphere of protection, and then moved on to the abbey. If we can believe the chronicler the processions indeed had positive effects. Several of the people that had been affected by the epidemic were miraculously cured, and after the procession, no one died in Soissons while the epidemic lasted.[98]

Catastrophe processions have not only left traces in medieval chronicles, they can also be found in contemporary liturgical Sources. Studying these, one gets a clearer picture of the frequency of such processions. Terence Bailey has analysed the distribution of rogation antiphons in twenty of the oldest French, Aquitanian, German, and Italian gradual manuscripts as well as in the concordances of Visigothic, Milanese, and Old Roman books. These sources are dated between the eighth and the twelfth centuries. Nearly all of these contain special antiphons for asking for rain or for delivery from floods or other natural disasters. The sole exception is found in the oldest of these manuscripts, the Mont-Blandin (near Ghent) Gradual.[99]

On the basis of his analysis, we may conclude that from the ninth century on processions with special prayers against drought, floods, and other natural disasters, were so common that it was customary to add special antiphons for such occasions to graduals. Indeed, Pierre-André Sigal claims that by the early eleventh century the custom of organising catastrophe processions with relics had become well established in the whole of western Christianity.[100]

During the High Middle Ages, the flow of sources describing catastrophe processions is continuous. Interesting examples are the processions organised in Paris in response to the flooding of the Seine and other catastrophes. In 1129–1130, there was an epidemic disease that killed masses of Parisians. The epidemic of 1129–1130 was ended with a procession and the intervention of saint Geneviève. Thereafter it became customary in Paris to carry her relics in procession from the monastery where they were normally kept across the river to the Notre-Dame.[101]

---

98. Pierre-André Segal, *L'homme et le miracle dans la France médiévale*, pp. 158–160.
99. Terence Bailey, *The Processions of Sarum and the Western Church*, pp. 121–129.
100. Pierre-André Segal, *L'homme et le miracle dans la France médiévale*, p. 157.
101. Stephen Wilson, '*Introduction*', in Saints and their Cults. Studies in Religious Sociology, Folklore and History, p. 24; P. Ferret, *L'abbaye de sainte-Geneviève et la congregation de France*. Tome I L'abbaye de sainte-Geneviève (Paris, 1883), pp. 309–310.

This was not the last of saint Geneviève's successive interventions. We know that her relics were again carried *processionaliter* in connection with the serious floods of 1206. After the relics had been brought into the Notre-Dame, and obligatory celebrations had been held the flood ceased. Then the relics of saint Geneviève were carried back to the abbey. Half an hour after the procession had crossed the bridge called le Petit-Pont, it collapsed into the river. Miraculously no one was on the bridge when it collapsed. This was perceived as another example of saint Geneviève's protection of the Parisians.[102]

Eudes de Châteauroux described Parisian processions in his sermon *In processione facta propter inundationem aquarum*. He re-told to his audience the biblical story of how the ark of the covenant was carried across the river Jordan (Joshua 3), and claimed that: '*Similarly, in a time of flood, the bodies of the saints are carried. Unless they refuse to move because of our sins, their merits will cause the flooding to cease when their bodies are carried to the scene.*' From the prayer that finished the sermon we learn that the relics carried in this particular procession included those of saint Geneviève.[103]

By the thirteenth century, the carrying of relics in processions to obtain protection and help in times of disaster was already an age-old custom. We even know that in Italy it was customary to leave some part of the saint's relics outside the main reliquary so that they could be more easily used in processions. When the bones of Saint Ansanus were transferred to Siena in 1107, one of his arms was reserved to be used as a portable relic against fire and lightning.[104]

In addition to the relics proper, miracle working holy pictures were also carried in catastrophe processions. The earliest known and one of the most important protective sacred images was the Hodegetria icon of the Virgin and Child in the church of Santa Maria Maggiore in Rome. According to tradition Saint Luke painted it. Gregory the Great had it carried in the plague procession of 590. After the plague of 590 it was always carried in Roman catastrophe processions, and it became known as *Salus populi Romani*.[105]

Matthew Paris tells in his *Chronica Maiora* that in late July and early August of 1258 there was a great famine and high-level mortality in England.

---

102. A detailed account of this procession and the miracle of Petit-Pont written by anonymous monk of the Sainte-Geneviève abbey is to be found in Paris BN ms. lat. 14859, f. 226r. A French translation is available in *Le rire du prédicateur*. Ed. Albert Lecoy de la Marche. Présentation de Jacques Berlioz (Brepols, 1999), pp. 116–117, 176–177.
103. Eudes de Châteauroux, *Sermo in processione facta propter inundationem aquarum*. Arras Bibl. mun. 137, f. 79v–80r. For the latin text of the sermon, see Appendix 2, A.
104. Diana Webb, *Patrons and Defenders. The Saints in Italian City-states* (London & New York, 1996), pp. 62–63.
105. Steven S. Ostrow, *Art and Spirituality in Counter-Reformation Rome. The Sistine and Pauline Chapels in S. Maria Maggiore* (Cambridge, 1995), pp. 120–124; Michele Bassi, 'La Panaya Odigitria e la Madonna di Constantinopoli', *Arte Christiana* 84 (1996), pp. 4–6.

The previous crop had been a bad one, and the current year's one was late due to continuous bad weather and rains. The poor were dying in numbers and even the rich would have died had not food been brought in from the continent. Having set the scene, Matthew went on to say that in the absence of any human help, people turned to divine aid. The chapter of Saint Albans abbey decided that all the people were to fast and organise a procession. They were to walk devotedly and barefooted to the parish church of Saint Mary. This procession was arranged on the feast of Saint Oswin (20 August) to ensure the help of the Saint. The example of Saint Albans was followed in London. Matthew ends his story by telling that, with the help of St. Mary ('*advocata nostra potentissima*'), the protomartyr Saint Alban, and other saints, the rains soon stopped, or at least became less severe.[106]

Here we have an example of a careful plan for maximising the effects of the procession. The population of the town was exhorted to fast and perform other penitential activities before the actual procession. The time of the procession was fixed on to the feast of Saint Oswin to secure this saint's help. And finally, the procession ended in the church of Saint Mary – *mater misericordiae* and the ultimate intercessor.

The most important point in this case was the timing. Matthew lets us know that it was still early August at latest ('*in confinio Julii et Augusti*') when the famine and rains were harassing people. Then the chapter of Saint Albans decided to arrange a procession. Alas, we do not know the exact date of this decision. However, it is quite likely that it happened sometime in the first half of August. Instead of acting as fast as possible, the chapter decided to opt for a more convenient day, i.e. Saint Oswin's feast. This is a significant detail when one bears in mind that every single day of delay could mean further loss of life. This suggests that the procession was not just a religious formality that was carried out more or less automatically in time of disaster. The monks of Saint Albans believed genuinely in the usefulness of the procession and wanted to make sure that everything was done under the best possible circumstances.

The next example is from late medieval Sweden, to bring some variety in period and geographical area. Here it is not a question of an actual procession, but rather of instructions how one should be arranged. The anonymous writer gave instructions how the realm can be saved from Divine wrath. Unfortunately, we do not know the exact nature of the disaster in question, but judging from the circumstances a plausible guess would be the plague. After an introduction about the sins of the people and the inevitable divine

---

106. Matthaei Parisiensis monachi Sancti Albani *Chronica Maiora*. Ed. Henry Richard Luard. Vol. V A.D. 1248 to A.D. 1259 (London, 1880), p. 710–712. 'Deficiente igitur humana solatio, ad divinum denuo recurritur. Statutum enim fuit in capitulo Sancti Albani, ut per officium archidiaconi, indicto solempni jejunio et communi in populo, per omnes ecclesias ejusdem villae, die sancti Oswaldi, scilicet nonis Augusti congregati cum summa devotione, conventum ad ecclesiam beatae Mariae de Pratis nudis pedibus processionaliter sequerentur, et ibidem Deum et Ejus Matrem humiliter deprecarentur, ut precibus martiris Sui et meritis tunc ibidem praesentis aure et aeris, populo suo miseratus, tribuere dignaretur commoditatem.'

The Salus populi *icon in Santa Maria Maggiore, Rome. From the days of Gregory the Great it was habitually carried in front of Roman processiones causa necessitatis.*

punishment, the preacher moved on to consider what should be done to avoid further punishments and restore God's favour.[107]

In addition to other measures, the preacher suggested a procession, though he never used that word. The processions (the preacher is addressing his instructions to all dioceses of Sweden) were to be organised in connection with votive Masses. For the sake of larger humility and devotion, the par-

---

107. Anonymous, *Sermo*. UUB C 226, f. 101v–102r.

ticipants of the Masses were to walk barefooted around their churches and cemeteries, singing hymns and praying. People were also urged to stay in the church until the end of the celebration if it was only possible without great inconvenience. Furthermore, they were to give alms to the poor according to their economic means. In addition to these measures, the preacher declared that a general fast with bread and water should be observed for seven consecutive Fridays. Those unable to fast were expected to give alms and say prayers instead.[108]

Here we see again that the procession as such was not considered to be sufficient action to placate God. In addition, there had to be other penitential measures to secure a positive outcome. People were to confess their sins and, more interestingly, they were also required to make satisfaction for them. This was done in the form of fasting, almsgiving, and prayers. All these measures are mentioned in any medieval *summa de penitentia*. As visible signs of humility, devotion, and penance the participants of the procession went barefooted.[109]

All these penitential activities were known customs in Sweden from the time of the *Black Death*. There is a 1349 letter from King Magnus Eriksson. It was addressed to the clergy and the laity of the diocese of Linköping. The letter opens with stating that God has sent great pain and sudden death to Sweden to punish the people for their grave sins. It is important to try to placate God and remove His wrath. This can be done, if every Friday all people come to their parish churches barefooted, make a procession around the church with the host, hear mass, and give offerings. Furthermore, everyone was supposed to fast with bread and water on Fridays.[110] Interestingly, there is no sign to prove any awareness of the dangers involved with public meetings in times of plague, though we do not know whether this was due to a lack of knowledge, or to king Magnus' belief that the protective power of processions was great enough to risk further contagions.

King Magnus' letter can be compared with various surviving exhortations to engage in public penance, prayers, and processions from England on the

---

108. Anonymous, *Sermo*. UUB C 226, f. 102v. 'Item omnes pro maiori humiliacione et deuocione nudis pedibus in prescriptis vij missarum diebus cimiteria sua et ecclesias cantando vel orando deuote, non confabulando perlustrant familia Domini domus in omnibus opidis et villis cimiteria et ecclesias....visitet et perlustret loca supradicta. Item vir et uxor expectent benediccionem et finem misse, si commode possint absque dampno. Item sufficientes dent vij elemosinas in quolibet illorum vij dierum vel v vel tres vel unam, prout sufficiunt, quia Deus non pensat muneris quantitatem, sed bonam voluntatem.—Item fiat ieiunium per vii sextas ferias in pane et aqua. Senes et decrepiti et egroti et debiles exempti sunt, quia ad ieiunia non astringantur. Sufficientes ex istis personis dent quinque vel tres elemosinas. Non sufficientes legat tot Pater noster et Aue Maria.'
109. The penitential nature of medieval processions has also been emphasised in the studies of liturgical history, see for example A.G. Martimort, 'Processions, pélerinages, jubilés', in A.G. Martimort, *L'Église en prière. Introduction à la liturgie* (Paris - Tournai - Rome - New York, 1961), p. 636.
110. *Diplomatarium Suecanum* 4515; Yngve Brilioth, *Svenska kyrkans historia*. Andra bandet. *Den senare medeltiden 1274–1521* (Uppsala, 1941), pp. 100–102.

advent of the *Black Death*. Among others, Bishop Edington of Winchester ordered the cathedral chapter to recite special prayers, most notably '*the long litany instituted against pestilences of this kind by the holy fathers.*'[111]

Giovanni Boccaccio describes in the *Introduzione* to the *Giornata prima* of his *Decamerone* the precautions taken by the Florentines against the *Black Death*. He writes:

> 'And there against no wisdom availing nor human foresight...nor yet humble supplications, not once but many times both in ordered processions (in processioni ordinate) and on other wise made unto God by devout persons, – about the coming in of the Spring of the aforesaid year, it began on horrible and miraculous wise to show forth its dolorous effects.'[112]

On the basis of the examples presented above we may safely conclude that processions were used as a means of combating natural disasters from the Early Middle Ages through the Early Modern Age. Furthermore, they were known in all Christendom. There were regional variations, but the basic liturgy remained the same.

There were clear theoretical models for the organisation of the processions, and allowing for small regional variations these models were on the whole carefully respected. Now that we have gone through some examples of actual processions, and established the continuity of this practise, it is time to analyse these processions more closely. The above-presented descriptions are often rather sparse on details. Consequently we shall have to look at other sources to obtain a more precise picture of what exactly happened during a procession.

How was a procession arranged? Sicardus Cremonensis gives a detailed description of processions in his late twelfth-century liturgical guidebook *Mitrale*. At the end of the thirteenth century Guillaume Durand incorporated its passage concerning processions into the enormously popular *Rationale divinorum officiorum*. Durand's book has survived in numerous manuscripts, as well as in numerous early printed editions. Hence Sicardus' procession description found its way all over Europe. Sicardus writes that the marching order was as follows: first came the clergy, then in a determined order the religious, nuns, novices, laymen, widows, and finally married women. He also presents a slightly alternative order. Both these orders however have one thing in common; the members of the clerical stand were always ahead of the lay people.[113]

We have seen that the participants of processions were expected to follow a dress code and certain behavioural habits. These are also mentioned in theoretical works devoted to such matters. Guillaume Durand wrote:

---

111. William J. Dohar, *The Black Death and Pastoral Leadership. The Diocese of Hereford in the Fourteenth Century* (Philadelphia, 1995), pp. 4–5.
112. Giovanni Boccaccio, *The Decameron*. Translated by John Payne (New York, 1930), p. 8. See also Elisabeth Carpentier, *Un ville devant la peste*, p. 168.
113. Sicardus Cremonensis, *Mitrale*, col. 368; Guillaume Durand, *Rationale divinorum officiorum* (Roma, 1477), ff. 235v–236r.

> '*Litanies are also held because of various other reasons, whence Pope Liberius instituted that in the case of war, famine, pestilence or any other such adversities are imminent there should always be litanies so that we can escape such adversities with the aid of supplications, prayers and fasting.*'[114]

Here we are made to understand that the participants of processions were supposed to have the right religious mentality, and that they were also supposed to fast. Nothing is said about going barefooted, but Sicardus Cremonensis noted that, in addition to fasting participants should wear penitential and mourning clothes ('*in poenitentiali et flebili habitu*'), which obviously included going barefooted. Sicardus emphasised also the importance of the participation of all members of the community. He wrote that all people; men, women, and servants should abstain from servile labour and participate in the processions until they were all over. As everyone had sinned, they should all do penance together.[115] It is un-certain if laypeople were always expected to participate. Noël Coulet has proposed that, at least in southern France, the processions were originally a clerical rite, but that there was a progressive growth of lay participation as the processions became a civic issue and were de-clericalised during the fourteenth century.[116] However, most of the evidence seems to confirm that lay participation was indeed ruling custom.

We have seen that relics were often carried in processions. Liturgical books confirm this. Guillaume Durand wrote that the crucifix and reliquaries of saints should be at the head of the procession, so that the war banner of the cross and the prayers of saints might expel demons from the way. In addition to the crucifix, there was supposed to be a banner carried to commemorate the victory of resurrection and the ascension of Christ.[117]

In some areas, it was also customary to carry a banner or statue presenting a dragon. Both Sicardus Cremonensis and Guillaume Durand explained that this dragon symbolised the devil. It was carried before the crucifix and banner of Christ's victory during the two first Rogation Days. During the last day it was carried behind them. The two first rogation days stood for the first two periods of world history, that is, the time before and during the law, whereas the last day stood for the last period, the time of grace. During the first two periods the devil was the ruler of this world, hence his banner was carried first

---

114. Guillaume Durand, *Rationale divinorum officiorum* (Roma, 1477), f. 235v. 'Fiunt etiam letanie propter plures alios causas unde Liberius papa statuit ut pro guerra, pro fame, pro pestilentia et huiusmodi adversitatibus semper litania fiat ut sic ista per supplicationes, orationes et ieiunia effugiamus.'
115. Sicardus Cremonensis, *Mitrale*, col. 369.
116. Noël Coulet, 'Processions, espace urbain, communaute civique', *Cahiers de Fanjeaux* 17 (1982). Liturgie et musique (IXe–XIVe siècle), p. 393.
117. Guillaume Durand, *Rationale divinorum officiorum* (Roma, 1477), f. 235r. 'Ceterum in processione ipsa procedunt crux et capsa reliquiarum sanctorum ut vexilla crucis et orationibus sanctorum demones expellantur.'; See also Sicardus Cremonensis, *Mitrale*, col. 368.

in the procession. Yet in the time of grace Christ had defeated him. After his defeat, the devil no longer was able to harm Christians openly. He could only try to seduce them to fall trough suggestions, and thus his banner was also kept behind the insignia of Christ and saints.[118] The early fifteenth century German preacher Johannes von Werden confirmed these details concerning the carrying of a dragon image as told by Sicardus and Guillaume, and specified that in his time this custom was mainly used in France.[119]

Diana Webb suggests that this curious presentation of a dragon may have signified also the plague that Gregory the Great had hoped to avert from Rome with the original Major Litanies.[120] Some folklorists and historians have proposed that the mocking parade of the dragon the city commemorated its own foundation in a region now purged of all traces of rurality and wild beasts. For those historians Rogation Day processions were essentially an urban phenomenon. According to André Vauchez *'clerical interpretation of the monsters in the procession precluded any other reading, particularly the obvious one which would establish a relationship between the attention paid to the tail of the monster, the organ in which its potency was concentrated, and fertility rites.'*[121] As interesting as these hypothesis are, in lack of confirming evidence it seems to be safer to believe the explanation put forward by Sicardus Cremonensis and Guillaume Durand.

Gary Dickson emphasises that the flagellant movement of 1260 in Perugia was originally a religious revival well within the limits of catholic orthodoxy. In it the old monastic habit of penitential flagellation was fused to penitential processions of the Church.[122] And indeed, the best sources that allow us to understand the real character of orthodox medieval penitential processions are those illuminated manuscripts that present scenes with participants of flagellant movements. Leaving aside the actual flagellation, we may observe

---

118. Guillaume Durand, *Rationale divinorum officiorum* (Roma, 1477), f. 236r. 'Consuevit quoque quedam draco cum cauda longo erecta inflata duobus primis diebus ante crucem et vexilla precedere ultima vero die quasi retro aspiciens cauda vacua atque depressa retro sequitur. Nempe draco iste significat diabolum qui per tria tempora, scilicet, ante legem, sub lege et tempore gratie que per hos tres dies significantur, homines fefellit et fefellere cupit.'; Sicardus Cremonensis, *Mitrale*, col. 368–369. 'In primis duobus erat quasi dominus orbis, ideoque princeps, vel deus mundi vocatur, inde est quod in primis duobus diebus cum inflata cauda precedet; in tempore vero gratie per Christum victus fuit, nec audet regnare patenter, sed homines seducit latenter, inde est quod in ultimo die sequitur cum cauda depressa.'
119. Johannes von Werden, *Dormi secure de sanctis* (Strasbourg, 1493). De rogationibus. Sermo 22, f. G3r. 'Unde in aliquibus ecclesiis et maxime gallicanis consuetudo habentur quod quidam draco cum longa cauda inflata plena palea uel aliquo huiusmodi in letaniis minoribus que fiunt tribus diebus ante ascensionem Domini, duobus primis diebus ante crucem portatur et tertio die cum cauda uacua post crucem defertur. Per quod significatur quod dyabolus in hoc mundo regnauit. In tertio autem die scilicet tempore gratie per passionem Christi de suo regno expulsus est.'
120. Diana Webb, *Patrons and Defenders. The Saints in Italian City-states*, p. 19.
121. André Vauchez, 'Liturgy and the Folk Culture in the *Golden Legend*', pp. 136–137.
122. Gary Dickson, 'The Flagellants of 1260 and the Crusades', *Journal of Medieval History* 15, no. 3 (1989), pp. 231–235.

that such pictures present all the features of penitential processions described by Guillaume Durand and Sicardus Cremonensis. There are barefooted penitents, crucifixes, and presentations of the dragon.[123]

We know from the ordinary Rogation Day processions that they either went around the church from where the procession started and returned there, or that they headed to some other church (known as the station church). In both cases, at the final destiny a Mass was eventually celebrated at the final destination.[124]

It seems that processions *pro causa necessitatis*, might occasionally have ended up at the place where the actual problem was situated, for instance the riverbank in the case of a flood. Nevertheless, in most cases the processions either returned to the place from where they originally started, or ended up in some station church, perhaps a church dedicated to a saint whose aid was summoned.

Sometimes the procession did not move from place A straight to place B, but rather went around the village or town in question "beating the boundaries of the parish". Walking around the walls of town made sense, because all the people of the community were living inside the walls. Thus the procession formed a sphere of protection against the plague, which unlike a flooding river, was something that men could not localise. Choosing a circular route was a common custom in processions performed because of epidemics.[125] The circular route was also used to mark the confines of the community, for a procession was seen as a collective act that defined the identity of the community over against that of neighbouring parishes.[126]

While the procession was on the move, antiphons were sung as well as the litany of the saints, and the seven penitential psalms were (according to the length of the passage). The lay participants were expected to show their contrition in other ways.[127] Here it is not possible to go into details about the exact psalms, hymns and prayers that were used, for even though the general outlook of religious processions remained very much the same in different parts of Europe, there were differences in local customs. Some prayers also

123. For such illuminations see for instance Gary Dickson, 'The Flagellants of 1260 and the Crusades', p. 228; Jean-Noël Biraben, *Les hommes et la peste*, Tome II. Pictures after page 160, pictures three and four; Norman Cohn, *The Pursuit of Millenium* (London, 1957), picture 6(a) facing page 144. In Salisbury, however, the sign of dragon was not used in case of *processiones causa necessitatis*, but only during the normal Rogation Day processions; *Processionale ad usum insignis ac praeclarae ecclesiae Sarum*. Ed. W.G. Henderson (Leeds, 1882), pp. 105.
124. John Harper, *The Forms and Orders of Western Liturgy from the Tenth to the Eighteenth Century*, p. 137; Terence Bailey, *The Processions of Sarum and the Western Church*, pp. 25–26; Guillaume Durand, *Rationale divinorum officiorum* (Roma, 1477), f. 236v. 'Post processionem cantatur missa in aliqua ecclesia.'
125. Pierre-André Segal, *L'homme et le miracle dans la France médiévale*, p. 160; Jean Delumeau, *Rassurer et proteger*, pp. 146–148; Noël Coulet, 'Processions, espace urbain, communaute civique', pp. 389–390.
126. Eamon Duffy, *The Stripping of the Altars. Traditional Religion in England 1400–1580* (New Haven and London, 1992), p. 136.
127. *Processionale ad usum insignis ac praeclarae ecclesiae Sarum*, pp. 105.

differed according to the problem in question.

To underline this variety of possibilities we can take an example. In the processions organised according to the Salisbury use there were different antiphons for different kinds of situations. For instance,

For rain:

> Aridaverunt montes, siccaverunt
> flumina, terra fructum negavit;
> dona nobis pluviam: non peccavit
> terra nec radices montium, sed nos
> peccavimus; parce nobis, Domine,
> dona nobis pluviam.

For the end of rain:

> Inundaverunt aque, Domine, super
> capita nostra; invocavimus nomen
> tuum de lacu novissimo ne avertas
> faciem tuam a singultu nostro.[128]

These antiphons and numerous others which have survived are yet another concrete example of the penitential mood of the processions. The first one emphasises the role of sin as a reason for the drought: '*It is not the land which has sinned, not the mountain valleys; it is we who have sinned; spare us, Lord, grant us rain.*' The second antiphon does not mention sin and penance explicitly, but their presence is obvious, for it says: '*do not avert your face from out tears.*'[129] Tears were considered to be the evident sign of contrition,[130] which was the first step in the penitential process. It was followed by confession and, lastly, satisfaction.

On the basis of the theoretical instructions and actual cases described above we may now present a general picture of medieval catastrophe processions. First of all, it is significant to note that none of the cases presented above were spontaneous actions taken in a state of great religious fervour, but rather well-planned and carefully coordinated operations, generally orchestrated by the ecclesiastical authorities. Sometimes the initiative of organising processions came from lay authorities, as was the case in the above-described case of Swedish King Magnus' letter.

---

128. Both these antiphons are cited in Terence Bailey, *The Processions of Sarum and the Western Church*, pp. 128–129.
129. The translations are by Terence Bailey; *The Processions of Sarum and the Western Church*, pp. 128–129.
130. Here it is enough to think about Mary Magdalen, an archtype of penitential saint. Thirteenth-century preachers took the biblical story of Mary Magdalen bathing Christ's feet with her tears as a sign of true contrition and pain because of one's sins. Thus in general tears were treated as a symbol of contrition; Katherine L. Jansen, 'Mary Magdalen and the Mendicants: The Preaching of Penance in the Late Middle Ages', *Journal of Medieval History* 21 (1995), pp. 5–6 and 11–12.

Let us look more carefully at who were the people on whose initiative these processions were held. According to Nicole Hermann-Mascard, processions, both ordinary feast day and *processiones causa necessitatis*, always needed to have the authorisation of the local bishop.[131] The role and acceptance of the bishop seems to have been important in many processions. In the case of Soissons, we find that the procession was inaugurated by the bishop with the co-operation of the abbot of Saint Médard abbey.

The organisation of the flood processions in Paris was rather similar. High town officials (*prévôt des marchands* and councillors) turned to the bishop and expressed their wish that the relics of saint Geneviève should be carried *processionaliter* to Notre-Dame. Then the issue was discussed in the parliament of Paris. If the decision was taken to arrange a procession, it was up to the bishop to ask the permission of taking out the relics from the abbey of Saint Geneviève. The abbey could, at least theoretically, deny it. In practice, the abbot asked the bishop whether it was a question of extreme necessity. After the bishop had confirmed this, the permission was given. Once all was clear and a time was set, a public sermon was held in the church of Saint-Étienne to inform the Parisians of the approaching event, and how they should prepare themselves for it.[132] The role of bishops was obvious also in above-mentioned processions, and in the public prayers organised in context of the *Black Death*. Not only were the bishops summoning people to participate in processions, but they also encouraged them with special indulgences.[133] The bishop's role in organising catastrophe processions was also decisive in the late fifteenth-century Angers.[134]

In several cases, however, bishops are not mentioned. Matthew Paris provides a good example with the procession organised by the monks of Saint Albans to stop continuous rains. The chapter carried out the planning and organisation, and no doubt, also by the abbot of Saint Albans monastery, though we do not know that for sure. This, of course, does not necessarily mean that the monastery did not ask the permission of the bishop.

In the two mentioned cases from late medieval Sweden, the instructions come from King Magnus Eriksson and the anonymous preacher of the Uppsala manuscript. The king gave orders to arrange penitential processions on his own right. In the case of the anonymous preacher there is no mention of Episcopal permission. The preacher merely said what needed to be done.

---

131. Nicole Hermann-Mascard, *Les reliques des saints. Formation coutumière d'un droit* (Paris, 1975), p. 223.
132. P. Ferret, *L'abbaye de sainte-Geneviève et la congregation de France*, pp. 350–351.
133. William J. Dohar, *The Black Death and Pastoral Leadership*, pp. 4–5.
134. Jean-Michel Matz, 'Le développement tardif d'une religion civique dans une ville épiscopale. Les processions à Angers (v. 1450–v. 1550)', in *La religion civique à l'époque médiévale et moderne (Chrétienté et islam)*. Sous la direction d'André Vauchez. Collection de l'École Francaise de Rome 213 (Roma, 1995), pp. 351–352, 356–357. Jean-Michel Matz, 'Le développement tardif d'une religion civique dans une ville épiscopale. Les processions à Angers (v. 1450–v. 1550)', in *La religion civique à l'époque médiévale et moderne (Chrétienté et islam)*. Sous la direction d'André Vauchez. Collection de l'École Francaise de Rome 213 (Roma, 1995)

As we do not know his identity, we can only speculate with what authority he did so. We only know that the manuscript was quite likely written in the Vadstena monastery in the beginning of the fifteenth century, probably by an anonymous Bridgettine monk. We do not know whether the text itself was written by that monk or was he merely copying another, older text.

When locusts attacked the city of Marseille and its surroundings threatening to cause major damage to crops, the elders of different guilds decided that there should be '*processiones ecclesiarum et intercessiones apud Deum et etiam per universum populum huius civitatis processiones sequentes cum omni contritione.*' Thus the initiative came from the part of the temporal authorities and participation was considered to be duty of every citizen.[135]

Were there any instances of processions held on the popular initiative or as expressions of popular devotion and religious commitment? It has been argued that the 1260 penitential processions of the flagellants in Perugia were inspired by a certain Raniero Fasani a layman and *frate della penanza*.[136] Whether the originator was Raniero Fasani, someone else, or just the public spirit does not really matter. The important thing is that despite the participation by some members of the clergy, the fagellant processions seem to have been essentially a lay movement. Nevertheless, one has to remember that the flagellants were an anomaly, not a common occurrence. Therefore, it is open to discussion whether these flagellant processions can be called processions in the proper sense of the word.

Occasionally, the initiative for organising penitential processions came from the mendicant preachers who saw catastrophes as a signs of God's wrath. A fine example is the pestilence sermon of Franciscan Bernardino de Busti, which is included in his model sermon collection *Rosarium sermonum*. Bernardino asked what a sinner ought to do in the face of pestilence, and said that taking flight was no protection against God's wrath, for His punishment follows sinners everywhere. After dismissing other possibilities, he provided the real solution: '*Go then, and reconcile you with God, and pray to the Blessed Virgin, so that she might intervene on behalf of you and this city.*'

Bernardino described in detail how reconciliation with God is possible, and presented the processions of Gregory the Great as an example to follow. Interestingly in Bernardino's version, Rome was not saved solely because of the penitential activities ordered by Pope Pelagius and carried out by his more famous successor Gregory the Great, but also because of the inter-

---

135. Noël Coulet, 'Dévotions communales: Marseille entre Saint Victor, Saint Lazare et Saint Louis (XIIIe–XVe siècle)', in *La religion civique à l'époque médiévale et moderne (Chrétienté et islam)*. Sous la direction d'André Vauchez. Collection de l'École Francaise de Rome 213 (Roma, 1995), p. 119.
136. André Vauchez, 'Medieval Penitents', in André Vauchez, *The Laity in the Middle Ages. Religious Beliefs and Devotional Practices*. Edited and Introduced by Daniel E. Bornstein (Notre Dame, Indiana, 1993), p. 123; Gary Dickson, 'The Flagellants of 1260 and the Crusades', p. 230.

vention of Holy Virgin.[137] Perhaps he felt it impossible to leave aside the *Mater misericordiae*, when preaching about such mercy. This Mariological emphasis is, of course, something one would expect from fifteenth-century Franciscan. Whether such exhortations, which no doubt were common during catastrophes, played any significant role in deciding the course of action, we cannot know.

Other questions which ought to be asked are whether people actually took an active part in these processions and did they believe in their efficiency. We have already discussed the problems connected with the possibilities of knowing the actual level of participation and the motives of the participants. As said, there are numerous chronicles and other sources, which do not hesitate to describe the multitudes of people who took to the streets with religious fervour. In the Parisian processions of 1412 there were tens of thousands of people. Frequently, the sources neglect to give absolute figures and use only expressions such as '*trés grande people*', '*tant de peuple que sans nombre*' or '*grant multitude*'.[138] One is tempted to think that either the sources are exaggerating or that people were not participating of their own free will, but were rather manipulated or forced to participate. Indeed, we know that during the Parisian processions of 1412 there were instances when attendance was compulsory.[139]

We do not know how typical the processions of 1412 were, yet there seems to have been far more processions than in an average year. However, even if participation was not normally obligatory, it was rather difficult to stay out if the majority joined in. It would have meant turning one's back to one's own community at the moment of danger, and in general, those not participating in the collective religious activities of the parish were perceived as bad neighbours.[140]

When it comes to the real motives and behaviour of participants, there is some fragmentary evidence that they did not always take processions very seriously, at least from the point of view of the clergy. In his Rogation Day sermon Johannes von Werden complained that in his time many people turned processions into a laughing matter and jokes, and that therefore God was punishing the world.[141]

In his second Rogation Day sermon Federico Pisano Visconti refers to the long walk the participants had already gone through, and adds that he is

---

137. Bernardino de Busti OFM, *Rosarium sermonum* (Venezia, 1498). Sermo de pestilentie signis, causis et remediis, f. 257v. 'Quomodo o peccator faceres si ueniret pestilentia? Si enim fugis ab hac ciuitate, Deus faceret corrumpi aera ubi fugies.[...] Vade ergo et reconcili te Deo et precare beatam Uirginem ut interpellat pro te et pro hac ciuitate.'
138. Jacques Chiffoleau, 'Les processions parisiennes de 1412. Analyse d'un rituel flamboyant', *Revue historique* 284 (1990), pp. 64–65.
139. Jacques Chiffoleau, 'Les processions parisiennes de 1412', p. 69.
140. Eamon Duffy, *The Stripping of the Altars*, p. 136.
141. Johannes von Werden, *Dormi secure de tempore* (Augsburg, 1485). In diebus rogationum, f. h5r. 'Sed tamen hodie multi sunt in processionibus istis qui uertunt hoc in risum et iocum, ideo Deus heu plagat mundum.'

therefore going to preach only briefly. He also exhorts his audience to pray to Saint Peter so that he might intervene on behalf of them in such a manner that the preacher may preach as planned in advance, and that the congregation will listen to him.[142] Apparently Federico was not totally convinced of his audience's stamina and good will in listening to a long sermon after the prolonged procession. This implies that not everyone was overtaken by fervent devotion when it came time to go *processionaliter*.

Johannes von Werden and Federico Pisano Visconti both referred to ordinary Rogation Day processions, not to *processiones causa necessitatis*. It is very likely that at the time of danger, the attitudes of the congregations were more appreciative and pious. When the procession was organised to remove an acute problem at hand people were bound to have been better motivated and to have been in the right mood for it.

This can be illustrated by the surviving descriptions of flagellant processions and other late medieval sources. The *Journal d'un bourgeois de Paris* describes processions organised because of the flood and cold weather in June 1427. According to the diary, it was so cold that there was not a single grapevine with flowers. This was, of course, was exceptional for June. The diary states that around that time there were pious processions in Paris and in the neighbouring villages. Men, women, children, young, and old attended these processions, and nearly everyone went barefooted. There were crosses and banners, and the participants were singing hymns and praises for the Lord.[143] This description seems to convey a genuine sense of piety and devotion.

Processions were nearly always organised in line with instructions from ready-made liturgical manuals. They closely followed the liturgy of Rogation days. Usually the initiative came from the higher clergy. Thus, catastrophe processions were not *ad hoc* expressions of popular religious fervour in times of need, but rather carefully planned and organised collective actions performed during a longer lasting catastrophe situation.

---

142. Federico Pisano Visconti, *Sermones*. In letaniis, sermo secundus. Firenze Biblioteca Medicea Laurenziana MS Plut. 33.Sin.1, f. 48v. 'Hodie dicere credimus breuiter de secundo, scilicet, spei, quia propter longam uiam quam fecimus ueniendo pedes huc ad beatum Petrum apostolum ad gradum, sumus aliquantulum fatigati. Tamen rogemus beatum Petrum cui Deus magnam dedit gratiam predicandi ut ipse pro nobis intercedat ad Dominum Ihesum Christum quod ea que breuiter predicare intendimus, sic predicemus et uos sic audiatis…'
143. *Journal d'un Bourgeois de Paris 1405–1449*. Publié par Alexandre Tuetey (Paris, 1881), p. 216. 'Et en ce temps faisoit on processions moult pitieuses et dedens Paris et aux villaiges….tant qu'ilz furent bien de v à vic personnes ou plus, femmes, enfens, vieilz et jeunes, la plus grant partie nudz pies, à croix et bannieres, chantant hymnes et louanges à Dieu nostre sire, pour la pitié de la grant eaue et pour la pitié de la froidure qu'il faisoit, car à ce jour n'eust on point trouvé une vigne en fleur.'

Sermons[144]

Larissa Taylor, who has studied preaching in late medieval and reformation France, writes about catastrophe sermons:

> '*Procession sermons and those given at the condemnation of a heretic were also common. But another "occasion" for preaching had largely disappeared by the end of the Middle Ages—that of charismatic, prophetically preaching during times of catastrophe.*'[145]

However, part of the difficulty with this comment is that it is neither easy nor advisable to draw a rigid distinction between 'procession' sermons and 'catastrophe' sermons. Moreover, while there is much evidence from England of bishop's mandates calling for prayers and processions at times of national or local emergency, the evidence for the sermons that were associated with the processions is much more vague and it is not clear to what extent these sermons always took place.[146] Nevertheless from surviving mandates it is clear that there was a considerable overlap between what is here called the 'catastrophe' sermon and the 'procession' sermon: a sermon about an earthquake is clearly a 'catastrophe' sermon, and a mandate for prayers and processions for the health of the king would clearly generate a 'procession' sermon, but a sermon against a prevailing plague may be a 'catastrophe' and 'procession' sermon combined. This potential confusion makes it even more important to emphasise that catastrophe sermons, as they will be called from here on, were simply a part of the catastrophe liturgy, which was developed on the basis of normal penitential liturgy.

The aim of this chapter is to establish the fact that catastrophe sermons had not disappeared by the end of the Middle Ages, not even in France. On the contrary, it was a fairly common custom to preach in connection with different catastrophes. This is confirmed by two arguments. The first one is that the rather small number of surviving catastrophe sermons does not actually prove that such sermons were uncommon. The second argument is that there are considerably more surviving catastrophe sermons than has previously been thought. They were simply not always written down under that name.

---

144. This chapter is partly based on my article 'Late Medieval Catastrophe Sermons: Vanishing Tradition or Common Custom?', *Medieval Sermon Studies* 45 (2001), pp. 58–74. Some parts of the text have been quoted as such and I would like to thank the editors for kindly allowing me to reproduce them here.
145. Larissa Taylor, *Soldiers of Christ. Preaching in Late Medieval and Reformation France* (Oxford, 1992), p. 19.
146. For references to such mandates in England see Peter Heath, *Church and Realm, 1272–1461* (London, 1992), pp. 107–110, 231, 279–280, and 284.

Actual Catastrophe sermons

We can gather information about catastrophe sermons in two different ways, that is, going through all kinds of secondary evidence, and reading the surviving sermons themselves. There is some research on secondary evidence for catastrophe sermons. Oliver Guyotjeannin, who has analysed the chronicle of Brother Salimbene de Adam, states that Salimbene's descriptions of natural catastrophes are in most cases also meant to serve as material for his fellow preachers. Salimbene gives them suitable *themae* to be used when preaching on such occasions.[147] Even if Salimbene's chronicle does not prove that these *themae* were ever used, it is obvious that Salimbene knew that his fellow Franciscans did indeed preach on such occasions. Otherwise, it would have been pointless to provide them with suitable *themae*.

In this context, it is also important to acknowledge the work of Herve Martin on preaching in late Medieval Northern France. He uses vast numbers of chronicles, as well as fiscal sources concerning payments to preachers. From these sources, he has managed to find information about 1147 sermons between the years 1350 and 1520 (i.e. roughly the period studied by Larissa Taylor). For 262 of these sermons he has been able to identify the context of preaching. Nine of these sermons were held in connection with some natural disaster (calamités, épidémies). On the basis of this evidence he concludes that sermons as a part of "*religion panique*" were fairly common in late medieval France.[148]

It should be remembered that absolute figures are always open to different interpretations, and it is rather hazardous to judge whether these sermons were fairly common or not. However, I am willing to postulate that Martin's evaluation is correct. There are even indications that catastrophe sermons were underrepresented in Martin's sources.

There are similar indirect sources from England. For example, in a study of the registers from the diocese of Lincoln, Alison McHardy has shown that there were fifty-one occasions during the period of the Hundred Years War (1337–1453) when special prayers were requested. Although most of these – thirty-four in total – concerned the war with France, some were against natural disasters such as repeated outbreaks of plague.[149]

It can be argued that catastrophe sermons were different compared to other sermons, because they were held in times of acute crisis. This may sound obvious and trivial, but it is not really. In times of acute disaster, it was not normally a question of hiring a famous preacher to deliver sermons to the people. Catastrophe sermons were meant to urge audiences into immediate

---

147. Oliver Guyotjeannin, *Salimbene de Adam un chroniquer franciscain* (Brepols, 1995), p. 275.
148. Herve Martin, *Le métier de prédicateur à la fin du Moyen Age 1350–1520*, pp. 549–551.
149. Alison K. McHardy, 'Liturgy and Propaganda in the Diocese of Lincoln during the Hundred Years War', *Studies in Church History*, 18 (1982), 215–227, especially p. 216.

contrition and penance, to avert the disaster. Hence, there was no time to seek out the most popular and famous preacher. It was more important to act fast. After all, what might have been lacking in the skill of the preacher was probably compensated for by heat of the moment. Under such dire circumstances, the audience was normally receptive and less interested in ridiculing a clumsy preacher or seeking aesthetic contemplation from the sermon.

This leads us to assume that members of the local clergy most likely delivered catastrophe sermons, unless some famous preacher happened to be conveniently present. It is highly questionable whether local priests or friars were paid for delivering catastrophe sermons. If they were not, then there were no fiscal records produced to tell modern scholars about these sermons.

There are also problems with using chronicles as sources for catastrophe sermons. Many chronicles usually report disasters and other unusual natural phenomena, but, only rarely do they allow us to know what was actually done about the situation. It was quite exceptional for a chronicler to write down that a sermon was given. The absence of such information does not really prove that such a sermon was not delivered. The very fact that such sermons occur at all in chronicles makes it very probable that they were actually fairly common.

It will suffice to present just one concrete example of a late medieval catastrophe sermon described in secondary sources. There was a major flood in Paris in 1426, and the so-called *Journal d'un Bourgeois de Paris* describes that this threat was dealt with by organising a traditional procession to Notre-Dame. A mass was held in honour of the Holy Virgin, and afterwards the Franciscan Friar Jacques de Touraine delivered a very pious sermon to the congregation.[150] Of course, we do not know what *frere* Jacques exactly preached, but it is sensible to assume that his sermon had something to do with the reason of the whole procession.

If we turn to the primary evidence, that is, the surviving medieval catastrophe sermons, we find that the corpus is not particularly large.[151] The corpus of surviving catastrophe sermons appears even smaller, if one compares it to the number of all surviving medieval sermons.[152] This would seem to imply that catastrophe preaching was indeed a vanishing art. However,

---

150. *Journal d'un Bourgeois de Paris 1405–1449*, p. 208. '...et revindrent par le pont Nostre-Dame en la grant eglise; et là chanterent une messe de la Vierge Marie moult devotement, et fist on ung moult piteux sermon, et le fist frere Jacques de Touraine, religieux de l'ordre Saint-Françoys.'
151. See Appendix 1.
152. If one takes into account only those sermons that were included in J.B. Schneyer's *Repertorium der lateinischen Sermones des Mittelalters für die Zeit von 1150–1350*, (Münster, 1969–1990), 11 vols, and in his unpublished archives that cover the years from c. 1350 to 1500, one has a catalogue of 150 000 surviving sermons. Despite the huge work done by Schneyer and his associates, the *Repertorium* is by no means complete. On Schneyer's unpublished materials see George Ferzoco, 'The Schneyer Archive', in *Medieval Sermon Studies* 39 (1997), pp. 6–8.

several questions need to be addressed before any rational conclusion can be drawn concerning the real numbers of catastrophe sermons and their importance. First of all, one might ask whether the number of catastrophe sermons is really as small as it seems.

The surviving medieval sermons have not come down to us according to a random selection taken from all the sermons that once existed, but according to a certain mechanism that preferred certain types of sermons to survive to others. The huge majority of surviving medieval sermons are contained in model sermon collections. These were in most cases organised according to the liturgical calendar. There are four important categories of such model sermon collections, namely *sermones de tempore/dominicales, sermones quadragesimales, sermones de sanctis* and *sermones de communi sanctorum*.[153]

It was difficult to fit catastrophe sermons into these collections, because floods, earthquakes and other such natural disasters obstinately refused to follow the liturgical cycle. Those rare exceptions that we find in these collections are often found in *sermones de communi sanctorum* collections, which frequently included sermons for different occasions, such as visitations, chapters, and the consecration of new churches.

All these arguments taken together make it obvious that the possibility for catastrophe sermons to make it into a model sermon collection, or to be recorded in fiscal sources and chronicles was rather small. Therefore one cannot argue that since very few medieval catastrophe sermons survive, such sermons were preached only rarely. In fact, all things considered, it seems reasonable to assume that such sermons were in reality rather common.

Two additional facts support this conclusion. The first one is that the few surviving sermons come from different centuries and from different regions of Europe. Eudes de Châteauroux preached in thirteenth-century France and Italy, whereas Bernardino da Busti wrote his sermons in Italy during the last quarter of the fifteenth century. We have even one example from late fourteenth- or early fifteenth-century Sweden. This seems to point to a custom that was spread throughout Christendom.

Secondly, we know that the habit of delivering catastrophe sermons outlived the Middle Ages. They are mentioned in sources concerning the Great Lisbon earthquake of 1755 and on many other occasions.[154] If the custom of holding catastrophe sermons had vanished, or become very uncommon during the later Middle Ages, it must have been re-invented at the beginning of the early modern period. I do not find this very plausible. It is far more logical to assume that the custom never died out.

---

153. Louis-Jacques Bataillon, 'Approaches to the Study of Medieval Sermons', *Leeds Studies in English*, new series 11, p. 20. Reprinted in L-J. Bataillon, *La prédication au XIIIe siècle en France et Italie*, I, pp. 19–35.
154. T.D. Kendrick, *The Lisbon Earthquake* (London, 1956), pp. 78–79. See also Emanuela Guidoboni, 'Riti di calamite: terremoti a Ferrara nel 1570–1574', *Quaderni storici* 55 (1984), pp. 112–120.

Now that we have established that the surviving evidence does not allow us to measure the frequency of catastrophe preaching, we may move on to another argument; one that supports the theory that catastrophe preaching was common.

Rogation Day Sermons

It has been argued that there is only a very small number of surviving catastrophe sermons. This is correct only if we count the sermons that are clearly titled as catastrophe sermons. However, this situation changes dramatically if we take into account other sermons that could have been used as catastrophe sermons. My hypothesis is that Rogation Day sermons were often written in such a manner, so that in case of an emergency they could easily be converted into catastrophe sermons. Systematic comparison between Rogation Day sermons and catastrophe sermons points in this direction.[155] Before examining this evidence in some detail, it is worthwhile to take a look at Rogation Day sermons on a more general level, for they are interesting to this study in their own right.

These sermons were meant to be delivered during the three Rogation Days before Ascension Day. Generally speaking, most of these sermons concentrated on two major issues, namely prayer and confession. People were instructed how to pray, where and when they were to do it and, most of all, what constituted the righteous and suitable subjects of prayer. A good example is Konrad Holtnicker's second Rogation Day sermon. It has a threefold division that is built around praying. The first part focuses on the true needs of the people as opposed to those things they falsely imagine to be their needs, such as temporal goods. The second part of the division is about how one should pray. The final part deals with the generosity of God who will surely concede anything to those who pray righteously.[156] This pattern in treating prayer is repeated with minor changes in numerous Rogation Day sermons.

Sometimes these sermons deal in a very detailed manner with the matter of confession. A good example is Konrad Holtnicker's seventh sermon *in rogationibus*. It very closely resembles a manual for penitents. It has a fourfold division. The first part tells audiences that they are supposed to confess to learned priests, who have the necessary skill to handle the sacrament. Konrad does not forget to say that in case of extreme necessity, that is, mortal danger, it is also possible to confess to a layman or, if there is not even a layman

---

155. Rogation Day sermons are marked with the signum T 34 in Schneyer's *Repertorium*. Those that are actually quoted in this book are indicated in the Sources section, but in addition to them I have read dozens of others that were not essentially different from the cases chosen to be presented as examples.

156. Konrad Holtnicker, *Sermones de tempore*. In rogationibus, sermo secundus. BAV. MS. Vat. Burghes. 180, ff. 88r–v. 'Sed circa petitionem orationem nostrarum attendere debemus nostram necessitatem, petitionis congruitatem, diuinam largitatem.'

available, directly to the supreme penitentiary, that is, God.

In the second part of the division, Konrad tells his audience that they should confess their own sins, not those of others. Furthermore, they should confess all their sins, even the venial ones. This must be done either according to the sins against the Ten Commandments, or according to the Seven Capital Sins and their progenies. The third part of the division informs audiences that they must confess while they are still in this world, for in the other world it will be too late. Conrad exhorts them to confess four times in a year. Echoing the famous 21st canon of the IV Lateran Council, he also reminds his audiences, that even if they are not willing to confess four times a year, they are nevertheless obliged to do so at least once a year. The fourth part of the sermon is about how one should confess, and there Conrad refers his readers to another sermon where he already had considered this subject.[157]

In many sermons, the topic of confession was neatly bridged together with the topic of praying by stating that God overlooks the prayers of sinners. The secret of effective prayer therefore lies in confessing ones sins before praying. In fact, confession can be seen as part of the proper praying process. Bertrand de Tour wrote in his sermon:

> '*Sins are impediments to a worthy prayer. God rejects the prayers of the sinner for they are not worthy of being heard. Hence God says to sinners in Isaiah 1: "And when you stretch forth your hands, I will turn away my eyes from you: and when you multiply prayer, I will not hear. For your hands are full of blood", that is, sin.*'

He gave the solution in the next passage:

> '*If a sinner wants to pray to God in a worthy manner he has to leave behind his sins and turn to God. No one can leave sins and turn to God unless through sacramental penance, one part of which is true conversion, which comes after true contrition and before real satisfaction of one's sins. Such a confessions therefore comes before worthy prayer, and if it does not, then the prayer is not worthy to be heard. Therefore let us confess one to another, as it is presented in above quoted epistle.*'[158]

---

157. Konrad Holtnicker, *Sermones de tempore*. In rogationibus, sermo septimus. BAV. MS. Vat. Burghes. 180, ff. 91r–v.
158. Bertrand de Tour, *Sermones de tempore de epistolis*. In rogationibus, sermo secundus. BAV. MS. Vat.lat. 1242, ff. 226r–v. 'Igitur peccata sunt impeditiva digne orationis, repellitur enim a Deo peccatorum oratio quia non est exauditione digna. Unde dicit Dominus peccatoribus Ysa. 1: "Cum extenditis manus uestras, auertam oculos meos a uobis et cum multiplicaueritis orationem, non exaudiam manus enim uestre sanguine plene sunt", id est, peccato.'; 'Si enim peccator uult digne orare Deum oportet ipsum peccata relinquire et conuerti ad Dominum. Peccatum autem non relinquitur, nec ad Deum quis conuertitur nisi per sacramentalem penitentiam cuius una pars est uera conuersio que supponit ueram contritionem et proponit ueram satisfactionem. Talis ergo confessio precedit dignam orationem, nisi non precedat, non est exauditione digna. Ergo confitemini alterutrum sicut supra in epistola est exposita.'

This way of connecting prayer and confession with the passage from the first chapter of Isaiah seems to be one of the common topoi of Rogation Day sermons. It can also be found in sermons of Conrad's fellow Franciscan Jean Rigaud,[159] and in the late medieval sermon collection of Johannes Herolt.[160]

Unlike that of Konrad Holtnicker, Bertrand de Tour's sermon does not read like a manual for sinners going to confession. Nevertheless, he does not fail to mention the three parts of the confessional process, namely contrition, confession and satisfaction. The emphasis on the sacrament was probably meant to encourage the audience to confess more often and more willingly, at least that is the impression one gets when reading large numbers of Rogation Day sermons.

Now that we have given a short description of the nature and functions of Rogation Day sermons, it is time to proceed with the stated hypothesis, namely that Rogation Day sermons were easily converted into catastrophe sermons. In fact, I am willing to hazard a guess that this was not just a theoretical possibility, but also the prevailing practise. This hypothesis is nearly impossible to prove categorically, but there are six arguments to justify such an assumption.

First of all, we may notice that the processions that were organised during the Rogation time were originally intended to protect people against natural disasters. As we have seen, these same litanies and processions were often adapted and used in connection with some major catastrophe. If the liturgy of Rogation time was easily converted to be used in case of natural cataclysms, then why not also Rogation time sermons, which, as we have seen, were often an integral part of that liturgy. Even if the sermons were not necessarily part of the liturgy, they nevertheless reflected and reinforced the same theological ideas as Rogation time liturgy.

The second argument is that in Rogation Day sermons preachers often dealt with natural disasters when reminding their audiences of the origins of the Litanies. It was customary to tell stories of the plague in Gregory the Great's Rome and different catastrophes in Mamertus' Vienne. Normally this was done at the beginning of the sermon to establish the historical background and the theological justification for the Litanies. When doing this, the preachers, accidentally or intentionally, influenced their audiences to deduce that what they were actually praying for God's protection against catastrophes, such as

---

159. Jean Rigaud, *Sermones de tempore*. In rogationibus, sermo secundus. BAV. MS. Vat.lat. 957, ff. 254r. 'Quia hiis diebus rogationum fiunt processiones et processiones sunt ordinate propter orationes et orationes non exaudientur nisi orantium fuerint pure mentes sicut dicitur Ysa. primo: "Cum multiplicaueritis orationes uestras non exaudiam, manus enim uestre sanguine plene sunt, lauamini mundi estote."'

160. Johannes Herolt, *Sermones discipuli de tempore* (Strasbourg, 1494). Sermo 64, in rogationibus, f. 236r. 'Et sic per oppositionem sunt quinque impedimenta quare oratio nostra non exaudiatur. Primum impedimentum orationis est peccatum orantis Isa. prima: "Cum multiplicaueritis oraciones uestras non exaudiam uos quia manus uestre sanguine plene sunt."'

the Plague in Rome in Gregory's time or the earthquakes in Mamertus' time.

A good example of sermons expounding the history of the Litanies is the first Rogation Day sermon by Federico Visconti Pisano, archbishop of Florence. It was delivered in vernacular sometime during his episcopate (1254–1277). Federico explains carefully all the details connected with the invention of Rogation Days by Gregory the Great and Mamertus of Vienne. Federico Visconti's sermon is very rare as it is one of the few Rogation Day sermons which we know for sure were actually delivered, not only written to serve as a model sermons.[161]

Federico was by no means the only preacher to tell the history of the Rogation Day Litanies. The nearly contemporary Franciscan preacher and theologian Bertrand de Tour expounded the same history in his first sermon *In rogationibus*.[162] Johannes Herolt explained in his sermon's introductory part why Rogation Days were celebrated by the Church, and what should be prayed for. He explained that there are three things that people ought to ask from God and His saints. Firstly, that God would end wars, which were especially common during spring, that is, at the time of the Rogation Days. Secondly, that He protects and multiplies the crops. Thirdly that He makes people ready and able to receive the Holy Spirit.[163] Here we can reason that protecting the fields would imply keeping floods, draughts and storms away. With another fifteenth century preacher known as Meffreth we get even more explicit information. He wrote that on Rogation Days the Church asks protection against epidemics, conservation of crops and rains to help them grow.[164]

---

161. Federico Visconti Pisano, *Sermones*. In letaniis ante ascensionem sermo primus. Firenze Biblioteca Laurenziana MS. Plut. 33.sin.1, ff. 47v–48r. The actual story is very similar to that told by Sicardus de Cremona in his *Mithrale* and before him by Iohannes Beleth in his *Summa de ecclesiasticis officiis*. It is quite likely that Federico used it as his source when explaining the history and meaning of Rogation Day processions to his audience.
162. Bertrand de Tour OFM, *Sermones de tempore de epistolis*. In rogationibus, sermo primus. BAV MS. Vat. Lat. 1042, 225r. 'Legimus in gestis romanorum pontificum quod beatus papa Gregorius contra pestem inquinariam que quodam pascali tempore nimis aflixit romanum populum instituit Rome letaniam, id est, rogationem seu processionem rogatoriam in festo sancti Marci euangeliste cum sollempni ieiunio perpetuis temporibus celebrari. In cronicis et autenticis legimus quod beatus Mamertus Uienensis episcopus contra pestes multiplices, que tunc multipliciter galliarum pertinebat populum, instituit tres diebus ante ascensionem Deo letanias, id est, processiones rogatorias cum sollempni ieiunio per omnes gallicanas ecclesias celebrari.'
163. Johannes Herolt, *Sermones discipuli de tempore* (Strasbourg, 1494). Sermo 64, in rogationibus, f. 233v–234r. 'Primo ut Deus bella sedat que in uere frequentius fiunt, secundo ut teneres fructus conservet et multiplicat, tercio ut ad redemptionem Spiritus Sancti abilitemur.'
164. Meffreth, *Hortulus regine* (sine loco, sine anno, BAV signum Inc. Barbe-rini. BBB.V.10), In diebus rogationum, f. hh3r. '...et principaliter quando pro totius ecclesie utilitate et auersione pestium et conseruatione frugum et datione pluuiarum postulamus.'

Johannes von Werden wrote that on Rogation Days we ought to pray for four things: remissions of our sins, divine grace, an eternal home in heaven, and lastly liberation from our tribulations. According to Johannes, these tribulations are hunger, pestilence, and wars. Then he continued with a very detailed description of the origins of the Litanies.[165] These specifications of just what people were actually supposed to pray for during the Litanies make it rather difficult to draw a line between Rogation Day sermons and catastrophe sermons. Both seem to be first and foremost concerned with natural disasters.

The third argument is that both sermon types use occasionally the same biblical passages as *themae*. This is significant because the *themae* for different liturgical times and different occasions overlapped rarely if ever. When we find that the same *themae* were used for both types of sermons, we can safely assume that these sermons were essentially interchangeable.

The *themae* for preaching were normally taken from the Gospel or Epistle readings of that particular Sunday. Gospel readings were often preferred over Epistle readings and the Rogation Day sermons are no exception to this rule. However, the choice of the *themae* in Rogation Day sermons is somewhat exceptional. Most preachers used the *thema* '*Petite et accipietis*' (John 16:24), whereas the actual reading of the day would have been Luke's version of the same speech of Jesus (Luke 11:5–13). The probable reason for this change is that John's laconic quotation was rhetorically more efficient than Luke's reading '*Petite et dabitur vobis*'. Even if the '*Petite et accipietis*' was by far the most common choice, there were also other possible *themae*. Some preachers, for instance, chose to use the theme '*Amice accomoda mihi tres panes*'.

In the case of Rogation Day sermons, we have a fairly large corpus of sermons using the Epistle reading as a source for the *thema*. The Epistle of the day was James 5:16–21 and the *themae* most frequently taken from it were '*Confitemini alterutrum peccata vestra*' and '*Elias oravit et caelum dedit pluviam*'.

If we look at the *themae* used in the few surviving catastrophe sermons, we find that some of the Rogation Day sermon *themae* were also used for catastrophe sermons. The Epistle text '*Elias oravit et caelum dedit pluviam*' is used in three out of thirty surviving catastrophe sermons. These are Nicolas de Gorran's sermon *Ad impetrandam pluviam*, Jacques de Lausanne's sermon *Ad impetrandam pluviam*, and Giovanni Regina da Napoli's sermon *In processione pro pluvia impetranda*.

Furthermore, two other catastrophe sermons use a variation of this *themae* taken from the same Epistle text, that is, sermons of Guillelmus de Sequavilla and Nicolas de Gorran's sermon *Ad impetrandam serenitatem*. If one looks

---

165. Johannes von Werden, *Dormi secure de tempore* (Augsburg, 1485). In diebus rogationum, f. h3v–h5r. 'Quarto dico quod debemus petere pro tribulationum liberatione, quia ecclesia diuersimode tribulatur nunc per famem, nun per pestilentiam, nunc per guerras.'

at these five sermons there are two interesting things to notice. The first is that Dominican friars wrote them all. Whether this is just a co-incidence or has some significance is impossible to establish here. It is, nevertheless, interesting. Another striking feature, far more relevant for the present purpose, is that all these sermons deal with the problems posed by drought or heavy rains.

This connection with only one category of natural disasters, that is, those involving water, leads one to wonder whether the fact that these sermons use common *themae* with Rogation Day sermons could be merely a co-incidence. James' letter simply happens to be a very good passage for anyone hunting for a suitable *thema* when preaching on floods or droughts. This passage would inevitably come up if a preacher were looking for the word *pluvia* in a biblical concordance. Even if we reject the possibility of mere co-incidence, it is only reasonable to point out that five sermons is hardly conclusive evidence.

The fourth argument to support the hypothesis that the Rogation Day sermons could have been used as catastrophe sermons is that the most important issues dealt with in these two genres of sermons are the same. Both strongly emphasise the meaning of penance and prayer. Sometimes the similarities are so striking that without seeing the title of the sermon it would be very hard to tell which sermon is which.

In his first sermon *Ad impetrandam pluviam*, the Dominican preacher Nicolas de Gorran writes that drought is a punishment from God brought upon us by our sins. Nicolas quotes Jeremiah to emphasise this relationship between sin and drought: '*Our sins have withholden good things from us.*'[166] The only way to find liberation from this punishment is to reject sin and beg God for mercy. This is achieved through penance and prayer. Even the *thema* of the sermon ('*If heaven shall be shut up, and there shall be no rain, because of their sins, and they, praying in this place, shall do penance to thy name, and shall be converted from their sins, by occasion of their afflictions*, 3 Kings 8:35') reflects this emphasis on penance and prayer.

Another Dominican, Giovanni Regina da Napoli, wrote that the roots of trees and plants could not draw water from dry soil. Therefore they cannot flourish if the earth is not irrigated. Such is also the case with sinners. They lack the humidity of Divine grace, and therefore, as an external sign of this, God will not let the rains fall upon them. The solution to the problem of drought was penance. Once the people have purified themselves from their sins, they are recommended to turn to God, to pray humbly for rain, and they will surely receive it. Giovanni rounds up his argument by quoting Mark 11:24: '*Therefore I say to you, all things, whatsoever you ask when ye pray, believe that you shall receive; and they shall come unto you.*'[167]

---

166. Jeremias 6:25.
167. Giovanni Regina da Napoli, *Sermones varii*. In processione pro pluuia impetranda. Napoli, Biblioteca Nazionale, VIII.Aa.11, ff. 70v–r. 'Humorem non autem possunt attrahere a terra nisi humectata per pluuiam uel aliam aquam, ergo nisi terra humectetur terre nascentia non possunt producere fructus...Sed nota quod sicut in febricante siccitas lingue est signum siccitatis interioris et caloris febrilis ergo et qua

These two sermons follow the typical pattern of Rogation Day sermons. Proof of this similarity can be obtained by comparing these two sermons with the *Sermo in rogationibus* by the contemporary fellow Dominican Aldobrandino da Toscanella. He used the theme *Confitemini alterutrum peccata vestra*, and divided it as follows:

> '*The most important reason for the deprivation of spiritual and temporal goods is sin. Jeremiah 5: "Our sins have withholden good things", the good in its spiritual category, and the good in the sense of abundance of temporal goods. Take heed that saint James with these words exhorts us principally to three things. Firstly to the hatred of sin through confession: "Confess your sins one to another."..... Secondly he exhorts us to gain good things through prayer: "Pray one for another, that you may be saved.".... Thirdly he exhorts us to accumulate merits...*'[168]

The similarities in approach between these three sermons are obvious. In fact, the only significant difference between Nicolas de Gorran's or Giovanni Regina da Napoli's sermons and that of Aldobrandino da Toscanella, or of any other typical Rogation Day sermon, is that in catastrophe sermons the threat is named (the lack of rain). It would have been easy to use Aldobrandino da Toscanella's sermon with slight modifications as a catastrophe sermon.

The fifth argument is that in addition to the central issues of prayer and penance, there are also similarities in numerous less important details, such as biblical quotations used as arguments and other literary topoi. Indeed, one such similarity can be seen in the above presented examples. Both Nicolas de Gorran's sermon *Ad impetrandam pluviam* and Aldobrandino da Toscanella's Rogation Day sermon quote the same passage of Jeremiah (5:25) when they argue that sin is the cause of temporal misfortunes. Pelbartus of Themeswar repeats this quotation in his Rogation Day sermon as well.[169]

---

curata per medicinam cessat et siccitas lingue, sic carentia pluuie exterioris est sepe propter carentiam humoris interioris diuine gracie et calorem inordinatum concupiscentie mundalium iuxta illud Ier. 3a: "Poluisti terram in fornicationibus tuis quam ob rem prohibite sunt scille pluuiarum et serotinus ymber non fuit." Ergo curatio per penitenciam sequitus pluuia temporalis si expedit et nostre saluti spirituali quam principalius debemus appetere.'; 'Marcus 11: "Omnia quecumque orantes petitis credite quia accipietis et eueniunt uobis." Ergo si a Deo petimus pluuiam per oracionem deuotam et saluti nostre expedit habere ipsam, ipsam ut causa prima, et celum ut causa secunda dabit nobis ipsam ...'

168. Aldobrandino da Toscanella OP, *Sermones de tempore*. In rogationibus. Biblioteca Apostolica Vaticana, MS Ottob.lat. 557, ff. 200v–201r. 'Confitemini alterutrum peccata uestra etc. Ja. 5. Principalis causa priuationis bonorum spiritualium et temporalium est peccatum. Ier. 5: "Peccata nostra prohibuerunt bonum", bonum in qua spirituale est genera, bonum temporale quod est terrenorum habundantia. Nota beatus Jacobus in uerbis prepositis ad tria principaliter nos hortatur. Primo ad peccatorum detestationem per confessionem quia "confitemini alterutrum peccata uestra.".... Secundo hortatur nos ad bonorum impetrationem per orationem quia "orate pro inuicem ut saluemini."...Tertio hortatur nos ad meritorum cumulationem...'

Another example of such a com-mon topos is the use of Jeremiah 3:2–3: '*And thou hast polluted the land with thy fornications and with thy wickedness. Therefore, the showers were withholden, and there was no lateward rain.*' Bertrand de Tour uses it in his second Rogation Day sermon when underlining the importance of penance to avoid earthly punish-ments from God.[170] Giovanni Regina da Napoli uses the very same passage in his sermon *In processione pro pluuia impetran-da*.[171] The only difference is that where Bertrand is discussing tem-poral misfortunes brought about by sin in general, Giovanni is concen-trating on one spe-cific form of catastrophe – hard rains.

A third example is the ano-nymous sermon *Pro serenitate uel sanitate* in MS Vat. Burghes. 138. The preacher is expounding the three conditions that need to be fulfilled so that people can ask favours from God without fear. The first condition is that the petitioner should be worthy to pray to God, for '*God is not in the habit of listening to others, John 9: "We knoth that God doth not hear sinners."*'[172] The Franciscan friar Nicolaus de Aquaevilla refers to the same passage in John in his Rogation Day sermon. Nicolaus is dealing with exactly the same subject. He presents three reasons why God does not always hear our prayers:

> '*It should be noted that God does not always listen to us nor does He always give to us what we ask. There are three reasons for this. The first is the indignity of the petitioner, because man in mortal sin does not deserve that God hears his prayers, hence John 20 says about the blind man whom the Lord gave sight and who, having got his sight back said angrily* [that is, being angry to the Pharisees who were interrogating him] *about Jesus: "We knoth that God doth not hear sinners."*'[173]

---

169. Pelbartus de Themeswar, *Sermones Pomerii de tempore* (Hagenauw, 1501), In rogationibus, sermo quartus, f. Y3v.
170. Bertrand de Tour, *Sermones de tempore de epistulis*. In rogationibus, sermo secundus. BAV. Vat.lat. 1242, f. 226r. 'Propter peccata enim prohibentur stille pluuiarum, scilicet, materialium Iere quarto (in fact 3:3).'
171. Giovanni Regina da Napoli, *Sermones varii*. In processione pro pluuia impetranda. Napoli Biblioteca Nazionale MS. VIII.Aa.11, f. 70v. 'sic carentie pluuie exterioris est sepe propter carentiam humoris interioris diuine gracie et calorem inordinatum concupiscentie mundalium iuxta illud Ier. 3a: "Poluisti terram in fornicationibus tuis quam ob rem prohibite sunt scille pluuiarum et scrotinus ymber non fuit."'
172. Anonymous, *Pro serenitate uel sanitate*. BAV. MS Burghes. 138, f. 233v. 'Prima dico dat petendi audaciam et hoc cum dicit "Petite" circa quod sciendum quod audaciter potest aliquis petere si petat iustus, hoc est si sit ex parte petentis dignitas, non enim consueuit Dominus alios exaudire, Jo. 20 [pro 9]: 'Scimus quia peccatores Deus non audit.''' According to Annelise Mayer's catalogue of Burghesian manuscripts this manuscript is from the fourteenth century and the writer is 'clericus Tolosanae'.
173. Nicolaus de Aquaevilla OFM, *Sermones de sanctis*. In rogationibus. BAV. MS Vat. lat. 1251, f. 194v. 'Sed notandum quod Dominus non exaudit nos semper nec dat nobis quod petimus et hoc propter tria. Primum est propter petentis indignitatem quia homo in mortali peccato existens non est dignus ut Dominus orationem suam inaudiat unde Jo. 20 [pro 9] dicit Dominus ille cecus illuminatus et iratus quam Dominus illuminauit: "Scimus quod Dominus, scilicet, in quantum peccatores non audit."'

Nicolaus and the anonymous preacher of the *Pro serenitate uel sanitate* were both writing of what could be called *The three obstacles of prayer* topos. It was very common in Rogation Day sermons. In thirteenth-century sermons, this topos is normally repeated in its original form, whereas in late medieval sermons one finds that the number of obstacles to prayer varies from one sermon to another, yet the original three were always included. The quotation of John 9:31 seems to have been an essential part of this topos. In addition to the sermon of Nicolaus de Aquaevilla, we find it included in Rogation Day sermons of Johannes Herolt and Pelbartus of Themeswar.[174]

Finally, there is a quotation from Isaiah. Bernardino Tomitano da Feltre writes in his sermon *De flagellis Dei et que sunt signa* that God allows some time for sinners to mend their ways, but once they have become evil enough, He does not want to listen to them anymore. Here Bernardino quotes Isaiah 1:15: '*And when you multiply prayer, I will not hear.*'[175] The same passage can be found in numerous Rogation Day sermons.[176]

The sixth, and final, argument is based upon two interesting sermons that establish direct and explicit connections between Rogation Day sermons and catastrophe sermons. The first one is the third Rogation Day sermon of the friar minor Jean Rigaud. It has the following title description: '*Theme from the same day of saint Mark during Rogation time. It can be applied*

---

174. Of the thirteenth-century sermons a good example is that of Franciscan Pierre de saint Benôit; *Sermones de tempore*. BAV. MS Vat.lat. 1253, f. 205v. 'Quoniam autem uerbum accipiendum est non uulgariter sed cum conditionibus debitis, uidendum est qualiter petitio nostra debet fieri ut sit exaudibilis. Scimus enim quid dixit "petites et non accipietis eo quod male petatis", Ja. 10. Ideo obseruandum sunt conditiones ex parte petentis, ex parte petitionis, ex parte modi petendi. Nam ex parte eius a quo petitur nullus potest esse defectus.' Of the Late medieval sermons Johannes Herolt names five obstacles of the prayer: 'Et sic per oppositam sunt quinque impedimenta quare oratio nostra non exaudiatur. Primum impedimentum orationis est peccatum orantis Isa. Primum: "Cum multiplicaveritis oraciones uestras non exaudiam uos quia manus uestre sanguine plene sunt." Ps.: "Si inquitates aspexi in corde meo non exaudiet." Joh. 9: "Scimus quod non exaudiet Deus peccatores."…Secundum impedimentum orationis est quando homo cum proposito non attente orat… Tercium quando petitur quod non est expeditus petenti… Quartus quando quis cum hesitatione petit et sic nichil impetrat… Quintus defectus perseverantie in orationis'; Johannes Herolt, Sermones de tempore Discipulus. BAV. Inc. Ross. 1273–1274. Sine anno, sine loco, ff. 236r–237v. Pelbartus de Themeswar produces no less than seven of them (1. orantis culpa propria, 2. Rogatorum indecentia, 3. Affectus negligentia, 4. Dubietatis diffidentia, 5. Ingratitudinis offensa, 6. Imperseverantia, 7. Aliorum pro quibus oratur malitia); Pelbartus de Themeswar, *Sermones Pomerii de tempore* (Hagenauw 1501), In rogationibus, sermo quartus, f. Y3v. 'Item Joh. 9: "Scimus quod Deus peccatores non exaudit."'
175. *Sermoni del Beato Bernardino Tomitano da Feltre*. A cura di P. Carlo Varischi da Milano. Tomo I (Milano, 1964), p. 279.
176. For example: Johannes Herolt, Sermones de tempore Discipulus. BAV. Inc. Ross. 1273–1274. Sine anno, sine loco, ff. 236r.; Pelbartus de Themeswar, *Sermones Pomerii de tempore* (Hagenauw, 1501), In rogationibus, sermo quartus, f. Y3v. 'Item Ysa. 1: "Cum multiplicaueritis orationem non exaudiam."'

whenever there is a procession for obtaining rain, or serenity, or because of any other tribulation.'[177]

The other sermon is the exact mirror image of Jean Rigaud's sermon. It is a catastrophe sermon delivered on Saint Mark's Day, that is, in connection with Rogation time. The Observant Franciscan friar Bernardino Tomitano da Feltre preached this sermon in the city of Pavia in 1493. The title of this sermon is *Feria quinta post secundam dominicam post pasca in die sancti Marci. De peste*. It was probably preached in connection with the Major Litany processions, for the first lines of the sermon include the common explanation why Litanies are organised in that time of the year.[178]

One must remember that thus far these two sermons are the only known cases that explicitly makes the connection between these two genres of sermons, although, there may very well be more in the numerous uncharted medieval sermon manuscripts. Therefore, considering all the evidence presented, it is plausible to assume that it was customary to use model sermons for Rogation Days also for natural disasters.

This would mean that the alleged disappearance of catastrophe sermons during the Late Middle Ages cannot be taken at face value. Some sources do provide information about catastrophe sermons that were actually held, and some catastrophe sermons have survived in written form. More importantly, however, in the form of Rogation Day sermons there was a nearly endless store of potential catastrophe sermons to be used in case of need. One might object that all this does not prove that these sermons were actually used for this purpose. There is not any positive evidence to prove the opposite. Considering the fact that other traditional means of reacting to catastrophes (i.e. specific masses, processions and prayers to saints) were used all the time, it seems more than plausible to assume that so were Rogation Day sermons. This becomes even more plausible if one takes into account that catastrophe sermons were widely used during the early modern age. It would be more than odd, if they had disappeared for two hundred years only to reappear with the dawn of the modern period.

Putting together the actual surviving catastrophe sermons and Rogation Day sermons in *de tempore* collections, we get a complete picture of the character of catastrophe sermons, and how often they were used. According to David d'Avray, there were two kinds of preaching. First of all there was revivalist preaching, designed to have an immediate effect on feelings and action. The actual message of these sermons was not the most important point; it was to produce desirable effect on the audience. Then there were

---

177. Jean Rigaud, *Sermones de tempore*. In rogationibus, sermo tertius. BAV. MS Vat. lat. 957, f. 255r. 'Thema de eodem die Marcis in rogationibus. Et potest applicari quandoque fit processio pro pluuiam uel serenitatem uel pro quocumque alia tribulatione.'
178. Bernardino Tomitano da Feltre OFM obs., Sermo in feria quinta post secundam dominicam post pasca in die sancti Marci. De peste. In *Sermoni del Beato Bernardino Tomitano da Feltre*. Tomo II. A cura di P. Carlo Varischi da Milano (Milano, 1964), pp. 265–273.

the model sermons that were repeated year in year out. They had a long-term impact on the listeners. The same or similar *topoi* were repeated time after time until they were transformed into popular assumptions.[179]

In a certain sense catastrophe sermons were an overlapping genre – they belonged to both of these groups of sermons. One might think that both Rogation Day sermons and actual catastrophe sermons were in fact all catastrophe sermons. The difference is in their timing. When preached in their original context, Rogation Day sermons were preventive measures against disasters. They circulated in model sermon collections in a standardised form. As such, they were routinely preached every year in connection with the *Rogationes*. One Rogation Day sermon did not differ very much from others. Furthermore, the contents of these sermons fitted in very well with the general teachings of the Church concerning sin and penance. Repeated every year at the same time, they produced a cumulative effect on the ideas and mentalities of the audience.

The actual catastrophe sermons, on the other hand, were reactions to something that had already happened. When preached in the hectic situation of a natural disaster they were most certainly intended to have an immediate effect on their listeners. Immediate conversion and penance were required to placate the wrath of God. Surviving a cataclysm demanded something very close to a religious revival, or even a true and proper revival such as the flagellant movements.

The Setting of Catastrophe Sermons

The surviving catastrophe sermons offer us some important insights into the role of sermons in catastrophe situations. They let us know what kinds of disasters provided an occasion for preaching, and they also provide us with some information on where, when, and how catastrophe sermons were delivered. The sermons used in this study can be divided into three categories.

The first category consists of sermons that were preached before any other spiritual activities were undertaken. Their function was to inform the people what was going to happen and why. We have already mentioned such sermons, when dealing with the Parisian processions. It was said that a public sermon was held in the church of Saint-Étienne to inform the Parisians about the impending religious event.

A good example of such an informative public sermon is Nicolas de Gorran's second sermon *Ad impetrandam serenitatem*. The *thema* of the sermon is taken from 3 Kings 18:44 '*Prepare thy chariot and go down, lest the rain prevent thee.*' Nicolas starts by saying that these are the words of

---

179. David L. d'Avray, 'Method in the Study of Medieval Sermons', in *Modern Questions about Medieval Sermons. Essays on Marriage, Death, History and Sanctity* by Nicole Bériou and David L. d'Avray. Biblioteca di "Medioevo Latino" 11 (Spoleto, 1994), pp. 8–9.

Elias to Achab, but they might as well be the words of Christ to the Church. He explains that these words stand for the three things that give prayer its efficiency, namely, unanimity, humility, and utility. The Church prepares its chariot when it comes together in an unanimous congregation.[180] By this Nicolas presumably means Mass.

With the words *go down*, the Lord means that the Church must act with humility. This is done by forming a devote procession. The sermon closes with Nicolas' exhortation that the people ought to prepare the chariot by coming unanimously together to go down by making a procession. All this is done '*lest the rain prevent thee.*' The rain preventing them was of course the flood, which prevented people from living a normal life and caused all kinds of inconveniences.[181] The length of the sermon is less than half of a modern printed page and does not provide many details. However, we can deduce from the sermon that it was preached, or was meant to be preached, to inform the audiences what had happened, and what kind of measures the Church was about to take. Most importantly, it informed them what was to be the role of the lay congregation in the up-coming liturgical activities. The people were informed about votive masses and processions.

Another rather curious sermon, if indeed it is a sermon at all, leads us to believe that, at least occasionally, a sermon was held before other measures to handle catastrophes comes from late medieval Sweden. It was probably written by a Brigettine monk from Vadstena Abbey.[182] The sermon was written in answer to some major catastrophe that affected the whole kingdom. Unfortunately, the preacher does not tell us the exact nature of the catastrophe. However, judging from the context, the most plausible candidate is that it was a plague epidemic.

---

180. Nicolas de Gorran, *Sermones de communi sanctorum*. Ad impetrandam serenitatem. Sermo secundus. UUB. C 18, f. 60r. '"Iunge currum tuum et descende ne preoccupet te pluuia." III Re. xviii. Uerbum est Helye ad Acab et potest esse uerbus Christi ad ecclesiam ubi hortatur ad tria que dant efficationem petitioni, scilicet quando fit unanimiter, humiliter, utiliter. Hortatur ergo primo ad unanimiter conueniendum ibi "iunge currum tuum". Tunc enim ecclesia currum iungit quando fit facta unanimis congregatio.'
181. Nicolas de Gorran, *Sermones de communi sanctorum*. Ad impetrandam serenitatem. Sermo secundus. UUB. C 18, f. 60r. 'Secundo ad humiliter procedendo ibi "et descende". Tunc descendit ecclesia quando fit humiliter processio et deuota [...]. Ergo "iunge currum tuum" faciendo sanctam et unanimem congregationem, "descende" faciendo deuotam et humilem processionem "ne preoccupet te pluuia" euadendo diuinam indignationem.'
182. On the dating and locating of this sermon, see Appendix 1. The problem of the generic definition of this text arises from the fact that there are numerous stylistically similar texts that were written in Vadstena Abbey, and they have been categorized as pastoral letters, even if the manuscripts sometimes have margin note calling them sermons. This problem has been studied in Alf Härdelin, 'Admonitions and Reprimands to Parochial Clergy. A "Pastoral Letter" from Vadstena', in *Master Golyas and Sweden. The Transformation of a Clerical Satire*. Edited by Olle Ferm and Bridget Morris (Stockholm, 1997), pp. 407–451. I would like to thank Doctor Stephan Borgehammar for drawing my attention to this essay.

This curious sermon starts with God punishing the kingdom of Sweden because of the sins of its inhabitants. Then the preacher relates what penitential action ought to be taken to ensure that God's punishment will cease. The preacher is merely stating the situation, that is, the imminence of the catastrophe, and then he proceeds to discuss what ought to be done.[183] The bottom line is that in this particular case the role of the sermon was to say what would be done, and thus it certainly preceded processions, alms, masses, and other concrete forms of action.

If one puts proper catastrophe sermons aside and turns to Rogation Day sermons, one finds that, in many cases, they seem to have been delivered before the processions commenced. As seen above, many of these sermons placed a lot of emphasis on explaining the history and importance of such processions. If one considers the first Rogation Day sermon of Federico Pisano Visconti, which was certainly preached to a live audience (*'In letaniis ante ascensionem quam idem dominus fecit in uulgari'*), one gets the impression that he is preaching about a procession that has not yet occurred.[184]

The second category consists of sermons, which were preached during the processions, either at the final destination, or in some station church along the road. The *Salisbury processionale* says that, once the procession had arrived at the stationary church, a mass was celebrated and in connection with it *'fiat sermo ad populum, si placuerit.'*[185] These words do not allow us to conclude that sermons were always held in connection with processions, as a matter of fact; they seem to have been delivered only when the clergy felt it was needed. Furthermore, they do not reveal the custom outside Salisbury. Yet there is further evidence in the form of surviving catastrophe sermons that were originally delivered in connection with catastrophe processions.

Eudes de Châteauroux, preached one such surviving catastrophe sermon probably in 1233, 1240 or 1242. It has come down to us in one single manuscript, in which the sermon carries the title *in processione facta propter inundationem aquarum*. As the title of the sermon indicates, it was delivered during a procession organised to stop looding. The internal evidence confirms this. The concluding prayer mentions the relics of saint Genevieve and those of other saints that had been carried to the place where Eudes was preaching. This must either have been some station church during the procession or, more likely, the ultimate destination of the procession, that is, the cathedral of Notre-Dame.[186] The latter possibility seems to be the most likely. In any case, the sermon was delivered well after the procession had started.

---

183. Anonymous, *Sermo*. UUB C 226, f. 102r.
184. Federico Pisano Visconti, *Sermones*. In letaniis, sermo primus. Firenze Biblioteca Medicea Laurenziana MS Plut. 33.sin.1, ff. 47v–48v.
185. *Processionale ad usum insignis ac praeclarae ecclesiae Sarum*, pp. 113–114.
186. Eudes de Châteauroux, *Sermones*. Sermo in processione facta propter inundationem aquarum. Arras Bibliothèque Municipal MS 137, f. 78v–80r. On the Latin text, see Appendix 2, A.

This is also the case with the early fourteenth-century sermon, *In processione pro pluvia impetranda*, from Dominican Giovanni Regina da Napoli. Again we can detect from the title given in the manuscript that the sermon was actually preached during a procession, not before. This is confirmed by the actual text of the sermon. Giovanni writes: '*We are all gathered here to ask God to give us rain. To achieve this we have organised a procession and sung Mass.*'[187] Obviously, Giovanni was preaching in a church where the procession had ended. One might also speculate that the sermon was delivered right after the Mass following the procession.

The topics dealt with in the sermon also indicate that the procession and the Mass had already taken place. Giovanni does not say anything about the procession. We have seen that, in the case of the sermons delivered before the processions, it was common to reflect on the procession, its meaning, and its proper performance. Giovanni's sermon is divided into three parts. The first one deals with the sinfulness of the congregation, the second is on the effects of prayer, whereas the third one contemplates the outcome of the process, when God has heard the prayers of the congregation.[188] Hence the prayers of the individual members of the congregation that are the actual subject of the sermon. This is hardly surprising, since all the possible collective actions had already been taken.

The last category of catastrophe sermons consists of those that took place after the actual catastrophe and after the immediate activities in response. Such sermons are Eudes de Châteauroux's *Propter timorem terremotu* and his *Sermo quando timetur de terremotu*. The latter one explicitly refers to an earthquake that had taken place recently ('*nuper*'). Judging from their contents, both of these sermons were delivered a few days after the actual catastrophe.[189] These sermons do not tell their audiences what they should do to save themselves and to bring the catastrophe to an end. They were merely explaining what had happened, and most of all why it had happened.

Votive Masses and Collective Prayers

Votive masses were another means of collective religious activity in times of acute danger. These were normally specific masses for a certain saint or for the Holy Virgin, but they could also designate masses in times of specific danger, such as natural disasters or wars.

The history of votive masses is nearly as old as the history of the Christian Church itself. Votive masses already existed in the early Church. The first written remnants of such masses are to be found in the *Sacramentarium*

---

187. Giovanni Regina da Napoli OP, *Sermones varii*. Napoli Biblioteca Nazionale VIII. Aa.11, f. 70r. 'Omnes ad presens sumus congregati ad rogandum Deum quod det nobis pluuiam pro quo facta est processio et cantata missa.'
188. Giovanni Regina da Napoli OP, *Sermones varii*. Napoli Biblioteca Nazionale VIII. Aa.11, ff. 70r–71r.
189. See Appendix 2, sermons B and D.

Gelasianum, most of which dates from the sixth century. The Old Gelasian sacramentary includes Masses *in tribulatione, tempore mortalitatis, pro mortalitate animalium, ad pluviam postulandam, ad poscendum serenitatem*, and *post tempestatem et fulgura*. The sacramentary thus includes most of the votive masses that were used during the late middle ages, and which are still part of the *Missale Romanum*.[190]

In medieval handbooks for the Mass, those masses already named in the Old Gelasian are nearly always included, whereas some others with a bearing on specific natural disasters were added. This is not the proper place to go through such sources extensively, but a few random sources will be given. At the time of Charlemagne, Alcuin supervised the revision of the sacramentary of Gallican Church. The new sacramentary included 44 votive masses, some of which are interesting from the point of view of this study: *missa de quacunque tribulatione, missa pro peste animalium, missa ad pluviam postulandam, missa ad postulandam serenitatem*, and *missa ad repellendam tempestatem*. In addition, the Archbishop Eudes de Cambrai (d. 1113) presented quite a few masses against natural disasters in his *Expositio in canonem missae*. Among these, we can, for instance, point to the mass *Contra nimiam aeris siccitatem vel tempestatem* and *contra pestem*.[191]

In order to study the earliest history of votive masses, one does not need to limit oneself to handbooks concerning the mass proper. Votive masses were in fact normal masses that included votive prayers; hence they can be studied by reading collections of early Episcopal prayers. The ancient Gallican liturgy traditionally incorporated an Episcopal blessing to the mass. This took part right before communion. Despite the romanisation of Gallican rites, this practice continued in the Frankish kingdom and, indeed, well beyond the Middle Ages until the reform of the missal by the Pope Pius V.[192]

The surviving pontificals allow us to see what kind of specific prayers were inserted into Mass during catastrophe situations. In practice, such prayers turned the normal mass into a votive Mass. Most surviving Episcopal prayers have been published in the *Corpus benedictionum pontificalium*. Among these Episcopal prayers two categories are of interest for the present study, namely, the prayers for Rogation Days and the prayers for specific occasions. These include numerous examples of prayers used in connection with natural disasters.[193]

To gain a better understanding of the character of votive Masses, we conclude this chapter by looking at a few late medieval votive Masses in

---

190. Adolph Franz, *Die Messe im deutchen Mittelalter. Beiträge zur Geschichte der Liturgie und des religiösen Volkslebens* (Freiburg im Breslau, 1902), p. 123; Cyrille Vogel, *Medieval Liturgy. An Introduction to the Sources*. Translated and revised by William Storey and Niels Rasmussen (Washington, 1986), pp. 66–68.
191. Adolph Franz, *Die Messe im deutchen Mittelalter*, pp. 119, 131–132.
192. Dom Edmond Moeller, 'Perspectives de recherche', in *Corpus benedictionum pontificalium*. CCSL 162 B (Turnhout, 1973), p. viii.
193. *Corpus benedictionum pontificalium*, passim.

greater detail. Perhaps the most famous votive Mass is that composed by Pope Clement VI to protect people from the great plague epidemic known today as the *Black Death*. It was copied extensively in fifteenth-century missals. This Mass is known by many names. It is called *Missa recordare contra pestem*, for it begins with words *Recordare domini testamentum tui*. Yet it is also known as *missa pro pestilentia vitanda, missa contra mortem subitaneam* and *pro morte hominum et pestilentia*. It was incorporated into the modern catholic Missal under the title *Pro vitanda mortalitate vel tempore pestilentiae*.[194]

The text of this Mass leaves no room for speculation about the cause and origin of the plague catastrophe. The text urges God to remember His promise and to stop His angels from destroying mankind, lest the world be desolate and all souls lost. It begs God to have mercy on his people, since it is well known that He does not want the death of sinners but rather their repentance. By listening to this mass, the people were showing their willingness to repent their sins and to do penance. Pope Clement VI conceded indulgences for everyone who participated in these masses, and ordered that the audience ought to carry lit candles in its hands (the actual amount of indulgences promised varies from one manuscript to another). If the participants did so, '*one could well believe that they were not in danger to be called by instant death.*'[195] *Missa recordare* was normally sung on five consecutive days. In addition to the mass, each day processions and sermons were organised to bring the populace into the right disposition and encourage penitential activities.[196]

We know a good deal about other votive Masses performed during acute catastrophes, to secure the protection of the God or the saints. Thus far these votive masses have not been studied in depth. Perhaps one reason for this lack of interest has been the view taken by some liturgists that medieval votive Masses were merely a corruption of Mass, and a form of superstition. A good illustration of this, not particularly understanding attitude towards medieval forms of spirituality, is the following statement of Cyrille Vogel: '*Also belonging to this category of popular deformations of the Mass are the all-too popular votive Masses...*' He continues to mention Masses for the Fourteen Holy Helpers, Masses of Saint Sebastian and Saint Roch against the pestilence, and several others as examples of such deformations.[197] However, these Masses did not constitute a deformation, but rather a sincere attempt to have control over something outside the means of human capability.

---

194. Adolph Franz, *Die Messe im deutchen Mittelalter*, pp. 183–184; Michael E. Goodich, *Violence and Miracle in the Fourteenth Century*, pp. 117–118.
195. *Missa pro vitanda mortalitatem.* BL Addit. 40146, f. 307r–v. '...et omnes illam audientes portare debent ardentem candelam in manibus et, ut pie credi potest, mors eis subitanea non uocabit.' A slightly different version of this text is published by Jules Viard; Jules Viard, 'La messe pour la peste,' *Bibliothèque de l'École des Chartes.* LXI année 1990, pp. 334–338.
196. Adolph Franz, *Die Messe im deutchen Mittelalter*, p. 188.
197. Cyrille Vogel, *Medieval Liturgy*, p. 163.

These votive masses were not attempts to corrupt the liturgical beauty of the Mass, but signs and sources of current reli-gion and spirituality. To judge them as deformations is anachronistic. Furthermore, it is certainly not very productive for historical research.

The cults and Masses mentioned by Vogel were extremely popular during the *Black Death* and the subsequent plague epidemics. In fact, the Late Middle Ages saw a multiplication of all sorts of pre-ventive cults.[198] The cult of the Fourteen Holy Helpers was popular in the Rhineland, and spread from there to the rest of the Germany, Hungary, and Scandinavia. The number of these helpers and their identity varied somewhat in dif-ferent sources. Several masses were dedi-cated to these holy helpers. One of these masses, surviving in the Bamberg manuscript, was even attributed to Pope Nicolaus V.

Eamon Duffy gives an example of a late medieval English equivalent of the cult of the Fourteen Holy Helpers. In the collections of the Fitzwilliam Museum there is an East Anglian Book of Hours that contains a verse devotion to nine martyrs with special intercessory po-wers, namely saints Giles, Christopher, Blaise, Denis and George, Margaret, Barbara, Katherine, and Martha the sis-ter of Lazarus.[199] Similar examples can be found in late medieval devotional books, liturgical manuals and church art everywhere in Europe.

Late Fifteenth-century version of the Missa recordare *in* Missale aboensis, *printed in Lübeck 1488 for the diocese of Turku in Sweden.*

198. Jacques Verger, 'Nouveaux fléaux, nouveaux recours', in *Les malheurs des temps. Histoire des fléaux et des calamités en France* (Paris, 1987), p. 217. For examples of votive masses that were actually organised during the plague epidemics, see Jean-Noël Biraben, *Les hommes et la peste*, tome II, pp. 64–65.
199. Eamon Duffy, *The Stripping of Altars*, p. 178.

Miniature presenting Saint Sebastian and a prayer dedicated to him. Italian book of hours, c. 1500. Uppsala Universitets Bibliotek Ms C 511, f. 147r. The prayer asks Saint Sebastian to repeat the miracle he performed in Lombardy and save people from the plague: 'O sancte Sebastiane, miles beatissime qui totam Lombardiam tuis meritis et precibus a mortifera peste liberasti. Rogamus te miseri peccatores, ut per sanctam pietatem tuam atque passionem quam pro fide domini nostri Iesu Christi substinuisti, nos ab ipsa peste et morte subitanea atque maligno hoste liberare digneris.'

In addition to the Fourteen Holy Helpers, several individual saints were venerated as special protectors against natural disasters. They too received special votive masses. The most important of these is saint Sebastian, who was considered to be a protector against plagues and other epidemics even before the outbreak of the *Black Death*. He held this special position due his martyrdom by being shot with arrows. The various epidemics were seen as arrows of divine wrath and so the mental link was established between these catastrophes and the martyrdom of Saint Sebastian.[200] According to a more recent tradition originating from Paulus Diaconus, Sebastian had actually saved the people of Rome and Pavia from a major epidemic. This legend was repeated in Jacopo da Varazze's enormously popular *Legenda*

---

200. Jean Delumeau, *La peur en Occident XIVe–XVIIIe siècles* (Paris, 1978), p. 107; Eamon Duffy, *The Stripping of Altars*, pp. 178–179.

Saint Roch, the primus inter pares *of plague saints. Even the iconographic presentation underlines the saint Roch's function as a protector against bubonic plague. The saint is shown in the form of a pilgrim filled with bubos. Etienne, Toulouse (Photo: Pekka Tolonen).*

aurea, and was reiterated in masses for saint Sebastian as an argument for his capacity to avert the plague.[201]

---

201. Adolph Franz, *Die Messe im Deutchen Mittelalter*, p. 179. Early sixteenth century mass reproduces this argument in a prayer included: 'Omnipotens sempiterne Deus, qui meritis et precibus beati Sebastiani martiris tui quondam generalem pestem ab hominibus mortiferam reuocasti: presta supplicibus tuis, ut qui pro consimili peste reuocanda ad ipsum tua confidencia confugimus, ipsius meritis et precibus ab ipsa peste et ab omni tribulacione liberemur.'; Iacopo da Varazze, *Legenda aurea*. Edizione critica a cura di Giovanni Paolo Maggioni. Tomo I (Firenze, 1998), p. 168. 'Legitur quoque in gestis Longobardorum quod tempore Gumberti regis Ytalie tota tanta peste percussa est ut uix unus alterum sufficeret sepelire et hec pestis maxime Rome ac Papie crassabatur....Tunc cuidam diuinitus reuelatum est quod nequaquam hec pestis cessaret donec sancto Sebastiono altare Papie construetur; Quod quidem constructum est in ecclesia sancti Petri in que dicitur ad uincula. Quo facto statim illa cessauit quassatio et illuc a Roma reliquie sancti Sebastiani sunt delate.'

We are talking about the plague and other epidemics, since it is often next to impossible to know the exact disease referred to in the sources, since chroniclers often did not describe the actual symptoms of the victims. They merely provide vague statement, such as '*Numerous people were killed by pestilence*'. The word pestilence (lat. *pestilentia*) could mean any epidemic disease whatsoever. One therefore has to keep in mind that Sebastian was not merely a plague saint, but a protector against all kinds of epidemics.

Saint Roch was another famous late medieval plague saint. Historically, he was a hermit who caught an epidemic disease himself, and thus became a natural protector against the plague. His cult was particularly popular in Germany, France and the Netherlands. The earliest traces of his cult can be found in the latter half of the fifteenth century, starting from 1468 in Italy and from 1480 in Germany. Thus Saint Roch was not a product of the *Black Death*, but of later outbreaks of the plague. This is sensible, because it was not useful to have a specific patron saint for protection against something unique. Only when the plague epidemics began to reappear at regular intervals did become necessary to have a patron saint to protect people against them.[202]

If we look at the prayers included in votive masses against natural disasters, we notice that the cause of the disaster nearly without exception was attributed to the sinfulness of mankind. As a rule, the prayers first acknowledge the rightfulness of God's sentence and punishment, and then appeal to His mercy, for God being a loving father does not want the death of sinners, but rather their conversion.[203] The masses of Saint Roch are no exception. One of the masses says: '*Have mercy on us Lord, and remove mercifully from us the whip of your anger, merited by our sins, because of the prayers and merits of Roch, your blessed confessor.*'[204] In addition to masses, the dangers of nature, especially storms, were addressed with separate prayers and blessings. Sometimes these prayers were connected with masses and processions; sometimes they were used separately against the immediate danger.[205]

Individual Reactions

In his classic book, *Religion and Decline of Magic*, Keith Thomas wrote of the hazards of life in the Middle Ages, and contemporary attitudes towards them: '*Poverty, sickness, and sudden disasters were thus familiar features of*

---

202. Heinrich Dormeier, 'Il culto dei santi a Milano in balia della peste (1576–1577)', pp. 238–240.
203. See for instance *Corpus Benedictionum Pontificalium*. Ed. Dom Edmond Moeller. Corpus Christianorum. Series Latina CLXII A (Turnhout, 1971), numbers 1018, 1019, 1175, 1239, and 1435.
204. Cited in Adolph Franz, *Die Messe im deutschen Mittelalter*, p. 182. 'Parce nobis, Dominus, et flagella ire tue, que peccata nostra merentur, precibus et meritis beatissimi confessoris tui Rocchi a nobis misericorditer auerte.'
205. For examples of such prayers and blessings between tenth and sixteenth century, see Adolph Franz, *Die kirchlichen Benediktionen im Mittelalter*, Band II, pp. 74–104.

the social environment of this period. But we must not make the anachronistic mistake of assuming that contemporaries were as daunted by them as we should be, were we suddenly pitch forked backwards in time.'[206]

Must we not indeed? It is important to note that the sources of the Middle Ages are not first hand reports, but rather reports from observers who sometimes were personally present when disasters happened and sometimes heard from others how people reacted. Thus, we do not know how the victims of disasters really felt and what they really thought. We only know how they appeared to feel and think in the eyes of contemporary observers. When it comes to the actions taken by individual persons in the middle of natural disasters, we are on a slightly more firm ground, for it is difficult to envisage why compilers of medieval chronicles would have imagined or falsified their reactions.

Not surprisingly, fear seems to have been the dominant feeling or reaction amongst disaster victims and survivors. Even simple natural phenomena, such as thunder and lightning were enough to scare the living day lights out of medieval people. Chronicles are filled with descriptions of the fear of thunder. In 1287 *'a little before dawn, on the morrow of the octave of Epiphany, there were sudden flashes of lightning at Bury St Edmunds, which terrified spectators not a little (non modicum).'*[207] We have a similar description of the effects of a particularly heavy storm on people in London a hundred years later (in 1392): *'...and then about the feast of St. Thomas the Apostle (21 December) a great storm over land and sea, so dreadful that it struck terror into men's hearts.'*[208]

Reactions to more serious natural disasters were quite similar. The forces of nature were inexhaustible sources of fear and panic. Salimbene de Adam describes an earthquake that took place in 1279 in Marches of Ancona: *'Such a fear occupied people in these parts that they did not dare to remain in their houses, not even the papal legate Lord Cardinal Latino* [Malabranca].'[209]

Earthquakes seem to have been such daunting disasters that people did not even try to find a means to fight them. They caused so much fear that people simply left their houses and towns in panic. Guido da Pisa describes the earthquake of 1117 in Northern Italy. He tells that in several towns houses and other buildings, including the famous amphitheatre of Verona, collapsed, causing such fear and panic that people left their homes unattended and went to live in nearby villages and suburbs.[210] Jacopo da Varazze says in

---

206. Keith Thomas, *Religion and the Decline of Magic*, p. 17.
207. *The Chronicle of Bury St Edmunds 1212–1301*, pp. 87–88.
208. *The Westminster Chronicle 1381–1394*, p. 511.
209. Salimbene de Adam, *Cronica*. Vol. II. Ed. Giuseppe Scalia. CCCM 125A (Turnhout, 1999), pp. 731–732.
210. Guido Pisanus, *Descriptio terremoti*. BAV. MS Vat.lat. f. 184r. 'In nomine Domini nostri Jhesu Christi eterni Dei anno ab incarnatione eius 1117 regnante Henrico quinto imperatore anno imperii eius in Ytalia sexto beatissimo quoque Paschali papa secundo in sancta et romana ecclesia residente, terremotus magnus, quales nostris

his Chronicle of Genoa that people left the city and slept in the fields during the earthquake of 1222.[211] Thirteenth-century *exemplum* collections provide further evidence to suggest that fleeing was considered to be the only remedy against earthquakes.[212]

Not even the highest church dignitaries were immune to paralysing fear and panic in the face of an earthquake. The Dominican Francesco Pipino da Bologna tells in his chronicle how on the First Advent Sunday of 1298 Pope Boniface VIII was celebrating Mass in Rieti cathedral when suddenly a violent earthquake shook the town. The church seemed to be on the verge of collapsing and the whole town was threatened to be swallowed by the earth. People in the church were extremely terrified and mortally stunned *(perterrita et stupefacta mortaliter)*. In the middle of the panic the supreme pontiff looked up for a moment and raised his hands towards heaven. Then he rose from his throne and fled with the people through the streets of town unharmed. They all left the town and settled in some minor suburbs nearby *'because it would have been tempting God to stay in danger'*. Several cardinals also took the sensible precaution of sleeping out in the open.[213] Francesco was contemporary to the events he describes. We know that in 1298 he was residing in the Dominican convent of Bologna.[214]

Giovanni Villani describes the reactions of Florentine citizens to the flood of 1333. He writes that all the people lived in great fear and that all the church bells were chiming continuously until the moment the water stopped rising. People were also banging basins and copper pots (as if to imitate the church bells) and crying to the Lord to have mercy on those in danger. This was quite reasonable behaviour, since it was a common belief that the sound of church bells had a specific power against demons and other dangers, such as thunder and lightning. The good citizens of Florence were simply assuming that

---

non fuerunt, Longobardiam, et Tusciam et usque ad Basim fruerit. Namque circa mediam noctem apud Pisam magnus terremotus fuit nichil mali, praeter solum timorem ferens. Die autem sequenti circa horam xi eiusdem diei terremota est a Deo graviter maxima pars turrium et edificiorum et campanilium cum graui damno dirueretur et scinderetur in quibus virorum quidam ac mulierum, ac puerorum subruti sunt et extincti. Quo timore ciues exterriti ex magna parte domos suas sine custode dimiserunt....Durauerit autem hic terremotus per dies 40 in quibus ciues relictis urbibus et domibus suis nullis adhibilis custodibus in uillis et in supurbis habitabant.'

211. Jacopo da Varazze, *Chronicon Genuense ab origine urbis usque ad annum 1297*. In L.A. Muratori, Rerum Italicarum Scriptores. Tomus IX (Milano, 1726), col. 46.
212. Jacques Berlioz, 'Les recits exemplaires, sources imprevues de l'histoire des catastrophes naturelles au Moyen-Age', p. 13.
213. *Chronicon fratris Francisci Pipini Bononiensis O.P.* In L.A. Muratori. Rerum Italicatum Scriptores. Tomus IX (Milano, 1726), col. 742. It is interesting to notice that Francesco justifies the escape of pope and curia in front of the danger arguing that staying would have been tempting God. This is an early example of the argument whether one should try to escape the danger or whether he should place himself on the mercy of God. During the Later Middle Ages this became an important issue, especially in connection with plague epidemics. Martin Luther wrote a tractate on the subject were he defended those who wanted to save themselves by fleeing.
214. *SOP* I, p. 392.

any noise resembling church bells was capable of chasing demons away.[215] Bernard Vincent has studied earthquakes in the Spanish province of Almeria during the Late Middle Ages and Early Modern Period. His conclusion is that the first reaction to earthquakes was always general panic. Only later, when their minds were starting to accommodate the situation, were people capable of rational action.[216]

When we move onto more serious disasters, the sources become even more explicit about the presence of fear and terror. When the plague hit Florence in 1348 *'there was such a fear that no one knew what to do'*, that is, the Florentines were paralysed by fear and unable to respond to the challenges of the situation.[217] The ultimate example comes from the chronicle of the Franciscan brother Detmar. He describes how the *Black Death* struck the city of Lübeck. On the Day of Saint Lawrence alone 2500 people were killed, and, as he added, most of them died from mere fear, for they were not used to such mortality without an apparent reason.[218] It is highly questionable whether brother Detmar was capable of diagnosing the cause of death of his fellow Lübeckians. Most of them (if any) probably did not die of fear, but there is no reason to doubt that people were frightened out of their wits.

All of these descriptions, and indeed many others, confirm the view presented by Jean Delumeau that fear, either in disguised or open form, was omnipresent in pre-modern Europe, that is, in a civilization technologically ill-equipped to confront menaces presented by a hostile environment.[219]

No matter how paralysing the fear sometimes was, something nevertheless, had to be done to overcome the threat and to secure at least some chance of survival. Earlier on, we have evaluated the possibilities of collective action. Typical for collective measures against natural disasters was that they were used in connection with disasters that allowed some time for preparations. People needed to be summoned to participate, and even when all this was accomplished, the actual performance of liturgical ceremonies did take a considerable amount of time.

---

215. Giovanni Villani, *Cronica* tomo VI, p. 5–6. '...onde tutta la gente vivea in grande paura, sonando al continuo per la città tutte le campane delle chiese, infino che non alzò l'acqua: e in ciascuna casa bacini o paiuoli, con grandi strida gridandosi a Dio misericordia misericordia per le genti ch'erano in pericolo,...' On the power of the church bells see Adolph Franz, *Die kirchlichen Benediktionen im Mittelalter*, p. 42.
216. Bernard Vincent, 'Les tremblements de terre dans la province d'Almeria', *AÉSC* 1974/3, p. 579.
217. *Cronaca fiorentina di Marchionne di Coppo Stefani*. Cited in Élisabeth Carpentier, Une ville devant la peste, p. 129, n. 4. 'Fu di tanta paura che niuno non sapea che si fare.'
218. *Chronik des Franciskaner Lesemeisters Detmar*. Herausgegeben von F.H. Grautoff. Erster Theil (Hamburg, 1829), 'In der stad tho Lubeke storven by eneme naturliken daghe sunti Laurentii, van der enen vesper tho der anderen XXV hundert volkes betolt. De lude ghinghen alse doden unde er sturven vele van anghste unde vruchdeten, wente se weren des unbewonet.'
219. Jean Delumeau, *La peur en Occident*, p. 31.

Here it is important to note that collective and individual ways of seeking Divine protection were by no means mutually exclusive. Even though the people did participate in collective processions and other liturgical ceremonies, they also tried to protect themselves on an individual basis. One of the most common ways of improving one's position before the Highest Judge was to amend one's life. At times of natural disaster it was common to pay more attention to charity. Offering help to the poor was a merituous act and might very well appease God's wrath, or at least guarantee personal survival through hard times.[220] Almsgiving was also considered to be one of the means of making satisfaction for one's sins provided that the individual in question had confessed formally to a priest. Thus almsgiving protected against God's punishment of sins, a punishment that, as we shall see, was often believed to take the form of natural disasters.

In many cases natural disasters did not allow enough time for individual persons or communities to take measures to appease God, but demanded immediate responses.[221] Earthquakes constitute a good example. They did not normally last long enough to arrange processions, specific masses, or the distribution of alms to the poor. In such a situation, all spiritual activities to ward off its disastrous effects had to be taken on an *ad hoc* basis.

In practice, the only spiritual means of protection available for individual persons in the case of acute distress were recourse to the holy places, saying commonly known prayers, and invoking the help of a particular saint. The earthquake of 1348 in Villach provides us with a good example of the first two means of protection. According to Florentine merchants, five hundred persons had sought the protection of the parish church of Saint James in Villach. The church collapsed and they were all killed.[222]

Here it is not essential to elaborate on the unhappy outcome, but the idea that people thought it safer to be in a church than outside. Jean-Noël Biraben states that during the early Middle Ages it was common to seek the protection of holy places where the presence of holy relics produced a powerful shield against evil. He wrongly believes that this custom had disappeared by the fourteenth century.[223] There is plenty of evidence suggesting that this custom not only survived to the fourteenth century, but that it outlasted the Middle Ages.

An example of the continuous trust in the power of relics and holy items was the earthquake of 1518 that virtually destroyed the Spanish town of Vera. Later on the citizens established a new hermitage in a parish church to commemorate the fact that during the earthquake the part of the church where the Holy Sacrament was kept had not collapsed.[224] Many victims of the Lisbon earthquake of 1755 sought also protection in churches.

---

220. Jean-Noël Biraben, *Les hommes et la peste*, p. 83.
221. Paul Slack, *The Impact of Plague in Tudor and Stuart England* (Oxford, 1990), p. 5.
222. A. Borst, *Das Erdbeben von 1348*, p. 538.
223. Jean-Noël Biraben, *Les hommes et la peste*, p. 83.
224. Miguel-Angel Ladero Quesada, 'Earthquakes in the Cities of Andalusia at the Beginning of the Modern Era', in *Stadtzerstörung und Wiederaufbau*, p. 101.

Giovanni da Parma wrote in his chronicle that the earthquake of 1348 lasted long enough for him to read slowly three times the *Pater noster* and three times the *Ave Maria*.[225] Similar cases are known from other places. For example, according to the official chronicler of Montpellier, the earthquake of 3 March 1374 lasted as long as it takes to read *miserere mei* prayer. Another earthquake that followed on 19 March lasted, according to a certain observer from Barcelona, roughly half of the time needed to read *Ave Maria*.[226] It is unlikely that these people chose to read these prayers merely to measure the time or just used the names of the prayers to measure time. Therefore, one might assume that they were seeking personal protection or spiritual reinforcement through prayer. Indeed, we know that people who participated in processions were also encouraged to recite those two prayers that were supposed to be familiar to all Christians, namely *Pater noster* and *Ave Maria*.[227]

Even if there are not many sources describing the rituals and prayers committed by individual persons in times of disaster, there are some normative sources that give us an idea of what people were expected to do in such circumstances. Vincent Ferrer informs his audience of four different means of praying when faced with a natural calamity. The first of his proposed methods was chanting the litanies. Yet he concedes that this was practical mainly for clerics, as not everyone would know them by heart.[228]

However, there were obviously quite a few laymen who had learned the Litanies, or at least parts of them. In his *Sermo quando timetur de terremotu* Eudes de Châteauroux writes:

> '*What should we do to evade them* (i.e. earthquakes)? *What is the best remedy? The prophet teaches us that when he promises:* "My cry shall come to his ears." *That is the effective remedy, and therefore people are accustomed to shout Kyrie eleison when they hear the sound of an earthquake. And it is a splendid habit! Kyrie eleison is interpreted to mean God have mercy. He who says so, does not excuse his doings, nor does he ask to be sentenced, but asks for mercy.*'[229]

Kyrie eleison of course constitutes the *incipit* part of the litanies. Alas, we do not know the people who were in the habit of saying *Kyrie eleison* when they heard the rumble of an earthquake. Were they the French fellow countrymen of Eudes, or perhaps the Italian inhabitants of Viterbo where he was

---

225. Quoted in A. Borst, 'Das Erdbeben von 1348', p. 536.
226. Carmen Batlle, 'Destructions naturelles des villes de la Couronne d'Aragon au Bas Moyen Âge', in *Stadtzerstörung und Wiederaufbau*, p. 72.
227. William J. Dohar, *The Black Death and Pastoral Leadership*, p. 5.
228. Vincent Ferrer, *Sermones aestivales*. Feria secunda rogationum, sermo II, p. 176. 'Sed quae orationes sunt dicendae?...Prima laetania in qua invocantur Pater, Filius, et Spiritus Sanctus, Virgo Maria et omnes sancti. Hoc maxime pertinet ad clericos, quia non omnes sciunt laetaniam.'
229. Eudes de Châteauroux, *Sermones varii*. Sermo quando timetur de terremotu. Pisa Cateriniana MS 21, f. 151r. On the Latin text see Appendix 2.

preaching? Were they happy to just say *Kyrie eleison*, or did they try to chant the litanies according to the advice of Vincent Ferrer? We do not know.

Vincent Ferrer's second way of prayer was chanting the *Canticum*, and making the sign of cross with each verse. If this was done devoutly while kneeling, the storm would move to a distant place or to a wasteland, without harming anyone and good weather would return. At least that is what Vincent tried to tell to his audience. The third way of praying was to say the Creed, making the sign of the cross with each of the twelve articles. While the first two means of prayer had been somewhat socially exclusive, Vincent reminds his audiences that everyone was supposed to know the Creed. The fourth way of praying was to be said when the storm was already breaking. The people ought to kneel, sign themselves with the cross and say out loud 'Jesus, Jesus, Jesus.' If this was done, the demons that brought about the storm would be expelled.[230]

Vincent, being a popular preacher in the best sense of the word, did not limit himself to advising learned members of clergy, but also provided common tricks for protection against storms, namely, reading the creed and using the name Jesus as a kind of magical invocation. Even if the sermon's minimalist style entices the reader to think, along the lines of Keith Thomas, that these measures were more magical than religious in the true sense of the word, one has to note that the preacher takes the existence of devotion for granted. The sermon only mentions its exterior signs, such as kneeling when praying. Vincent is not suggesting magical means to expel the demons, but various possible prayers. This is not to say that medieval religion on a popular level from time to time was not superstitious and magical, but such tendencies are easily exaggerated when reading small source passages taken out of their proper context.

Nevertheless, there seems to have been a wide spread belief that the name of Jesus worked as a protective spell, or as an invocation against the demons. There is a nearly contemporary example from Bernardino da Siena's Sienese Lenten sermons in 1425.[231] One eyewitness, who wrote down all these sermons, accidentally recorded for posterity what happened when Bernardino preached about the holy name of Jesus. When the sermon was over, the audience (all 30 000 of them according to our witness) started shouting

---

230. Vincent Ferrer, *Sermones aestivales*. Feria secunda rogationum, sermo II, p. 176. 'Secunda oratio est canticum. Quicumque vult salvus esse, faciendo crucem in qualibet versu. Probatum est quod si devote dicatur genibus flexis pro mala nube vel spargitur, vel vadit ad desertum locum ne noceat et revertitur bonum tempus. Tertius modus est dicere Credo in Deum, quod omnes tenemini scire, in quo sunt duodecim articuli fidei, faciendo magnam crucem contra tempestatem in quolibet articulo. Quartus gradus est, de quo nullus potest se excusare, quando iam incipit tempestas, genibus flexis, cum signo crucis contra tempestatem, sic dicendo Iesus, Iesus, Iesus et sic expellentur daemones et malum tempus.'
231. Especially in the Later Middle Ages it was a custom that bigger cities hired some well known preacher to deliver Lenten sermons, that is, to preach in every day during the Lent.

rhythmically the name of Jesus. Immediately a certain lady who had been possessed ('*indemoniata*') for fourteen years was freed from her demons.[232]

We do not know how common it was for ordinary people to pray. Neither do we know whether the prayers in question were those suggested by Vincent Ferrer. Judging from the surviving evidence, the most common individual response to different problems and disasters was to turn to the saints for help. This help was not expected to be free. Normally, invoking the help of a saint took the form of an agreement between the saint and the individual in question. If the saint were kind enough to intercede, the invoker would do something for the saint in return.[233] These commitments usually were about votive gifts and pilgrimages. Sometimes they could even imply conversion and entry into a religious order.

One has to remember that, when dealing with saints and natural disasters we are operating very much on the level of speculation. In miracle collections surprisingly few cases have anything to do with natural disasters, unless one assumes that healing miracles in many cases imply some kind of epidemic disease. Most miracles recorded in these collections dealt with kinds of healings. André Vauchez has studied eight canonization processes in full. According to his analysis, 86% of all miracles in the period 1201–1300 dealt with matters of healing. This percentage went down to 69,4% for the period 1301–1407. Possible cases of protection against natural disasters would be found in Vauchez's category deliverance and protection, which grew from the 3.2% to 11.8% for the latter Middle Ages.[234] Alas, Vauchez's table does not allow us to judge how many of these miracles had something to do with natural disasters.

Vauchez's results are confirmed by other studies on medieval miracles. Ronald C. Finucane estimates that over nine-tenths of the miracles were cures for human illnesses. He adds that in modern terms, shrines were faith-healing centres.[235] Gérard Veyssière whose study concentrates on the Provence, has analysed around seven hundred miracles. 550 of these miracles, that is, roughly 80%, were cases of miraculous healing.[236] Christian Krötzl, who has counted miracles of eight Scandinavian saints, concludes that 87,6% of all the cases in their miracle collections were healing stories.[237]

---

232. San Bernardino da Siena, *Le prediche volgari*. Publicate dal padre Ciro Cannarozzi O.F.M. Predicazione del 1425 in Siena, vol. secundo (Firenze, 1958), p. 158.
233. André Vauchez, *La sainteté en Occident*, p. 530; Jean Delumeau, *Rassurer et proteger*, p. 225.
234. André Vauchez, *La sainteté en Occident*, p. 547.
235. Ronald C. Finucane, *Miracles and Pilgrims. Popular Beliefs in Medieval England* (New York, 1995; first published in 1977), p. 59.
236. Gérard Veyssière, 'Miracles et merveilles en Provence', ín *Miracles, prodiges et merveilles au Moyen Age*. XXVe congrès de la S.H.M.E.S. (Paris, 1995), p. 199.
237. These calculations are from a databank Krötzl gathered for his book *Pilger, Mirakel und Alltag. Formen des Verhaltens im skandinavischen Mittelalter*. Studia Historica 46 (Tampere, 1994). These figures were eventually left out of the book. I would like to thank Doctor Krötzl for kindly letting me use them.

Modern equivalent of medieval votive gifts. Notre Dame la Noire, Toulouse. (Photo: Pekka Tolonen).

Nature is mentioned rather frequently in miracle story collections, especially in stories about storms and shipwrecks that were avoided thanks to the intercession of saints. A stereotypical example is the testimony of several sailors in the canonisation process of Thomas de Cantilupe. Their ship had barely parted from the harbour, when it was attacked by a violent storm, which kept them in its grip for several days. By that time, the men were already '*despairing for their lives*'. Since there was no priest aboard, they confessed to each other and prepared to die. At the moment of despair all the hands prayed unanimously to God and Saint Thomas, and vowed to make a pilgrimage to his shrine if they were saved. Then they said the *Pater noster* and *Ave Maria* aloud many times. Needless to say, by the evening the wind changed and the storm calmed down.[238] A typical Scandinavian variety of these kinds of miracles is a story about winter fishermen trapped by suddenly fractured ice floats. These are the stories most often found in miracle collections and canonisation enquiries, whereas miracles concerning floods, earthquakes and the like are conspicuous by their absence.

Such is also the conclusion of Philippe Jansen. He has examined thirty-four texts related to saints who lived and worked in the Marches of Ancona in the thirteenth and fourteenth centuries. All of these texts were written before the sixteenth century. Jansen points out that the central regions of Italy, namely Tuscany, Umbria and the March are areas where natural disasters are rather frequent. Despite this fact, there are no cases where a saint would have intervened in the face of natural disaster. There are a few cases where saints had something to do with the forces of nature, but even there the point was not saving people from natural disasters. For example, blessed Giovanni Bono stopped rain, not to protect crops or people against flood, but to prevent the rain from destroying the wall of a hermitage. Earthquakes, the most common natural disaster of the area, are mentioned only once – when blessed Jacopo da Venezia cured a man who was forced to sleep outdoors because of the earthquake of 1473. He had caught pneumonia![239]

Jansen gives two explanations for this unexpected absence of saintly interventions. According to him, it was not important for the saints whether they should cure one person, or save a whole town from the earthquake. The point was to fight evil by performing miracles, not the size of the miracles in question. Furthermore, he points out that saints' miracles during the Middle Ages were first and foremost an individual affair. Saints cured individual plague victims. They did not stop entire epidemics. Collective miracles start to appear in hagiographical literature only in the beginning of the modern age. Jansen mentions the deeds of Carlo Borromeo, the archbishop of Milan as an example of such later collective miracles.[240]

If we accept the explanation of Jansen, it would seem that the problem lies with the nature of hagiographic material. It is not that saints were not evoked in the middle of a danger caused by natural disaster. It is just that such cases never found their way into miracle collections. This can be confirmed by other sources, which occasionally let us know that the Holy Virgin and the saints were indeed invoked in such situations.

A good example is a story told in the chronicle of the Dominican friar Francesco Pipino da Bologna. When an earthquake struck Antioch in 1169, a certain Hermannus was in the church of saint Peter in the said city. The

---

238. *Processum canonizationis, Thomas de Cantilupe.* BAV. MS Vat.lat. 4015, ff.209v–210v.
239. Philippe Jansen, 'Literature hagiographique et catastrophes aux XIIIe–XIVe siècles: Les raisons d'une réalité absente', *Sources Travaux Historiques* no. 33 (1993). Histoire des catastrophes naturelles. Paysages-environment, pp. 25–35.
240. Philippe Jansen, 'Literature hagiographique et catastrophes aux XIIIe–XIVe siècles', pp. 29–35.

roof collapsed and more than a hundred and forty people were buried alive under the rubble. Hermannus was one of them, and at the moment of despair he decided to invoke the help of Our Lady in Rochamador. Hermannus said that all along he had the feeling that his prayers had been heard. Indeed, even though he was completely covered by bricks and almost suffocated, he was found in time and survived.[241] It is worth noting that this story was written down in a chronicle, not in a saint's *vita*.

In addition to Jansen's explanation why miracles connected to natural disasters are not included in saint's miracle collections, one might add André Vauchez's theory. According to him, medieval editors of miracle collections habitually preferred miracles that appear in the Bible, and especially those, which the New Testament attributes to Christ and his apostles.[242] Hence gaining protection from floods, or from earthquakes obviously was not a stereotypical miracle one would expect to find in miracle collections. On the other hand, miracles related to sea storms were included in miracle collections because there exists a corresponding Gospel story of Christ stilling the tempest at sea (Matthew 8:24–27; Mark 4:37–40; Luke 8:23–25).

When we look at post medieval sources we find more evidence to support the hypothesis that natural disasters are absent in miracle collections due to hagiographic conventions, not because saints were not invoked in such situations. We have plenty of well-documented evidence from 1588 onwards – the year when the *Sacra Congregazione dei Riti* was established. After any significant catastrophe such as a plague, an earthquake or a volcanic eruption, numerous requests of canonisation reached the congregation. Dioceses, universities, monasteries and other communities in need of new protectors sent these.[243] These miracles were always well documented and give us new insights into the history of sanctity. However, one can only speculate whether the importance of natural disasters in these supplications was a novelty, or whether the saints had always been invoked in such situations.

Some medieval evidence also allows us a glimpse of individuals invoking the help of saints, Christ or God during a natural disaster. Reading through several volumes of the *Archivio della Sacra Penitenzieria Apostolica*, I came across the following supplications.[244] In the last of these, that is, volume 9, the following supplication came up:

Rome xvi kal. Ianuarii

Jacobus Lodouici de Gambara laicus Brixensis diocesis. Timore terremotus ductus uouit aliquam religionem intrare quam minime expressit et demum post certum tempus spatium illud votum in mente sua ratum habuit et

---

241. Francesco Pipino da Bologna, *Chronicon*, col. 626–627.
242. André Vauchez, *La sainteté en Occident*, p. 546.
243. Sara Cabibbo, *Il paradiso del Magnifico Regno*, p. 90.
244. Volumes 7–10, that is, the years of 1459–1462 in the beginning of the pontificate of Pius II.

tandem mutato proposito matrimonium cum quadam muliere contraxit et consumauit. Petit igitur absolui de transgressione uoti.

Fiat de speciali Philippus sancti Laurenti in Lucina[245]

Before analysing this document, it is good to remember that the medieval part of this archive contains dozens of volumes. The first surviving volume of the Penitentiary archives covers the years 1409–1411. The continuous series begins from the year 1438. Few individual volumes are missing but there are no significant gaps. Volume 75 covers the fourth year of the pontificate of Clement VII (1526–1527).[246] Hence the medieval part of the archive is, depending on how the Middle Ages is defined, roughly seventy volumes. It is quite likely that a thorough search of these volumes would unearth more cases dealing with natural disasters than the ones mentioned above.

The case transcribed above is the supplication of a certain Jacopo Lodovico da Gambara, a layman from the diocese of Brescia. He had made a vow to enter a monastery or a convent if he survived the earthquake. The vow was not made publicly, and after the danger subsided, Jacopo changed his mind and got married. The vow, however, was binding even when committed in the privacy of one's own thoughts. Jacopo therefore was obliged to seek absolution for breaking his vow.

The details of the earthquake in question were either not recorded in Jacopo supplication, or they were simply not copied in extenso by the papal scribe. Since the supplication is dated 17 December 1461 we, nevertheless, may assume that the earthquake in question was the great earthquake of 1456.[247] It affected mostly the Southern parts of Italy, but shock waves of the earthquake were felt in many places far away from the epicentre. Brescia, the diocese where in Jacopo was living was also affected. Furthermore, it is possible that Jacopo was travelling somewhere in the South during the earthquake.

There is another interesting case from Northern Italy. Angerinna de Rectoris, a laywoman from the diocese of Milan explained that she was a widow and living in Milan when the plague struck the town. Angerinna made a vow that she would remain chaste for the rest of her life – presumably in exchange for staying alive through the epidemic. Once the plague had passed she

---

245. *Penitenzieria ap.* 9, f. 217r.
246. On the history of the Papal Penitentiary and its archives, see Kirsi Salonen, *The Penitentiary as a Well of Grace in the Late Middle Ages. The Example of the Province of Uppsala 1448–1527*. Annales Academiae Scientiarum Fennicae 313 (Saarijärvi, 2001); L. Schmugge, Patrick Hersberger and Béatrice Wiggenhauser, *Die Supplikenregister der päpstlichen Pönitentiarie aus der Zeit Pius' II. (1458–1464)* (Tübingen, 1996), pp. 4–56. On the exact details of the Penitentiary volumes before 1527, see Kirsi Salonen, *The Penitentiary as a Well of Grace*, Appendix 1.
247. See Bruno Figliuolo, *Il terremoto del 1456*. Tomo I (Edizioni Studi Storici Meridionali, 1998.

changed her mind and got married.[248] The document is dated 17 February 1460. The epidemic Angerinna is referring to must be that of 1451–1452, since there are no other known plague epidemics from that area that would fit in with the date of the supplication.[249]

These two documents are rarities in many ways. Not many reactions of individual men and women in connection with natural disasters have survived. These documents are even more interesting as they were not produced for hagiographical purposes, but for obtaining absolution for the breaking of an oath. Therefore they are in a sense more reliable testimonies of the religious attitudes of individual persons than miracle stories included in *vita et miracula* collections.

Our sample of the *Penitenzieria Apostolica* for three years of Pius II's papacy produced only two documents. As such, this does not prove much about the religious conventions and mentalities of the Late Middle Ages. Nevertheless I believe that these two cases were not exceptional. If there are at least two cases of persons who failed to keep their share of the bargain, that is, failed to enter a convent and keep chaste, there must have been many others who did what they had promised. Salimbene de Adam provides an exemplum of such case in his *Cronica*. Roberto da Reggio, Bishop of Brescia had barely survived the earthquake of 1222. The bishop had barely left his room when it collapsed. Afterwards he made an oath that he will remain chaste and abstain from meat until the end of his life.[250]

There were also quite likely people who had not fulfilled their votum, but who nevertheless, did not seek dispensation from the Penitentiary. Neither of these categories of people can be found in the archives of *Penitenzieria apostolica,* or in any other surviving sources. Furthermore, hagiographical sources provide thousands of cases in which similar vows were taken in exchange for a cure from disease, or some similar problem. The very existence of these two documents proves that the same bargaining method was used in connection with natural disasters.

Sadly, the Penitenzieria archives do not reveal with whom Jacopo and Angerinna were making their bargain. Did they turn to the saints, the Holy Virgin, or even to God himself? It was not recorded for it was not relevant from the point of view of the sin committed – the breaking of an oath. The scribes only noted the relevant parts of the supplication, and the identity of the desired helper was not among them.

---

248. *Penitenzieria ap.* 8, f. 116r–v. 'Exponit quod cum uidua esset et pestis in dicta ciuitate uigeret, uouit castitatem tenere que post peste mutato proposito matrimonium cum quodam contraxit et consummauit. Supplicat igitur quatenus ipsum a transgressione uoti absolui mandare dignemini. Fiat de speciali. Philippus sancti Laurentii in Lucina.
249. Jean-Noël Biraben, *Les hommes et la peste*. Tome I, p. 396.
250. Salimbene de Adam, *Cronica* I a. 1168–1249. Edidit Giuseppe Scalia. CCCM 125 (Turnhout, 1998), pp. 50, 271–272. For further examples, see Jean-Noël Biraben, *Les hommes et la peste*, p. 83.

Prayers and invoking the help of saints were not the only available spiritual means of securing one's safety. From the Later Middle Ages, we have lots of evidence of private masses, personal prayers, portable reliquaries, and all sorts of amulets that were meant to protect their owner.[251] In addition, there is evidence of superstitious means of personal protection. Vincent Ferrer gave his audiences a few words of warning concerning these practices. He states that many people, women especially, do many stupid things in catastrophe situations. They make noise with kettles or bowls, and burn stinking herbs to chase demons away. Vincent condemns such practices as useless, since the demons do not fear loud voices and they are too well accustomed to the evil stench of hell to be scared by the smelly fumes of burning herbs.[252] We have already seen that the similar banging of kettles was also used to drive away the demons in Florence during the flood of 1333.

All this seems to imply that devotion was taking a more individualistic form. There seems to have been a rising tendency to seek additional protection with personal devotion, even when public processions continued to be organised. It might be that the calamitous fourteenth century made the traditional measures of protection seem to be inadequate in front of continuous dangers and worsening natural conditions. On the other hand, it may be just another aspect of the emerging 'European individualism' debated by historians for some time now.[253] Be that as it may, there is evidence for a significantly increasing popularity of protective cults during the Later Middle Ages.[254]

---

251. J. Verger, 'Nouveaux fléaux, nouveaux recours', pp. 218–219. On the amulets and talismans used as protection against the plague, see Jean-Noël Biraben, *Les hommes et la peste*, pp. 58–62.
252. Vincent Ferrer, *Sermones aestivales*. Feria secunda rogationum, sermo secundus (antverpiae, 1572), 176. '...multae personas tunc faciunt multas stultitias, maxime mulieres, quando venit illud malum tempus faciunt sonum in caldario vel in pelvi ad terrendum daemones, sed ipsi nichil curant, sicut nec equus tubacinarii terretus ad sonum tubae quia assuefactus est. Alii comburent herbas foetentes, sed ipsi sunt iam assueti de inferni foetoribus. Alii ponunt alias truffas et stultitie sunt.'
253. See for example Colin Morris, *The Discovery of the Individual 1050–1200* (London, 1972); Richard D. Logan, 'A Conception of the Self in the Later Middle Ages', *Journal of Medieval History* 3/1986; Aaron Gurevich, *The Origins of European Individualism* (Oxford, 1995);
254. J. Verger, *Nouveaux fléaux, nouveaux recours*, p. 217.

4 The Aftermath – Explaining and Surviving Natural Disasters

When the acute danger was over and people were coming out of their shelters to estimate their losses, they started to look for explanations for what had happened. Writers of annals and chronicles, theologians, and quite likely ordinary persons as well, started to wonder what had caused the disaster. Medieval society produced different models to explain natural disasters. Jean Delumeau analysed them in his study about the explanations for the *Black Death*. He distinguished three major explanatory categories typical to the different strata of society.

The first explanatory category was that of learned natural philosophers. According to them, the Plague was caused by celestial phenomena, such as comets and conjunctions of the planets, or putrefied vapours. The second one was that of ordinary people. They were inclined to find scapegoats and were convinced that someone caused the Plague on purpose. The guilty persons had to be discovered and duly punished. The third one was that of the preachers. They taught that God was angered by the sinfulness of mankind, and had decided to have revenge on them. Therefore it was advisable to try to placate Him by doing penance.[255]

Delumeau's categories are useful not only for understanding the *Black Death*, but also for understanding the reactions of people to other natural disasters. However, this model should not be seen a monolith. It was not the case that only the learned accepted scientific explanations. This would have been rather peculiar considering they were mostly members of the clergy. The ordinary people likewise were not always searching for scapegoats. Sometimes they adopted the other explanations. In short, Delumeau's explanatory categories were not limited to the socio-educational strata of society distinguished by him. Nevertheless, these categories may have originated from these different groups, and they certainly were predominant in them.

Furthermore, more often than not, these various explanatory categories are found together in different combinations. We cannot honestly say that

---

255. Jean Delumeau, *La peur en Occident XIVe–XVIIIe siècles*, p. 129.

there were significant groups who believed that natural disasters were caused by spiritual powers only. Neither can we identify significant groups who believed that natural disasters were caused by natural causes only. Most people were aware of all three major explanatory categories, but chose to emphasise one of them, while still acknowledging the feasibility of the other ones. The following chapters analyse the sources in the light of Delumeau's categories although major attention is also given to the religious explanations, for as Piero Morburgo has detailed in his essay on the plague, in the end the emphasis on founding explanations for different disasters was always laid on two major issues, firstly the relationship between God and nature and secondly on the sinfulness on men and the necessity of his redemption.[256]

Scapegoats and Political Explanations

Since this book deals mainly with religious responses to natural disasters, Delumeaus's first explanatory category, the scapegoats will be passed over with just few remarks. The search of the scapegoats lead inevitably to violent acts towards persons and social groups that in the eyes of later historians were nothing more than innocent scapegoats.

According to Emanuela Guidoboni the need to find scapegoats who could be blamed was typical in connection with natural disasters. She writes that the need to find scapegoats to explain disasters was by no means a Christian speciality, but a universally diffused way of responding to serious calamities. Finding a scapegoat would restore the cognitive order disturbed by the catastrophe.[257] Thus the possibility of pointing out a guilty party would return the community to its usual state. Guidoboni's primary evidence dealt with a sixteenth-century earthquake in Ferrara, Italy, but his ideas are equally relevant for evidence concerning medieval natural disasters.

The potential scapegoats were normally found between two broad categories. They were either foreigners within Christendom, such as Jews, Muslims (in Spain and Sicily), and Heretics, or the black sheep of the Christian community such as notorious sinners and, especially during the Late Middle Ages, witches. Witchcraft and traditional folk healing methods were slowly demonised during the last two centuries of the Middle Ages even though the larger scale witch-hunts belonged to the early modern age.[258]

Before that time witchcraft and natural magic were seen as merely superstitious practices, sinful yes, but not dangerous or necessitating serious persecution. A good example of the earlier attitude is exhibited by the thir-

---

256. Piero Morburgo, 'La peste: dinamiche di interpretazione storiografica', in *The Regulation of Evil. Social and Cultural Attitudes to Epidemics in the Late Middle Ages*. Edited by Agostino Paravicini Bagliani and Francesco Santi. Micrologus' Library 2 (Firenze, 1998), p. 42.
257. Emanuela Guidoboni, 'Riti di calamitè: terremoti a Ferrara nel 1570–1574', p. 116.
258. František Graus, *Pest-Geißler-Judenmorde. Das 14. Jahrhundert als Krisenzeit*, pp.151–152; Jean-Noël Biraben, *Les hommes et la peste*, tome I, pp. 57–65.

teenth century inquisitor Étienne de Bourbon, who did not bother to persecute old women healers and diviners ('*vetulae*'), since he considered them to be merely simpletons who did not know what they were doing.[259]

People who did not belong to the community were considered unreliable. They were always potential scapegoats. Here it is not necessary to relate the details; enough has been written about the Jews causing the *Black Death* by poisoning the wells as well as about other potential scapegoats for famine and plague.[260] What needs emphasis is that the search for scapegoats was not by any means limited to the *Black Death*. Similar tragedies took place in connection with other major disasters, some of them well before the *Black Death*; the Jews, to mention but one example, were accused of the great earthquake of 1348 and consequently a large number of them were burned alive.[261]

One must keep in mind that blaming some minority group was not always a sign of mass psychosis. Such accusations were also raised for political reasons, especially when other Christians were accused. One means of medieval propaganda was to claim that the sins committed by the political opponents were the cause of natural disasters. If propagated well enough, such accusations could, of course, give birth to sufficient indignation and anger or redirect the already existing emotions of disaster victims towards chosen scapegoats and thus cause violent reactions.

Let us look at few practical examples of blaming political or religious adversaries for the occurrence of natural disasters. The first example plays with the political and ideological differences between the Apostolic See and Frederic II. Salimbene de Adam wrote:

> '*In that year* [1284] *God struck the Pisans with pestilence, and many people died, according to the words written in Amos VIII* [8:3]: "*Many shall die*"—*The sword of God's wrath killed Pisans because they had rebelled against the Church for a long time and captured in the sea the prelates on their way to Council, which was convocated by the late pope Gregory IX.*'[262]

Salimbene referred to the event of 3 May 1241, when the Pisans captured the Genovese fleet carrying money and delegates to the General Council summoned by Gregory IX. The Pisans were supporting the cause of Frederic II and thought that by intercepting the delegates they could prevent the Council from taking place. Among those captured were two cardinals and

---

259. Jean-Claude Schmitt, *Le Saint Lévrier*, pp. 55–57.
260. See for instance František Graus, *Pest-Geißler-Judenmorde. Das 14. Jahrhundert als Krisenzeit*, passim.; Friedrich Battenberg, *Das Europäiche Zeitalter der Juden. Band I: Von den Anfängen bis 1650* (Darmstadt, 1990), pp. 120–122; Richard Kieckhefer, *European Witch Trials. Their Foundations in Popular and Learned Culture, 1300–1500* (London, 1976), pp. 76–77; Jean Delumeau, *La peur en Occident XIVe–XVIIIe siècles*, p. 131; Jean-Noël Biraben, *Les hommes et la peste en France et dans les pays européens et méditerranées*. Tome I, pp. 57–65.
261. Arno Borst, 'Das Erdbeben von 1348', p. 539; František Graus, *Pest-Geißler-Judenmorde. Das 14. Jahrhundert als Krisenzeit*, pp. 157–158.
262. Salimbene de Adam, *Cronica*. Volume secundo, pp. 780–781.

several bishops. Due to the absence of the captives and the difficulties met by many other delegates on the road the Council never took place.[263] These events occurred more than forty years before the above-mentioned pestilence broke out. God obviously was in no hurry to take vengeance.

In another passage Salimbene de Adam described the flood of 1284 in Venice, and makes a casual comment about its cause:

> *'And the lord Bernardino, Cardinal of the Roman curia and legate, who then lived in Bologna said that this disaster happened to Venetians because they were excommunicated at the time.'*[264]

The Cardinal in question is Bernardino, cardinal of Porto. He had been nominated to work as papal legate in central Italy, to drum up support for the Guelfs, and to arrange the preaching of crusade against the Aragonese. The Venetians were excommunicated because they supported the king of Aragon, Peter III against Charles of Anjou, the paragon of the papal see. The issue in question was who should rule the kingdom of Sicily.[265]

Not only were the enemies of the Church blamed for political reasons. Occasionally, the scapegoat was found inside the Church. A good example is to be found in Matthew Paris' *Chronica Majora*. Matthew shows all through his chronicle his feelings about the papal taxation of the English church. There are literally dozens of passages where he complains about the avarice and exactions of the Roman curia. Therefore it does not come as a surprise that he should see the avarice of the Roman curia as a reason for Divine wrath. In 1250, the Northern Sea rose unexpectedly. The English coastal areas round Harlburn, Lincoln, and Winchester suffered badly. The inundation of the sea was also felt in the Dutch shores. After describing the damage Matthew says: *'Is there any reason to wonder that such things happen, when the Roman curia which should be the fountain of all justice, is instead a source of unspoken enormities.'*[266]

If one looks at the examples in which some other person or community is blamed for a disaster, one notices that in most cases such disasters are described from a considerable geographical or chronological distance. The chronicler is not personally involved in the disaster, but has heard about it through second-hand sources. The central motive for producing an account of the disaster is not the disaster itself, but rather the political message that can be connected to it, or, as in the case of Tyre's earthquake reported by Étienne de Bourbon, a need to teach a moral lesson. This is not to say that the

---

263. D. Abulafia, *Frederick II a Medieval Emperor* (London, 1988), p. 346–347.
264. Salimbene de Adam, *Cronica*. Volume secundo, p. 799.
265. Steven Runciman, *The Sicilian Vespers. A History of the Mediterranean World in the Later Thirteenth Century* (Cambridge, 1992; first published in 1958), pp. 242–243; Christoph T. Maier, *Preaching the Crusades. Mendicant friars and the cross in the thirteenth century* (Cambridge, 1994), pp. 86–87.
266. Matthew Paris, *Chronica Maiora*. Vol. V, p. 176–177. 'Et quid mirum? A Romana enim curia, quae fons esse totius iustitiae teneretur, enormitates irrecitabiles emanerunt.'

chroniclers were not concerned about the disaster, and about the loss of life. They indeed were and often produced a detailed description of the damage done. Nevertheless, these sources lack the feel of personal involvement.

Scientific Explanations

Natural philosophers and other learned persons sought to give rational explanations to natural disasters. According to them such phenomena could be explained, at least partially, according to the laws of nature created by God in the beginning. Hence not all the disasters were the result of God's direct intervention. Some natural events were used to forecast disasters, such as comets and constellations of the planets whereas others were used to explain their causes.

Almost all the appearances of comets were thought to predict some major catastrophe, either a natural disaster or a man-made disaster such as war. Dominican Aegidius de Lessines crystallised the function of comets as messengers of bad news in his *De essentia, motu et significatione cometarum* from the latter half of the thirteenth century. He wrote that comets are a sign rather than a cause of disasters. Since they are made of the element of fire, they predict mainly evil things such as floods, earthquakes, and the destruction of cities.[267]

Academic astrologers in Paris took the view that the *Black Death* was caused by the unhappy constellation of Jupiter, Saturn and Mars that had taken place in 1345. On the other hand, there were also sceptics who were not willing to believe in the influence of comets. Matteo Villani commented on several explanations of the plague proposed by astrologers by writing that there had been numerous similar constellations of the planets and yet nothing had happened before.[268] Nevertheless, it is obvious that astrological explanations did enjoy considerable popularity among the learned circles.

So prevalent were the religious explanations, that whenever scientific explanations as causes for natural disasters were put forward, they were almost without exception accompanied by religious ones. Giovanni Villani's description of the 1333 flood in Florence reminds us of this fact. Villani writes:

> '*On 1st November 1333 the rain began. It poured for four days and four nights, with fearful lightning and thunder; and the river rose, and rose, until the water broke down walls, then buildings, and ended by carrying*

---

267. Aegidius de Lectinis, *De essentia, motu et significatione cometarum*. In Latin Treatises on Comets Between 1238 and 1368 A.D. Edited by Lynn Thorndike (Chicago, 1950), 155–258. Aegidius was not alone in his opinion; comets were similarly presented as evil omens in several other contemporary treatises edited by Thorndike. See also Jean-Noël Biraben, *Les hommes et la peste*, tome II, pp. 9–14.
268. Piero Morburgo, 'La peste: dinamiche di interpretazione storiografica', p. 44.

> *away the three main bridges, all this with inestimable ruin and loss of life....*
> *It was agreed that this flood was the worst catastrophe in the history of*
> *Florence. And it its aftermath a question arose, and was put to the learned*
> *friars and theologians, and to the natural philosophers and astrologers:*
> *namely, whether the flood had occurred through the course of nature or*
> *by the judgement of God.'*[269]

It is understandable that the Florentines were upset about the flood. Villani compares the flood of 1333 to the earlier flood of 1269. According to the old people who were trustworthy witnesses and who had personally seen the earlier the flood of 1269 the present one was without any doubt worse. The floods of 1333 were not only a problem for Florence, but there are numerous sources from other cities of Central Italy, such as Parma, Bologna and Ferrara, that testify to the enormous effects of the disaster.[270]

Villani not only posed the problem of different explanations, but he also answered it. The very chapter in his chronicle that is entitled *D'una grande questione in Firenze, se'l detto diluvio venne per giudicio di Dio o per corso naturale* starts with expounding thoroughly what the astrologers had said about the unfavourable astrological signs, that is, bad constellations of the planets and the eclipse of the sun. These were interpreted as causes of the flood. The lengthy description with its complex details reveals that Villani was himself interested in astrology.[271]

Then he moved on to the explanation presented by the theologians of the city. They, as Villani writes, responded saintly and reasonably that the astrologers might very well be right up to a certain point, but not altogether. If God had not wanted the flood to happen, it would not have taken place, regardless of the conjunctions of the planets or other signs of zodiac. God, being the Creator, has ultimate power over nature. He had created the world out of nothing, and He is therefore completely capable to remake, change, shape, or undo it as He sees fit.[272]

In this the Florentine theologians followed the reasoning of Thomas Aquinas. Thomas had concluded that the established natural laws under normal circumstances operated perfectly well, God nevertheless was capable and omnipotent to change them and work miracles.[273] This idea of Thomas was by no means original; he merely presented it in impeccable scientific language.

---

269. Translated by Alexander Murray in his *Reason and Society in the Middle Ages* (Oxford, 1991; 1st published in 1978), p. 1.
270. see Laurence Moulinier e Odile Redon, '"Pareano aperte le cataratte del cielo": le ipotesi di Giovanni Villani sull'inondazione del 1333 a Firenze', in *Miracoli. Dai segni alla storia*. A cura di Sofia Boesch Gajano e Marilena Modica (Roma, 2000), p. 139.
271. Giovanni Villani, *Cronica*, tomo VI, pp. 13–16.
272. Giovanni Villani, *Cronica*, tomo VI, pp. 16–17. '...e chi ha podere di fare la cosa, pur materialmente parlando, la può mutare e disfare, maggiormente Iddio può tutto fare, e alterare, mutare, e disfare.'
273. Alexander Murray, *Reason and Society in the Middle Ages*, p. 12.

Villani's listing of the reasons for natural disaster is in many ways representative.

We find similar combinations of natural and supernatural explanations in many earlier sources. A good example is Matthew Paris' description of two earthquakes: one in England (in 1247), and another in Savoy (in 1248). About the first one he writes:

> *In this same year, on the ides of February, that is on the eve of St. Valentine's day [13 February], an earthquake was felt in various places in England, especially at London and above all on the banks of the River Thames. It shook many buildings and was extremely damaging and terrible. It was thought to be significant because earthquakes are unusual and unnatural in these western countries since the solid mass of England lacks those underground caverns and deep cavities in which, according to philosophers, they are usually generated, nor could any reason for it be discovered....*[274]

In this passage Matthew notes that according to scientific opinion earthquakes are not common in England. He is relying on the authority of Aristotle and the commentaries on his *Meteorologics*. Thomas Aquinas' commentary makes clear that earthquakes were believed to occur because of vaporisation of water in deep underground caverns. If there are holes in the ground the steam can come out harmlessly and cause winds, but if such holes are absent, pressures build up and finally cause earthquakes. The most seriously affected areas according to Aristotle and Aquinas were coastal regions, in particular those places where the sea was believed to go under the land, as was the case in Sicily.[275] Isidore of Seville already put this Aristotelian explanation of earthquakes forward in his *De natura rerum*. It received much wider audience through Vincent de Beauvais' enormously popular *Speculum naturale* and numerous other popular writings in the late medieval period.[276] This Aristotelian explanation with comments from Aquinas continued to be an accepted scientific model well into the early modern age. Marcello Bonito used it to explain earthquakes as late as in 1688.[277]

Matthew Paris implies that even when such underground caverns were lacking people were keen to find some natural explanation for the earthquake.

---

274. Matthaei Parisiensis monachi Sancti Albani *Chronica Maiora*. Ed. Henry Richard Luard. Vol. IV A.D. 1240 to A.D. 1247 (London, 1877), 'Quia edificia multa concutiens dampnosus extitit et nimium terribilis, quia, ut credebatur, significatibus et insolutus in his partibus occidentalibus, necnon et innaturalis, cum solidus Angliae cavernis terrestribus et profundis traconibus ac concavitatibus, in quibus secundum philosophos solet terraemotus generari, careat.' Translation by Richard Vaughan in *Chronicles of Matthew Paris. Monastic Life in the Thriteenth Century*. Edited, translated and with an introduction by Richard Vaughan (Gloucester, 1986), p. 91.
275. Thomas Aquinas OP, *In libros Aristotelis Meteorologicorum expositio*, II, 1. XIV.
276. Isidore of Seville, *De natura rerum* (PL 83), Cap. XLVI De terremotu; Vincent de Beauvais, *Speculum naturale* (Douai, 1624; repr. Graz, 1964), col. 387; Aegidius de Lectinis, *De essentia, motu et significatione cometarum*, p. 137; Oliver Guyotjeannin, *Salimbene de Adam un chroniqueur franciscain*, p. 280, n. 35.
277. Marcello Bonito, *Terra tremante*, pp. 4–21.

Only when natural explanations could not be found did the people finally turn to supernatural explanations. Matthew describes the case of Savoy in a following manner:

> '*At this time, in the region of Savoy, namely in the valley of Maurianne, certain towns, five in fact, were overwhelmed and swallowed up, with their cowsheds, sheepcotes and mills, by the neighbouring mountains and crags, which, as a result of a horrible earthquake in some caverns inside them, were torn away and pulled out from their normal place. Many say that three religious houses were struck down there but one chapel escaped. It is not known if the destruction of the mountains which raged so horribly in that place occurred miraculously or naturally, but because about nine thousand persons and an incalculable number of animals were destroyed, it seems to have happened miraculously rather than through natural causes.*'[278]

Here we have the perfect example of harmony between scientific explanations and those relying on divine intervention. In the first place Matthew describes what happened, and tells that it was caused by the movement of some underground caverns. Having stated this completely valid and at that time accepted geological cause of earthquake, he nevertheless concludes that it was caused by miraculous means. He sees no problem whatsoever in connecting the scientific explanation with that of Divine wrath.

Matthew Paris' story is a classical example of the inadequacies of medieval scientific explanations. The first thing he had misunderstood was the nature of the catastrophe itself. It was not an earthquake, but the collapse of a part of mount Granier that buried several villages in Savoy.[279]

A similar combination of natural science and religion is found in Thomas de Cantimpre's *Liber de natura rerum*. Thomas gives natural explanations for floods, which according to him were especially frequent in the East. During warm weather water could vaporize into steam and rise up into the clouds. The heat of the sun evaporated even the small amount of water that did get

---

278. Matthew Paris, *Chronica Maiora*. Vol. V, p. 30–31. 'Eodemque tempore, in partibus Sabaudiae, in vallibus videlicet Moriani, quaedam villae, scilicet quinque, cum suis bastaribus, caulis, et molendinis adjacentibus, obrutae sunt et absorptae, montibus et scopulis, qui vicini erant, de loco creationis suae, facto horribili terrae motu per quasdam sui cavernas, avulsis et revolutis. Multi dicunt tres domos religiosorum ibi oppressas fuisse, sed unum presbyterium ibi fuisse liberatum. Nescitur tamen si miraculose vel naturaliter illa montium ruina facta in pagos memoratos adeo horribiliter desaevit. Sed quia hominum circiter novem milia oppressit, et animalia, quorum non est numerus aestimabilis, videtur quod potius miraculose quam casualiter evenisset.' Translation by by Richard Vaughan in *Chronicles of Matthew Paris*, p. 150.
279. See Jacques Berlioz, *Catastrophes naturelles et calamités au Moyen Age*, chapitre IV, pp. 57–139. This chapter of the book deals exclusively with the collapse of Mount Granier and was originally published as an independent article. Berlioz assumes convincingly that Matthew Paris constructed the idea of an earthquake by combining whatever second hand information he had on the disaster with his natural philosophical learning, mainly Aristotle.

through. This caused huge under-ground water concentrations. When these water storages became too large, the water simply found its way out with pressure and this caused floods. After this explanation Thomas described Noah's flood, which was caused by God as a revenge for the corruption of mankind. The natural processes described earlier could not explain the latter flood, according to Thomas. The reason of Noah's flood was the huge mass of water, which God had in creation placed above the firmament that was brought down to earth when the floodgates of heaven were opened.[280]

Turning towards the homiletic evidence we find more examples of the intermingling natural and theological explanations. Cardinal Eudes de Châteauroux preached in Viterbo sometime after the earthquake of 1269. He commented that philosophers and scholars were in a habit of discussing the reasons of earthquakes, thunder and lightning and how they can be foretold. He then put forward the Aristotelian standard explanation for earthquakes and lightning. He even took the trouble of explaining this rather complicated theory in a more easily understandable way. He said that the heat closed within under ground caverns that finally erupts violently causing earthquakes can be understood by thinking about chestnuts. When they are roasted the vapour of the heat builds up inside them until the pressure breaks their shells.

Despite all this commitment to scientific arguments, Eudes soon nullified them by writing that it is useless to search for natural explanations of earthquakes and lightning or the signs preceding them. We should all know that the real cause (*causa efficiens, causa finalis*) for such disasters are God's wrath, and the signs preceding them are the sins of men.[281]

Another good example is Vincent Ferrer's second Rogation Day sermon. At first, Vincent gives a scientific explanation why Rogation time is the natural period for seeking divine aid against natural disasters. He reveals that during that period the earth starts to get warmer, and finally becomes hot. This implies that large amounts of vapour rise to the upper spheres of atmosphere. There the air is colder which causes the vapours to condensate producing thunder and lightning, which finally reach the earth with disastrous consequences, such as the destruction of crops, vineyards, fruits and other temporal goods. This apparently natural process is turned into a theological explanation by adding that God has the supreme control over nature. Therefore, to guarantee that nature was kept under control and showed benevolent face to mankind, the holy fathers had decreed that Rogation time, more than any other moment of the year, was the period when men ought to pray to God to intercede.[282]

---

280. Thomas de Cantimbre, *Liber de natura rerum*, L. 16, 5.
281. Eudes de Châteauroux, *Sermones*. Sermo quando timetur de terremotu. Pisa Cateriniana MS 21, f. 150v–151r. For the Latin text, see Appendix 2, D.
282. Vincent Ferrer, *Sermones aestivales*. Feria secunda rogationum, sermo II, pp. 174–175. 'Ideo facimus modo istas processiones, et magis in isto tempore paschali quam in alio, duplici ratione. Prima est naturalis. Secunda theologicalis. Quantum ad primam, quia in isto tempore sol ascendit per Zodaicum et sic ascendendo trahit

Vincent, being a Dominican preacher, not surprisingly seemed to adopt the view of Thomas Aquinas mentioned earlier. God does not normally make things happen in nature. He has laid down the laws and basic principles according to which nature works. Nevertheless, being omnipotent, He is capable of intervention whenever and if He so chooses.

Jean-Claude Schmitt has reached the same conclusion by studying diseases and healing in the Middle Ages. He writes that religious readings of disease did not exclude the idea of natural causes, yet these were always subordinate to the Divine plan. Hence there was no place for scientific causalities in the modern sense, that is, causalities that could be verified and falsified experimentally.[283] There was no need for them as God was omnipotent, and His actions were not limited by natural laws and causalities laid down by Him.

One might add that this predilecture of a mixture of supernatural and scientific explanations was not typical for the Middle Ages only. It remained fashionable well into the modern period. Paul Slack writes about the causes of the plague in the early modern period: *'The explanatory system within which the plague was set had been handed down from the past. In essentials it had been established at the time of the Black Death.'* In fact, as we shall see later on, it had been around centuries before the *Black Death*. Slack observes that while God was seen to be the first cause of the plague, He normally worked through secondary causes. Thus Supernatural and natural explanations for epidemics were interlocking parts of a single interpretative chain.[284]

Late medieval plague epidemics forced different writers of pastoral literature to pay more focused attention to the problem of tribulations. In 1493 the Observant Franciscan Bernardino Tomitano da Feltre was preaching on the Plague in Padua. In his rather long sermon, Bernardino mentions all the standard scientific explanations, starting with astrology and finishing with the obligatory quotations from Aristotle. Even though Bernardino accepts without arguing the importance of the planets and everything said in the *Meteorologics*, he nevertheless leaves the final word to God, stating that nothing agonising in this world happens against the will of God.[285]

Perhaps even more interesting is the plague sermon by his namesake and fellow Franciscan Bernardino da Busti. He thoroughly analysed different

> ad se vapores terre, quia terra nunc calefit, et fervet et mittit sursum vapores, et vapores in media regione aëris que est frigida, quia non est ibi reverberatio radiosum solarium ut in terra, ingrassantur, condensantur et congelantur in lapides, generantur tornitrua, et fulgura, et tunc lapides cadent et destruunt et devastant bona terrenalia, blade, vineas, fructus etc. Ideo est ordinatum a sanctis patribus, quod in isto tempore maxime christiani faciant istas processiones, et orando currant ad Dominum qui super totam naturam habet dominium, ut velit naturam refraenare et bonum terrena nobis concedere.'

283. Jean-Claude Schmitt, 'Religione e guarigione nell'Occidente medievale', p. 289.
284. Paul Slack, *The Impact of Plague in Tudor and Stuart England* (London, 1985), pp. 22–29.
285. *Sermoni del beato Bernardino Tomitano da Feltre*. A cura di P. Carlo Varischi da Milano. Tomo II (Milano, 1964), p. 266.

opinions on the reasons and predictability of epidemics in his sermon on the *pestilentie signis, causis et remediis*. Bernardino was writing in the latter half of the fifteenth, or in the beginning of the sixteenth century when society was under the continuous threat of plague epidemics.[286] Bernardino's plague sermon turned out to be extremely pragmatic. One might even call it a 'how to survive a plague' manual. It is very likely that Bernardino was not thinking exclusively about the salvation of souls, but also wanted to give his readers some practical advice. This combination of practical advice and religious instruction was fairly common in the early modern period.

Bernardino starts arguing whether it is possible to know in advance when God will punish mankind. He quotes Saint Paul (Romans 12:33): '*O the depth of the riches of the wisdom and of the knowledge of God! How incomprehensible are his judgements, and unsearchable his ways.*' Some people, says Bernardino, use this biblical quotation to prove that it is impossible for mortals to know when and how God is going to punish them. According to Bernardino, this is true as far as one is discussing the exact moment and the means of punishment. There are some signs, however, that allow us to deduce that Divine punishment is imminent, as it is said in Luke 21:25: '*There shall be signs in the sun and in the moon and in the stars.*'

Some people argue against this with the words of Jeremiah (10:2): '*Be not afraid of the signs of heaven which the heathens fear.*' Nicolaus de Lyra responds to this by saying that it is superstitious and heretical to argue that constellations of stars and signs of heaven could affect the rational mind and turn it to sin, as is also attested by the third book of Thomas' *Summa contra gentiles*. Nevertheless, Bernardino adds, the constellations of the stars and movement of the heavenly objects do affect physical phenomena such as droughts, rains, winds, sterility, sickness and epidemics.

Having established the theoretical basis of his opinions, Bernardino proceeded to the actual message of his sermon, that is, signs, reasons for, and remedies for epidemics, and wrote:

> '*And when such epidemics are to come, no one can know for sure, since that information is only in possession of God, and He can send them within a moment without any preceding signs. However, when they come because of natural causes, most often through heavenly and atmospheric bodies, it is possible to know from certain signs when it is going to happen.*'[287]

---

286. Bernardino joined the Franciscan order in c. 1475 and the first edition of his *Rosarium sermonum* came out of print in 1496, thus they were obviously written between these two dates.
287. Bernardino da Busti OFM, *Rosarium sermonum* (Venezia, 1498). Sermo de pestilentie signis, causis et remediis, f. 256r–v. 'Paulus ad Ro. 11o inquit: "O altitudo diuitiarum sapientie et scientie Dei, quam incomprehensibilia sunt iudicia eius, et inuestigabiles uie eius." Ex quibus uerbis quidam uoluerunt dicere quod de iudiciis Dei futuris nullam possumus habere cognitionem, quod uerum est de cognitione demonstratiua et certa. Possumus tamen coniecturare ex aliquibus indiciis quando Dominus uelit mittere flagella sua in hoc mundo. Imo et de die iudiciis futuro signa aliqua nobis Deus prius demonstrabit iuxta illud Saluatoris Luce 21o: "Erunt signa in sole, luna

Thus we see that Bernardino would seem to argue that natural disasters can happen through completely natural causes, in which case they can, at least with some kind of accuracy, be foretold by means of astrology and natural philosophical observation. They can, however, also happen through the will of God, and in that case there is no way of foretelling when they are going to happen. For God, being omnipotent can make them happen without the customary warning signs. Bernardino's interpretation is much more moralistic than the scientifically oriented opinions of Thomas Aquinas and Vincent de Beauvais. Yet the essential message is the same: There are natural laws that apply for the disasters, but God, when He so wishes, is above them.

Apocalyptic Explanations

> 'Then he said to them: "Nation shall rise against nation, and kingdom against kingdom. And there shall be great earthquakes in diverse places and pestilences and famines and terrors from heaven; and there shall be great signs."'
> (St Luke 21:10–11).

During the Middle Ages the idea of the end of world and the coming of Antichrist was always present. The world was growing old, and the eventual end could lurk just around the corner. In this generally apocalyptical atmosphere there were times when apocalyptic expectations were even more fashionable and concrete than usual. The most important of these were the change of the millennium, the first half of the thirteenth century, and the immediate aftermath of the *Black Death*.

If we look at the peak times of apocalyptic thinking we see several explanatory factors. The change of the millennium hardly needs further elucidation. Full thousand years simply seemed to be convenient time span for the coming of the Antichrist or the second coming of Christ. The middle of the thirteenth century, especially the year 1260, was interpreted as a potential moment of apocalyptic cataclysm, thanks to the popular prophesies of the Calabrian abbot Joachim of Fiore. The first half of the thirteenth century was the hay day of Joachimism. Clerics as well as laymen, were preparing for the last days and the coming of the Anti-Christ when 1260, the crucial year in the prophecies of Joachim was approaching. These apocalyptic expectations were only reinforced by the early thirteenth-century pseudo-Joachite writings and the catastrophic situation in Italy just before the decisive year 1260. In 1258 there had been a serious famine, and the following year saw the outbreak of epidemics in many parts of the country.[288]

---

288. Richard Kenneth Emerson, *Antichrist in the Middle Ages. A Study of Medieval Apocalypticism, Art, and Literature* (Manchester, 1981), pp. 60–61; Norman Cohn, *The Pursuit of Millenium*, pp. 38, 126.

The flagellant movements of 1260 prove that this expectation of the last days was not monopolised by clerics who had first hand knowledge of Joachim's writings. The fear for the approaching Antichrist and the end of the world was substantial enough to drive large numbers of people to the streets. They wore penitential clothes, they sang penitential songs, and flogged themselves. Norman Cohn points out that the famine of 1258, the following outburst of epidemic diseases, as well as the ravages of incessant warfare were seen through Joachim's and pseudo-Joachite prophesies. He implies that this combination of virulent Joachimism and hard times was the driving force behind the flagellant movement of 1260.[289]

Although the eminent historian Raoul Manselli questions this representation, Marjorie Reeves and Gary Dickson seem to provide sufficient corroborative evidence to uphold Cohn's vision. It might not have been a question of pure Joachism in the theological sense. Yet the role of prophetic and apocalyptic expectations in the flagellant movement seems undeniable. The flagellants fed on a widespread apocalyptic mood, which derived from many sources, but certainly was tainted with Joachimist prophecies.[290]

Joachim of Fiore's grim prophecies were supported by the onslaught of the Mongols against the Christendom. It had started in 1241–1242, when Mongol forces devastated large parts of Eastern Europe causing serious loss of population. All too conveniently from the point of view of Joachim's prophesies they were by the time of 1260 expected to renew their attack, and had indeed done so in Poland. The hordes of attacking nomads were sometimes interpreted to be the armies of Gog and Magog mentioned in the Apocalypse.[291]

In light of all this, it is no surprise that all natural and man-made disasters occurring within a close range of the key year 1260 were seen as sure signs of the end. One might add that apocalyptic expectations were by no means limited to Italy. The English Benedictine monk Matthew Paris reflected on the general apocalyptic mood by ending his account of the year 1248 with the following statement: *'The end of the world is apparent from many indicating arguments. These are: "Nation shall rise against nation, and there shall be earthquakes in diverse places and such things."'* Matthew paraphrased Luke 21:10–11. Hence he quite likely had in mind *'pestilences, famines and terrors from heaven.'*[292]

---

289. Norman Cohn, *The Pursuit of Millenium*, pp. 126–127.
290. Marjorie Reeves, *The Influence of Prophecy in the Later Middle Ages. A Study in Joachimism* (University of Notre Dame Press, 1993; first published in Oxford 1969), pp. 54–55; Gary Dickson, 'The Flagellants of 1260 and the Crusades', *Journal of Medieval History* 3/1989, pp. 253–258; Aaron Gurevich, *The Origins of European Individualism*, p. 201.
291. Antti Ruotsala, *Europeans and Mongols in the Middle of the Thirteenth Century: Encountering the Other*. Annales Academiae Scientiarum Fennicae, ser. Humaniora 314 (Helsinki, 2001), pp. 33–35;Gary Dickson, 'The Flagellants of 1260 and the Crusades', pp. 248–249.
292. Matthew Paris, *Chronica Maiora*. Vol. V, p. 47. 'Mundi finis multiplicibus argumenti indicatibus, ut sunt, surget gens contra gentem, et terrae motus erunt per loca et consimilia.'

Similar evidence can be gathered from other sources from the first half of the thirteenth century. Jacques Berlioz gives a few examples of eschatological motivated stories in *exemplum* collections. He indicates, however, that non-eschatological explanations for natural disasters were far more common in preaching materials, and ventures that apocalyptic themes were rather hazardous in connection with sermons.[293] The preachers did not want to give rise to any apocalyptic movement because experience had thought that such movements were not easy to control. Once out of ecclesiastical control, apocalyptic movements tended to cause all sorts of public disturbance, such as pogroms against the Jews and violent riots.

The passing of the crucial decade of the 1260's relaxed the general atmosphere in Europe. Nevertheless, apocalyptic theories remained popular through the late medieval period, also during better times. Cardinal Eudes de Châteauroux preached in Viterbo after the earthquake of 1269. He took his theme from Isaiah 24:18–19: '*The floodgates from on high are opened, and the foundations of the earth shall be shaken. With breaking shall the earth be broken, with crushing shall the earth be crushed, with trembling shall the earth be moved. With shaking shall the earth be shaken as a drunken man.*' It is difficult to imagine a more suitable Bible quotation when preaching about an earthquake. Having stated his *thema*, Eudes continues: '*God made this threat through Isaiah the prophet. It will be completed and have its consummation in the end of the world when the day of the final judgement approaches.*'[294] Here we see Eudes painting the damage and destruction caused to Viterbo with apocalyptic words from Isaiah. He reminds his audience that such scenes are preparing us for the last times.

The waning of Joachim's popularity caused a decline in eschatological expectations. They became fashionable again in the latter half of the fourteenth century. There were several reasons for pessimistic outbursts and apocalyptic fear in those decades. The economic situation in Europe had declined after the reasonably prosperous thirteenth century. A worsening climate caused crop failures and lower yield ratios. There had been serious food shortages from the beginning of the century and the catastrophe became complete with the coming of the *Black Death* and the subsequent outbursts of plague. There was also a religious crisis. The papacy had moved to Avignon, and when it returned to its natural post in Rome the exile was followed by a schism. One cannot forget the importance of the hundred years war that caused additional damage to France. In addition, the fifteenth century saw the military advance of the Turks who, according to the pattern established during the Mongol attack of the 1240's, were seen as precursors of the last times.[295]

---

293 Jacques Berlioz, 'Les recits exemplaires, sources imprevues de l'histoire des catastrophes naturelles au Moyen-Age', pp. 22–23.
294 Eudes de Châteauroux, *Sermones.* Sermo exhortatorius propter terremotum qui media nocte factus est Viterbii et in multis locis. Pisa conv. S. Catharinae 21, f. 147v. On the Latin text, see Appendix 2, C.
295 Jean Delumeau, *La peur en Occident XIVe–XVIIIe siècles*, p. 211. On the history of eschatological thinking during and after the Black Death see Robert E. Lerner,

With these darkening perspectives in mind, it might be useful to take a look at a contemporary chronicle and its views of the last times. The Franciscan Johannes Winterthur describes two important events around the middle of the fourteenth century, namely the earthquake of 1348 and the *Black Death*. The most interesting aspect in this passage of his chronicle, however, is not the description of the actual events, but the explanation given to them:

> *'The aforementioned events, that is, the earthquake and the pestilence are evil precursors of the maelstroms and storms of the last days according to the words of the Saviour in the Gospel: "And there shall be great earthquakes in diverse places and pestilences and famines etc."'*[296]

Johannes is referring to the Luke 21:13, a Gospel passage that discusses the signs of the end of the world. It is quite obvious that he was convinced that the great pestilence and other natural disasters of the time signified of the approaching end. Nor was he alone with his ideas. These mid-fourteenth-century earthquakes in Carinthia and Italy were generally interpreted to be 'messianic woes' which were to usher in the Last Days.[297] It should be remembered, however, that by the latter half of the fourteenth century, referring to the world's end in connection with natural disasters had become a well-established topos amongst medieval chroniclers. Nevertheless, given the other evidence, such as popular contemporary militant millenarian movements, we may safely assume that a considerable number of people genuinely believed that the end was at hand. The same attitude can be observed even in the sixteenth-century sources. Miguel-Angel Ladero Quesada who has studied Andalusian earthquakes between 1487 and 1534 writes that fear of the Apocalypse was always a factor in explaining earthquakes.[298]

In an intriguing argument, Robert E. Lerner holds that the crucial function of eschatological prophesies and interpretations of the *Black Death* was a comforting one. According to him, eschatological writings, and rumours were *'intended to give comfort by providing certainties in the face of uncertainty and must have helped frightened Europeans get about their work.'*[299]

'The Black Death and Western European Eschatological Mentalities', *American Historical Review* 3/1981. On the outbreaks plague epidemics after the Black Death see Jean-Noël Biraben, *Les hommes et la peste en France et dans les pays européens et méditerranéens*. Tome I, Annexe IV.
296. Johannes von Winterthur, *Chronica*. In Die Chronik Johanns von Winterthur. Herausgegeben von Friedrich Baethgen. MGH. Scriptores Rerum Germanicarum. Nova Series tomus III (Berlin, 1924), p. 276.
297. Norman Cohn, *The Pursuit of Millenium*, p. 135.
298. Miguel-Angel Ladero Quesada, 'Earthquakes in the Cities of Andalusia', p. 100.
299. Robert E. Lerner, 'The Black Death and Western European Eschatological Mentalities', p. 552.

World history was predestined and planned by God. Disasters such as the *Black Death* were merely before-written chapters in a great story moving towards its logical conclusion. Seeing things in the context of a Divine plan offered some comfort to people who had either lost their families or friends during the plague, or were simply devastated by the measure of destruction caused by it. According to Lerner's interpretation, eschatological writings created order out of chaos and gave a definitive and understandable meaning to the plague. The human catastrophe that was otherwise way beyond reason became understandable and maybe even acceptable as a part of a Divine plan.

Divine Intervention

God's Punishment

Despite the popularity of apocalyptic explanations for natural disasters, not all ecclesiastical writers were keen to speculate about the last days. Many preferred to see the workings of Divine providence on a more restricted local level. They took the view that natural disasters were indeed products of Divine intervention but did not interpret them necessarily as signs of the approaching end of the world. God was merely punishing sinners for their misdeeds and this punishment was measured out locally.

All the historians of the *Black Death* and following plague epidemics acknowledge that such disasters were explained as Divine punishments for the sins of man. Some medieval preachers and theologians were keen to blame mankind as a whole; others were satisfied with geographically more limited groups of sinners, that is, people living in the affected community. Explaining natural disasters as a sign of Divine wrath was by no means a medieval invention. Its history goes back to the earliest history of mankind. Jean-Noël Biraben refers to several examples in Greek mythology and in the *Old Testament*.[300]

Scholars of comparative religion and anthropology have long since established the idea that explaining natural, or for that matter other, disasters with Divine intervention was and is typical for all "primitive" societies. In fact, one line of anthropology has been to classify societies according to their level of rationality. All societies were envisaged to develop from magic through religion to the ultimate goal that is scientific rationality. According to this theory some primitive societies of today are now on a level of development the western society used to be once.[301]

---

300. Jean-Noël Biraben, *Les hommes et la peste en France et dans les pays européens et méditerranées*. Tome II. Les hommes face à la peste, pp. 7–8. See also František Graus, *Pest-Geißler-Judenmorde. Das 14. Jahrhundert als Krisenzeit*, p. 13; Piero Morburgo, 'La peste: dinamiche di interpretazione storiografica', p. 41.
301. I.C. Jarvie, *Rationality and Relativism. In Search of a Philosophy and History of Anthropology* (London, 1984), p. 28. This theory of levels of rationalism is no longer generally accepted among anthropologists. See also Mircea Eliade, *The Myth of Eternal Return* (Princeton, 1974), p. 96.

It is important to notice that the explanation of divine wrath as a cause of natural disasters is not fundamentally different from the eschatological explanation. Indeed these two seem to be related. One is a micro-level explanation suitable for explaining local disaster and its impacts upon the community, whereas the other is macro-level explanation, which can be used to explain all natural disasters in generic way; they are simply heralds of the approaching end of the world.

Even the redeeming activities and remedies suggested by these explanations were the same. People were exhorted to do penance while there still was time. The micro-level explanations stressed that penitential activities could be a means to save the community from the actual disaster. For the macro-level explanation, the actual disaster was not of a particular importance. It was merely one in the chain of many similar events, some of which already had happened, whereas some still had to come. What was important was the historical culmination point predicted by these disasters. It was for the final reckoning that mankind was urged to do penance, not to obtain salvation from the present menace.

These micro- and macro-level explanations were not mutually exclusive. While natural disasters were interpreted as heralds of the approaching end, their immediate effects might still be lessened with the proper penitential attitude and concrete acts of satisfaction. It is this way of thinking that allows us to understand why the flagellants of 1260 were crying out loud for peace and mercy.[302] It was quite reasonable for them to believe that God would show some mercy for the chosen ones when the last days would come. After all, Jesus himself had promised in Matthew 24:22 that *'for the sake of the elect those days will be shortened.'*

Among the numerous preachers that gave both macro- and micro-level explanations of divine intervention we can single out Eudes de Châteauroux. Earlier we quoted the apocalyptic passage of his *Sermo exhortatorius propter timorem terremotum*. Having presented an apocalyptic, macro-level explanation for earthquakes, Eudes continues with micro-level explanation on the level of individual cases:

> *'Nevertheless, it has been fulfilled many times in particular cases and we are afraid that we being sinners, it is again fulfilled in our times, for the prophet explains the cause of this threat in the words immediately the preceding aforementioned words* [that is, in the words of Isaiah preceding the *thema* of the sermon]*: "My secret to myself, my secret to myself. Woe is me! The prevaricators have prevaricated: and with the prevarication of transgressors they have prevaricated. Fear and the pit and the snare are upon thee, O thou inhabitant of the earth. And it shall come to pass, that he that shall flee from the noise of the fear shall fall into the pit: and he that rid himself out of the pit shall be taken in the snare: for the flood gates from on high etc."*

---

302. Gary Dickson, 'The Flagellants of 1260 and the Crusades', p. 255.

> *For our transgressions have been multiplied, and therefore the wrath of God has flown over men bringing along famine, pestilence, sword, lightning and storms, earthquakes and other kinds of scourges from God so that even brute animals such as lions, wolfs and even insensitive elements are seen to in surge against the mindless. They will in surge as vengeance against offences of the wretched men who will not cease provoking God. Let it be that this is secret for the people who do not understand that such things come because the wrath of God, the Lord informs this to his friends and He did told it to prophets. Therefore Isaiah says: "My secret to myself, my secret to myself", for it was revealed to him, if to no one else, that God sends aforementioned punishments to sinners also in the present world, and much greater ones in the future, and therefore he said twice my secret to myself.*'[303]

Here we see that Eudes first evokes the images of the final judgement and then continues with showing that God punishes the sinners also in this world. As such punishments, Eudes mentions in particular the most common natural disasters and wars. He does not claim that natural disasters happen exclusively because of sins, but when reading between the lines we get the impression that this it is exactly what he means.

Later in the same sermon Eudes hints at the sins he thought were the specific reasons of God's wrath. It is quite likely that this discussion was meant to be understood in a generic fashion. It was not addressed to the inhabitants of Viterbo and other towns that suffered from the earthquake. This is obvious because Eudes chose sins that were treated in all treatises of moral theology. He takes from Isaiah the words fear, pit, and snare. He links them with the three sins of 1st John 2:16, that is, concupiscence of flesh, concupiscence of eyes and the pride of life. These three forms of concupiscence according to strong medieval tradition were connected with the three capital sins of lechery, avarice, and pride. Within the framework of Seven Capital sins these three were considered to be the most important or dangerous ones, the other four, namely wrath, envy, sloth, and gluttony were given far less attention.[304]

When medieval man tried to understand natural disasters, the Bible was the first place to turn to. Archetypical stories, such as Noah's flood and the destruction of Sodom and Gomorrah were referred to time and time again. For example, when Gregory of Tours and Paulus Diaconus described contemporary floods in their chronicles, they turned to the example of Noah's flood, and later writers followed their example. It was only natural that these stories were used to give meaning to contemporary natural disasters for, as Saint Augustine had written: '*In the Old Testament the New lies hid;*

---

303. Eudes de Châteauroux, *Sermones*. Sermo exhortatorius propter terremotum qui media nocte factus est Viterbii et in multis locis. Pisa Catariniana MS 21, f. 147v–148r. See Appendix 2, C.
304. Eudes de Châteauroux, *Sermones*. Sermo exhortatorius propter terremotum qui media nocte factus est Viterbii et in multis locis. Pisa Catariniana MS 21, f.148r. See Appendix 2, C.

in the New Testament the meaning of the Old becomes clear.'[305] In the medieval exegetical and ecclesiological tradition the New Testament era not only covered the events described in it, but incorporated the history of the Church until the Final Judgement. The writings of the Old Testament were a storage from which man was encouraged to seek parallels and typological explanations for contemporary events and problems.

Sometimes the examples or archetypical stories of the Old Testament are openly mentioned, at other moments their influence can be read between the lines. An example of the latter is the description of Giovanni Villani concerning the above-mentioned flood of 1333 in Florence. He wrote that it rained continuously four days and four nights. The water rose to unforeseen levels so that it seemed that the floodgates of heaven had been opened ('*...che pareano aperte le cataratte del cielo...*').[306] When he wrote this passage, Villani obviously had in mind the passage of Genesis that describes the beginning of the flood, that is, Genesis 7:11. In the Vulgate text it reads: '*...rupti sunt omnes fontes abyssi magnae et cataractae caeli apertae sunt.*' The source and inspiration of his language most likely was immediately recognised by his readers, who therefore were able to read a part of his message that may be lost to modern readers who are less familiar with biblical language. Using Noah's flood as a point of comparison when describing floods was by Villani's time a well-established literary convention. Numerous influential earlier historians, such as Gregory of Tours and Paulus Diaconus, had used it.[307]

The general tone or the moral lesson of these two Old Testament stories, that is Noah's flood and Sodom and Gomorrah, directed the opinions of theologians. Natural disasters were perceived as a sign of God's wrath towards sinners. Any other explanation would have been extremely difficult to argument with recourse to the Bible.

Consequently there is no lack of sources describing natural disasters as the revenge of God for the sins of mankind as whole, or more specific groups. Some of these sources have been indicated in different books concerning the history of death.[308] Numerous others are found in manuscript and early printed sources. The French Dominican Étienne de Bourbon presented in his book *Tractatus de diversis materiis predicabilibus* a short description of an earthquake that took place in Tyre. The passage that interests us is found in a section of Étienne's book dealing with the seven capital sins. Having named the subspecies of the sin of lechery (simple fornication, sacrilege,

---

305. see Laurence Moulinier e Odile Redon, '"Pareano aperte le cataratte del cielo": le ipotesi di Giovanni Villani sull'inondazione del 1333 a Firenze', p. 138; Norman Cohn, *Noah's Flood*, p. 23.
306. *Cronica di Giovanni Villani*, tomo VI (Firenze, 1823), p. 5. For a more specific analysis of this passage of Villani, see Laurence Moulinier e Odile Redon, '"Pareano aperte le cataratte del cielo": le ipotesi di Giovanni Villani sull'inondazione del 1333 a Firenze,' pp. 137–154.
307. Laurence Moulinier e Odile Redon, '"Pareano aperte le cataratte del cielo"', p. 138.
308. See for example Christopher Daniel, *Death and Burial in Medieval England 1066–1550* (London, 1999; 1st published 1997), pp. 75–76.

adultery, incest, and sins against the nature), Étienne underlines the dangers of sin against the nature (*peccatum contra naturam*) by telling a story of an earthquake in the form of an *exemplum*. According to a person whom Étienne knew well and who was present in Tyre during the earthquake, many people were crushed to death because they had been practising this abominable vice when the houses collapsed. Étienne compared the faith of the Tyre victims to those of sodomites of Genesis 19.[309]

The earthquake described in Étienne's *exemplum* was not dreamt up to convince his readers. It actually had happened and is also mentioned by other sources, such as Jacques de Vitry's *Historia Orientalis*. It was customary that a certain measure of truthfulness was required from *exemplum* stories. This has been shown with regard to the exemplum collection of Étienne de Bourbon. Several of his *exempla* have been studied critically and found to be based on real historical events.[310] Étienne de Bourbon was not the only one to attribute the earthquake to the sinfulness of man. Francesco Pipino da Bologna described it in his *Chronicon* and explained it with the *exigentibus peccatis hominum* topos.[311]

There is another interesting story among the *exempla* of Étienne de Bourbon, namely, the history of the collapse of Mount Granier in Savoy in 1248.

---

309. Anton Lecoy de la Marche, *Anecdotes historiques, légendes et apoloques tirés du recueil inédit d'Étienne de Bourbon, dominicain du XIIIe siècle* (Paris, 1877), no. 464, ss. 400–401. On other examples of explaining natural disasters with Divine wrath within the exemplum genre, see Jacques Berlioz, 'Les recits exemplaires, sources imprevues de l'histoire des catastrophes naturelles au Moyen Age', pp. 17–22.

310. Jacques Berlioz, *Catastrophes narurelles et calamités au Moyen Age*, pp. 34–35. Here it is enough to mention three studies on the historicity of Étienne's *exempla*. Jacques Berlioz's articles *L'effondrement du mont Granier en Savoie (fin 1248). Production, transmission et réception des récits historiques et légendaires (XIIIe–XVIIe siècles)* and *1219 la catastrophe du lac d'Oisans* have been re-printed in his *Catastrophes naturelles et calamités au Moyen Age*. Jean-Claude Schmitt's classic study *Le Saint Levrier. Guinefort, guérisseur d'enfants depuis le XIIIe siècle* also deals with the historical reality behind one of Étienne's *exemplum* stories.

311. Francesco Pipino da Bologna, *Chronicon*, col. 626. 'Anno Domini 1169 qui fuit annus Friderici Imperatoris 16. in partibus Orientis et in Terra promissionis, exigentibus peccatis hominum, terraemotus multas urbes, ecclesias, oppida et villas subruit et innumera populorum millia hians terra deglutivit et aedificiorum casu morituros operuit.' *Peccatis exigentibus hominum* was a common and ancient topos or literary formula used to express the causality of human sin and divine punishment. It had been used already by Gregory VII and Orderic Vitalis. There are numerous examples of its use in different connections, for example the chroniclers of crusades used it to explain how it was possible that battles were lost in the holy war against infidels. It was the sinfulness of some crusaders that endangered the whole campaign and made them worthless to act as instruments of Divine plan. See Elisabeth Siberry, *Criticism of Crusading 1095–1274* (Oxford, 1985), pp. 69–72. One stumbles into it also in different chronicles and catastrophe sermons, for example Eudes de Châteauroux uses it in his Sermo exhortatorius qui media nocte factus est Uiterbii et in multis locis: 'Nichilominus iam multociens particulariter impleta est et timemus, ne temporibus nostris peccatis nostris exigentibus in parte impleatur; Pisa Cateriniana MS 21, f. 147v. See also Antti Ruotsala, *Europeans and Mongols*, p. 62, n. 12.

We have already seen that the English Benedictine chronicler Matthew of Paris moved between natural and supernatural explanations when describing this catastrophe. His contemporary Étienne de Bourbon had no problems deciding that the earthquake was caused by Divine wrath. His *exemplum* makes the priest Jacques Benevais, a member of the count of Savoy's retinue, responsible for the Divinely induced earthquake. Jacques had managed to lay his hands on the profits and lands of a priory just below Mount Granier by promising in exchange that he would persuade his master to join the papal party. Jacques and his accomplices had driven away the prior and the convent and were celebrating their success in the empty priory when God's vengeance (literally) fell upon them in the night.[312]

Medieval sermon literature provides numerous additional examples. Federico Pisano Visconti stated in his first Rogation Day sermon that God sends three types of tribulations to mankind as punishment of their sins, namely, pestilence, famine, and the sword.[313] The Dominican friar Aldobrandino da Toscanella wrote laconically that sin is the principal reason for our loss of spiritual and temporal goods.[314] His confrere Jacques de Lausanne preached about drought. He implied that where physical rain is absent, spiritual rain, that is, rain of grace, would be missing as well. Jacques compared the state of sin to disease. When man is suffering from fever and internal dryness, his mouth is also unusually dry. Similarly, the sickness of sin causes drought.[315]

One of the most enlighting sermons is Jacques de Lausanne's *De pluvia vel pro alio tribulatione*. The title suggests that we are dealing with a model sermon. Nevertheless, the text implies, as is also obvious from the context that it was originally delivered in connection with a flood. Jacques compared God to an archer who has drawn his bow and is waiting to let the arrow go to punish the sinners. The only way to avoid the archer's punishment is to be on the side of the string, not on the side of the arch, that is behind rather than in front of the bow.

God's punishment, which in this sermon is compared to an arrow, comes sooner or later, when the archer has grown tired of keeping his bow ready,

---

312. The *exemplum* is edited in Jacques Berlioz, *Catastrophes naturelles et calamités au Moyen Age*, p. 133. Berlioz analyses moral and political contexts of this *exemplum* in pages 108–113.
313. Federico Pisano Visconti, *Sermones*. In letaniis, sermo primus. Firenze Biblioteca Medicea Laurenziana MS Plut.33.sin.1, f. 48r. 'uel propter alia tria genera tribulationis quos Deus inmittit propter peccata populorum, uidelicet pestilentie, famis et gladii.'
314. Aldobrandino da Toscanella, *Sermones de tempore*. In rogationibus, sermo de epistolarum. BAV. MS Ottob. lat. 557, f. 200v. 'Principalis causa priuationis bonorum spiritualium et temporalium est peccatum.'
315. Jacques de Lausanne OP, *Sermones de communi sanctorum*. Sermo ad impetrandam pluviam. BAV MS Vat.lat. 1250 II, f. 152r–v. 'Ille defectus pluuie corporalis uenit ex defectu pluuie spirituales, scilicet, gracie Ier. 3: "Polluisti terram fornicationibus tuis et malitiis propterea prohibite sunt scille pluuiarum." Sicut enim siccitas in lingua infirmi et indicat calorem inordinatum et siccitatem interius, sic siccitas aque temporalis prouenit ex siccitate et peccato spirituali anime.'

that is, when the time of mercy and doing penitence has gone. If no sooner, it inevitably comes with the final judgement. However, God punishes also on a smaller scale before Judgement day. It is such smaller-scale punishment that the sermon is all about:

> '*Therefore God, willing to punish the vices of these days seems to be willing to bring on a new deluge. We all are gathered here that we might find a remedy against this deluge, and we do not see other chance but appeal to God the archer so that he turns away from us the arch of his vengeance and turns to us the string of his mercy. This is the advice of Malachias: "And now beseech ye the face of God, that He may have mercy on you (for by your hand hath this been done).*"'[316]

It is obvious that the original delivery of the sermon was connected with a religious meeting organised because of a flood, such as a mass in some station church before or after the procession. It is interesting to note that the preacher did alter the text of Malachias to make it a better fit for the occasion. Where the original text simply says that *by your hand hath this been done*, the version given by our preacher replaces the word *this* ('*hoc*') with the words *this bad weather* ('*hic malum tempus*'). Such alteration of the biblical text was a common device to emphasise the homiletic message. A little trick like this sufficed to make the audience see more clearly the connection between their sinful activities and the bad weather and flooding.

An anonymous sermon *pro pluvia* on the theme *Dimitte peccata eorum et da pluviam super terram* takes King Salomon and uses him as an exemplary figure to drive home the lesson of sin as a cause of disaster. The preacher starts by introducing King Salomon. He tells that the king said numerous prayers to God, but amongst them were three very special ones. One was to obtain victory in battle, another against pestilence, and the third one to procure rains:

> '*A third one for the rains. If heaven shall be shut up, and no rain will fall because of the sins of the people and the drought will lead to famine and lack of food in the land, this happens so that people may recognise their sins, invoke the generous Lord so that He may forgive sins of the people, and He may find it proper to concede rain to land. For this third prayer Salomon said the above-mentioned words*, which *we have very conveniently quoted here, for we see that because of our sins the sky is closed so that it will not rain on us. We see also such severe drought around us that famine is already setting on the land as well as shortage of food, and if He who only can help us will not come to our rescue, we fear more and more after*

---

316. Jacques de Lausanne OP, *De pluvia vel pro alio tribulatione*. BAV. MS Vat.lat. 1261, f. 162r–163r. 'Immo Dominus contra uoragines uitiorum uidetur diebus istis uelle facere nouum diluuium aquarum. Ad hoc autem sumus hic congregati omnes ut contra hoc diluuium inueniamus remedium et non uidemus aliud nisi ut recurreamus ad sagitandum Deum ut archum sue uindicte a nobis auertat et cordam sue misericordie ad nos conuertat. Hoc consilium dat Malachias propheta: "Nunc deprecamini uultum Domini ut misereatur uestri, de manu enim uestra factum est hic malum tempus."'

each day. Therefore we must follow the example of that king who was so devote and so humble, and pray with these words: "Forgive their sins and give rain upon land."'[317]

This sermon leaves very little room for speculation concerning the cause of the drought: people's sinfulness, nothing more, nothing less.

The Dominican friar Jacques de Lausanne wrote about a drought in his sermon *Ad impetrandam pluviam*. He also made a comparison between bodily illness and sin. Just as the tongue of sick people is often dry because of the inordinate bodily temperature and internal dryness, drought of temporal waters in a similar fashion comes from the dryness and sins of soul. He quotes Psalm 142 to verify this message: '*My soul is as earth without water unto thee.*'[318] Psalm 142 *Exaudi Domine* was one of the seven penitential Psalms that were sung during the catastrophe processions. Thus the context made the connection between sin and drought even stronger in the minds of the listeners than the outspoken words of the preacher. The comparison between bodily sickness and sins as a sickness of the soul was a medieval commonplace.

The sources are in most cases written by members of the clergy. Sometimes, however, they allow us to know to what extent the explanation of natural disasters with recourse to divine wrath was accepted by the population at large. For example, sometimes we get to know that the people took the liberty of deciding who were to blame without consulting the church. The Cistercian Abbot Johannes von Viktring, who described the epidemic of 1267 in Austria, wrote in his *Liber certarum historiarum*:

> '*In the year of our Lord 1267 there came pestilence and hunger, destruction of cities and villages all over Austria. They were so bad that a large share of the population and almost all the cattle died miserably. Ordinary people claimed commonly that this epidemic was brought about by God because of the illicit matrimony of the king.*'[319]

---

317. Anonymous, *Sermones*. Pro pluvia. BAV. MS Vat. Burghes. 138, f. 232r. 'Terciam pro pluuia ut, scilicet, si propter peccata populi claudentur celum ne plueret et sic per siccitatem orietur fames et caristia in terra et propter recognoscent peccata sua, inuocarent Dominum largitorem ut dimitteret peccata populi et dignaretur concedere pluuiam terre. Et in hac peticione tercia dixit uerbum propositum quod est hic conuenienter assumptum, uidemus enim propter peccata nostra celum clausum ne pluet nobis et uidemus tantam siccitatem quod iam fames incipit multa et eciam caristia. Et nisi succurrat ille qui succurrere potest, timemus cotidie de maior propter quod ad exemplum et similitudinem regis illius tunc tam deuoti, tunc tam humilis debemus dicere uerbum istud: "Dimitte peccata eorum et da pluuia."'
318. Jacques de Lausanne OP, *Sermones de communi sanctorum*. Ad impetrandam pluviam. BAV. MS Vat.lat. 1250 II, f. 152r. 'Sicut enim siccitas in lingua infirmi et indicat calorem inordinatum et siccitatem interius, sic siccitas aque temporalis prouenit ex siccitate et peccato spirituali anime Ps: "Anima mea quasi terra sitiens ad te semper."'
319. Johannes von Viktring, *Liber certarum historiarum*. Ed. Fedorus Schneider. Tomus I. MGH Scriptores Rerum Germanicarum 1. (Hannover-Leipzig, 1909), p. 170.

The population, or at least a considerable part of it, felt that the epidemic and famine were brought about by the sin of the king. Whether this attitude had developed spontaneously among the population or whether it was a product of ecclesiastical propaganda, we do not know. However, it seems obvious that the explanation of the clergy was appreciated and shared to some extent by the lay population.

Here we may remember the Florentine flood of 1333. Giovanni Villani repeats in his *Cronica* the considered opinion of the local theologians. They explained that God uses nature as a means to punish the sins of mankind, and He has the power to send his punishment according to the laws of nature, in supernatural means, and even against the laws of nature. However, the really interesting part is Villani's personal opinion. He took the view that the flood was indeed caused by the outrageous sins of the Florentines, and that the whole city would probably have perished, had there not been the prayers of holy men and the religious communities, as well as the liberal alms given by the Florentines. These were good enough to invite God's mercy and stop the flood.[320]

Villani did not limit himself to commenting on the particular flood in Florence. On a more general level he wrote:

> *'But to return to our original question and its solution, and keeping in mind the above stated examples, which are true and clear, we may say that all the pestilences, battles, sackings and floods, arsons and persecutions, shipwrecks and exiles come upon us with the permission of Divine justice, to wash away our sins. Sometimes they come according to natural order, sometimes supernaturally, as Divine power sees fit.'*[321]

A few important elements in Villani's account deserve specific emphasis. At first it is interesting that he took such a great interest in theological reasoning. After all, Villani was not member of the clergy, but a normal Florentine merchant. His description of the theologians' arguments is very detailed, and he does not limit himself to retelling their general arguments, but also repeats faithfully all the biblical quotations and other finesses used to argue the case. If Villani's chronicle can be used as indicative for lay opinion on general, it would seem that at least in Florence, many people were deeply interested in the possible causes of the disaster. They were not willing to fatalistically accept what had happened, but were actively seeking to know the causes of their misfortune.

The story of Villani shows that at least some laymen took pains to listen, learn, and understood theological reasoning. What is even more important, they accepted the clerical theory of Divine punishment of sins as a cause of the catastrophe. Villani tells us that majority of the population turned to penance and took communion to placate God's wrath.[322] In Florence at least,

---

320. *Cronica di Giovanni Villani*, tomo VI, pp. 13–24.
321. *Cronica di Giovanni Villani*, tomo VI, pp. 21–22.
322. *Cronica di Giovanni Villani*, tomo VI, p. 13. 'In Firenze ebbe del detto diluvio

astrologists, natural philosophers, and their followers were in the minority. The majority of the people believed that the disaster was brought upon them by their sins.

Divine punishment for the sins was the first explanation proposed in connection with the series of earthquakes that ravished the kingdom of Aragon in 1374. Penitential processions in three consecutive days were organised in the city of Barcelona soon after the worst of these earthquakes had struck in the night between 2 and 3 Mars. The most important relics from the churches were carried along the streets and the turnout of the crowd was exceptionally numerous. Not only were the citizens and clergy present, but also the royal family and nobility. It is obvious from the sources that both ecclesiastical and lay authorities believed that the earthquake was caused by the sins of people. Equal measures were taken in other Aragonian towns, such as Tortosa and Cervera. In Cervera, the particular sins were mentioned. A common opinion was that earthquake was caused by the evil habit of making oaths in the name of God, Holy Virgin or the saints or because of other blasphemies. Such practices were forbidden on the penalty of fine of ten gold pieces.[323]

The fifteenth-century preachers shared the opinions of their thirteenth-century predecessors. The German preacher Johannes von Werden continued to attribute natural disasters to divine punishment. He wrote that according to the Holy Scripture and Petrus Lombardus all the misery originates from sin, that is, it is a punishment for sin. Johannes specifies that misery in this context mean storms, disagreements, sterility of the soil etc. Naturally, the problems connected to agriculture, such as lack of fertility, are emphasised, since we are dealing with a Rogation Day sermon.[324]

The Italian Franciscan friar Bernardino da Busti, as we have seen above, took the view that natural disasters can sometimes be caused by totally natural reasons without any Divine intervention. Nevertheless, he stressed repeatedly that they also occur because of the sinfulness of the victims. Bernardino shouted theatrically to sinners: '*O you wretched! Why do not you fear to offend God?*' Then he moved on to explain that the plague and the corruption of the air (and indeed any other adversities in this world) are in most cases sent by God without any preceding warning signs when He is angered by our vices. Bernardino offered two examples. The first one was from the early Christian writers and the latter, concerning a plague in

---

grande ammirazione e tremore per tutte genti, dubitando non fosse giudicio di Dio per le nostre peccata, che poichè bassò il diluvio più di appresso non finava di piovere con continui tuoni e baleni molto spaventovoli; per la qual cosa le più delle genti di Firenze ricorsono alla penitenzia e communicazione, e fu bene fatto per appaciare l'ira di Dio.'

323. Carmen Batlle, 'Destructions naturelles des villes de la Couronne d'Aragon au Bas Moyen Âge', pp. 73–74.
324. Johannes von Werden, *Dormi secure de sanctis* (Strasbourg, 1493). De rogationibus. Sermo 22, f. G2v. 'Dicit magister li. II dis. IV quod ex peccato miseria est, scilicet fieri tempestates siue discordias siue sterilitates terre et huiusmodi etc., ut patet in sacra scriptura qualiter omnia talia acciderunt propter peccatum.'

Milan, came possibly from his personal experience. Bernardino told that in 1451, an extremely lethal pestilence struck the city of Milan and during it *'innumerable men died every day'*. The air was so polluted that if one took a piece of warm bread from the oven in the morning and put it out, it was totally spoiled by the evening.[325]

Having established that disasters fell upon mankind because God was angered by its sins, Bernardino moved on to discuss in more detail the sins that in his time were sufficiently upsetting God to make Him punish mankind with the plague. He started by saying that God indeed punishes men because of numerous sins, but that he will, for the sake of brevity, discuss only a few of these sins. As often happens when a speaker or preacher lets his audience know he is not going to speak for long, Bernardino launches into a description of sins that lasts for several pages. These included: sacrilege and vain glory among the clergy, idolatry, contempt of preaching, not paying tithes, gluttony, complaining about God, spreading rumours about others, unjust wars, deceitful business, fraudulent contracts, and ingratitude. The worst four sins, which Bernardino described with more detail, were abomination of Divine mandates, pride, robbery, and dishonest self-indulgence. In connection of the last one Bernardino emphasised sodomy more than anything else.[326] Starting from Bernardino da Siena, sodomy had been one of the favourite subjects of fifteenth-century Italian preachers.

Demons on the Loose

There exists a slightly different version of this explanation of Divine punishment. In the above-mentioned examples, God was punishing the sinners directly by letting or causing nature to punish them. Some writers chose to believe that God was not personally punishing sinners with the help of nature, but He merely withdrew his protection and allowed the demons occupying

---

325. Bernardino de Busti OFM, *Rosarium sermonum* (Venezia, 1498). Sermo de pestilentie signis, causis et remediis, f. 257v. 'O miseri peccatores! Quare non timetes offendere Deum? Pestilentia enim et corruptio aeris multotiens mittitur a Deo nullis signis precedentibus, quando nobis irascitur pro uiciis nostris ut enim refert Horosius libro tertio et Augustinus libro quinto *De ciuitate Dei* capitulo 18o anno ab urbe condita 481o ingens pestilentia urbem Romam intrauit et sybilla consulta respondit illam pestem ira Dei illatam. In ciuitate quoque Mediolani in 1451 horribilissima pestis adeo perualuit ut quasi innumerabiles homines quotidie morerentur. Tantaque erat corruptio aeris et morbositas quod accipientes panem recentem et callidum tunc coactum et ponentes mane ad aerem postea in sero reperiebant totam morcidam.' On the last part of the division of his sermon, Bernardino returns to this theme and remarks that he is not only speaking of the pestilence, but the sermon can be applied to cover other adversities in this life too: 'Cum igitur ut supradictum est ex Diuina iustitia propter peccatum disponatur unusquisque ad pestem et cetera aduersa...'; f. 260v.
326. Bernardino da Busti OFM, *Rosarium sermonum* (Venezia, 1498). Sermo de pestilentie signis, causis et remediis, f. 257v–2260v.

nature to have their own way. This demonological explanation is encountered mostly in sources written by or ultimately addressed to ordinary lay people.

Vincent de Beauvais wrote in his enormously popular encyclopaedia *Speculum naturale* that the demons were expelled from heaven after the mutiny of Lucifer against God. They settled in the air to wait for the final judgement. From there they tempt people and cause storms. Vincent added that according to pagan philosophers and learned doctors the air is as full of demons as there are tiny dust particles in the sun's rays.[327]

Preachers and moralists were quick to adopt this demonological explanation in their writings. Vincent Ferrer told his audience why they should organise processions and prayers in Rogation time. One of the reasons he mentioned was that when God had created heaven and earth, Lucifer and some other fallen angels started a rebellion against Him and were expelled from Heaven. Some of them went to hell where they torture sinners, others went to earth where they tempt us, and yet others stayed in the middle layers of the atmosphere. There they plot against people to destroy their crops, and thus to drive them to despair so that they will sin against God with impatience and blasphemies. According to Vincent, demons would have the power to destroy the whole world if God did not limit their activities.[328] Therefore it was essential to organise Rogation Day processions and litanies. If prayers would cease and God would withhold His protection, the demons would be free to have their way with mankind.

In essence this explanation of natural disasters is very similar to the above-mentioned explanation of God's wrath. Even if it is the demons that do the damage and cause the disasters, they are only operating because God allows them to (*'Deo permittente'*). Why does God permit them to destroy crops and do other damage to Christians? There are two obvious explanations, to tempt people and to punish the sinners.

We meet another example of this explanation in the pages of Villani's chronicle. In the middle of explaining completely rational theological reasons for the flood, he retold an *exemplum* story he had heard from the abbot of Vallambrosa monastery, who was, as Villani notes a religious and trustworthy man (*'uomo religioso e degno di fede'*). While praying, a certain hermit had

---

327. Vincent de Beauvais, *Speculum naturale*, col. 306.
328. Vincent Ferrer, *Sermones aestivales*. Feria secunda rogationum, sermo II, p. 176. 'Ab initio, postquam Deus in celo empyreo creavit sanctos angelos, Lucifer qui erat maior, peccavit contra Dominum cum magna multitudine angelorum. Credo quod plures sint quam sint folia arborum in mundo, qui ex peccato facti sunt daemones, quos Deus eiecit de paradiso. Et aliqui ceciderunt in infernum ad cruciandum animas damnatas, aliqui autem remanserunt circa nos ad tentandum, sed tot manserunt in media regione aëris et in tanto numero sicut sunt atomi in radio solis. Et quid faciunt ibi? Tenent consilium contra nos, quando blada sunt colligenda, et vinum, impediunt naturam qui possunt ex posse naturali, Deo permittente, destruere totum orbem, et mittunt lapides et destruunt omnia bona, ut christiani peccent contra Dominum per impatientiam et blasphemias. Propter hoc modo oramus ut Dominus compescat daemonum malitias.'

heard the infernal rumble as if there were numerous men riding in a state of fury. He made the sign of the cross, opened his shutter, and saw a multitude of terrible black horsemen galloping by. One of them said to the hermit: *'We are going to Florence to drown its inhabitants because of their sins, if God permits it.'*[329]

The black horsemen were demons. It was a common topos of *exemplum* literature to present them in a form of black horsemen.[330] The whole story is a very conventional *exemplum* story. It is so conventional that it makes one wonder whether the abbot of Vallambrosa had been affected by *exemplum* literature when telling the story to Villani. But leaving aside the form of the story, it is important to note that here again the supreme power of God is emphasised. The demons are able to drown the people of Florence only if God permits them to do it ('*se Iddio il concederà*'). Thus the common point with Villani's (or Vallambrosa abbot's) story and Vincent Ferrer's more theologically oriented explanation is that while the demons indeed are the executors of the actual destruction, they are only able to work within the limits laid down by God.

Even though the devil and demons were considered to have the power to bring on natural disasters, if not freely then at least with the permission of God, they were perceived as explanations very rarely when compared to the cases of direct divine intervention. Most commonly they are encountered in connection with one specific type of natural disasters, that is, storms and heavy winds as seen above. These were traditionally perceived as the work of demons.

Causality of Punishment

So far we have discussed the explanations of natural disasters, and found out that they were either explained by divine wrath or scientifically, but even the latter explanation could include an element of divine intervention. Now it is time to see how this model of natural disasters explained how God's anger was operationalised and turned into something that nearly matches a mathematical equation, or a sentence of systematic logic. We start with the *Sermo propter timorem terre motus* by cardinal Eudes de Châteauroux.[331] The very first chapter of the sermon makes this point in a manner, which leaves no doubt whatsoever:

> *'"The earth shook and trembled: the foundations of the mountains were troubled and were moved." [Ps. 17:8]. Job says in the fifth chapter [Job 5:6]: "Nothing upon earth is done without a cause: and sorrow doth not spring out of the ground." And in Thimeo: "Nothing is done without a legitimate cause preceding it." Truly in earth there is no pestilence, no*

---

329. *Cronica di Giovanni Villani*, tomo VI, p. 22.
330. See Frederic C. Tubach, *Index exemplorum. A Handbook of Medieval Religious Tales*. FF Communications No. 204 (Helsinki, 1981), no. 1618, 1619, and 3703.
331. See Appendix 1.

famine, no earthquake that happens without a cause, but nearly all the bad that happens is brought upon us by our sins.'[332]

At the end of his sermon Eudes also gave some advice to his readers concerning the remedies for natural disasters:

'If we get angry with ourselves the wrath of God will cease, and then He will establish the pillars of earth, that is, make the earth stabile and suitable for the habitations of men, and remove the earthquakes and other things that are against us. Let us then pray that we shall do penance for our sins so that we may make the face of God happy and serene again, and desist from our sins, for when the cause ends, so ends the effect. In this help us Lord Jesus Christ who shall live for evermore. Amen.'[333]

The attention of the reader is drawn immediately to the piece of impeccable logic: *'When the cause ends, so ends the effect.'* (lat. cessante causa cessabit et effectus). This quotation suggests a straightforward causality relation between sinfulness and natural disasters according to the following scheme:

sin = causa
natural disaster = effectus

Whenever there is *causa*, then there is also *effectus*. When the *causa* has been removed, the *effectus* will equally be removed. This inputs reason into the system. Instead of dealing with unpredicted and random occurrences, natural disasters turn out to be a part of the logical world order, which can be, if not controlled, then at least explained in a satisfactory manner. Order is made out of chaos.

It could be objected that too much is being made of a rather limited corpus of sources in claiming that natural disasters were always and almost mechanically explained with sin. This might be the case if we would have to rely on the substance of the sermons only; however, the similarities are not limited to what is said, they can also be found in the manner of presentation. Let us turn back to the catch phrase *'When the cause ends, so ends the effect.'* It is significant that the same sentence or something closely resembling it can also be found in many other catastrophe sermons – so frequently that it cannot be a mere co-incidence.

Eudes de Châteauroux himself repeats it in another catastrophe sermon – *Sermo in processione facta propter inundationem aquarum.*[334] The sermon begins with an exposition of the Genesis story on the creation of the world. *'In the beginning God created heaven, and earth. And earth was void and empty, and darkness was upon the face of the deep.'* Eudes asks rhetorically

---

332. Eudes de Châteauroux, *Sermo propter timorem terremotus.* Arras Bibliothèque Municip. MS 137, ff. 88r–v. For the Latin text see Appendix 2, B.
333. Ibid. f. 88v. For the Latin text see Appendix 2,B.
334. Eudes de de Châteauroux, *Sermo in processione facta propter inundationem aquarum.* Arras Bibl. mun. 137, ff. 78v–80r. For the Latin text see Appendix 2,A.

why God allowed waters to rule the earth in the beginning and answers '*because the world was void, that is, not bearing fruit and empty of inhabitants, and therefore there was no damage doing so nor anything to wonder about that he left earth be occupied by waters.*' Then Eudes comes to the bottom line of his argument:

> '*In a similar manner there is nothing to wonder about the floods that come now, rather it is a miracle that God does not cover the earth with a new deluge because it is void and empty, truly void because it does not produce fruit, for in present times the earth does produce no or very little fruit. In these days the prophesy of third chapter of Habacuc seems to be fulfilled: 'For the fig-tree shall not blossom: and there shall be no spring in the vines. The labour of the olive-tree shall fail: and the fields shall yield no food. The flock be cut off from the fold; and there shall be no herd in the stalls.*'

Then follows a substantially large part of the sermon where Eudes explains his quotation from Habacuc. The fig tree signifies priests and the religious, the vines stand for prelates and princes, the olive-tree means burghers, and the fields are peasants. The sins of these social groups are the reason why the earth does not bear fruit and deserves to be punished with floods. Not surprisingly, Eudes draws on the deluge in the time of Noah as a parallel case from the Old Testament to show his audience what could happen, if man keeps sinning in a similar manner. For Eudes it is only reasonable that nature, which is a servant of God, should punish those who sin against God, just like the servants of a temporal lord punish those who insult their master. Every element of nature does this punishing according to its means: earth through earthquakes, water through floods, air through storms, and fire through lightning. This idea implies that Eudes too held the position that catastrophes happened according to the normal laws of nature, but yet in accordance with the will of God.

Having stated the true cause of the flood Eudes moved on to the encouraging part of his sermon. He wrote that God has mercy on the great multitude of sinners if he can find a few righteous amongst their number '*and if our sins that are the springs of the abyss would come to an end, then the punishments inflicted on us by God would also come to end, that is, the floodgates of the heaven would be closed.*' This sentence is formulated exactly according to the model of *cessante causa cesset et effectus*. Only the word *causa* is changed to words *peccata nostra* and the word *effectus* with word *pene*.

It has been possible to find several other, even more obvious examples of the *cessante causa cessat et effectus* -topos in sermon literature. They prove that it was widely used and remained fashionable over an extended period of time. The following examples come from three different centuries. The first case is a late thirteenth-century sermon by Nicolas de Gorran titled *Ad impetrandum serenitatem*. This sermon starts as follows:

"'And He brought the wind upon the earth, and the waters were abated" Gen. X [Genesis 8,1]. It has been known for ages that the waters started flooding because of the flood of sins. Similarly it happens that the rain comes pouring down because of the flood of sins. When the cause is removed the effect goes away easily too. Therefore those who make penance will receive divine favour so that their temporal adversities cease, as can be understood from what is said above, and where the receiving of divine favour is handled in words: "And He brought the wind."'[335]

An anonymous Swedish late fourteenth- or early fifteenth-century preacher used this phrase as a *thema* of his sermon! It says in the margin of the manuscript *Item sermo*, the actual text starts with the words: *'Who doubts that when the cause is removed the effect will pass away, that is, people would stop sinning, God would also cease punishing the kingdom* [the kingdom of Sweden that is].'[336]

Bernardino da Busti used this same topos in his sermon *de pestilentie signis, causis et remediis,* written in the last quarter of the fifteenth century. He wrote that since it now is well established that the cause of pestilence is sin, it is possible to remove the pestilence by removing the sin. He quotes Aristotle to make this point and continues to argue it: *'Elsewhere it is said that when the reason is removed, so is the effect....thus as sin, as stated above, is the cause of pestilence, therefore if the sin is removed so will be also the pestilence...Oh you sinners, if you do not want that God sends you pestilence, or if you do want him to stop one that He has already sent to you, stop sinning and the pestilence will also stop.'*[337]

It seems beyond any doubt that the *cessante causa cessat et effectus* was a common feature of catastrophe sermons. The interesting question is: where did the notion come from? Considering the fact that the relation between sin and natural disasters was established as a completely predictable law, it should come as no surprise that it should have been described in juridical jargon. There is a close parallel in Gratian's *Decretals*, although the context is

---

335. Nicolas de Gorran OP, *Sermones de communi sanctorum et de occasionibus*. Ad impetrandum serenitatem sermo primus. UUB. C 18, f. 60r. 'Adduxit spiritum super terram et imminute sunt aque Gen. X. Antiquitus propter diluuium peccatorum factum est diluuium aquarum, sic et modo propter inundationes peccatorum fiunt inundationes pluuiarum et **quia cessante causa facilius cessat et effectus**, ideo penitentibus diuina condescendit benignitas ut mundana cessat aduersitas sicut patet in uerbo proposito ubi tangitur diuine benignitatis condescentio quia: "adduxit spiritum."'
336. Anonymous, *Sermo*. UUB. C 226, f. 101v. '***Quis dubitat de hoc quod cessante causa cesset et eius effectus**. Igitur, si cessarent homines peccare, cessaret et Deus regnum perlagare.*'
337. Bernardino da Busti OFM, *Rosarium sermonum* (Venezia, 1498). Sermo de pestilentie signis, causis et remediis, f. 260v. 'Cum igitur, ut supradictum est ex diuina iustitia propter peccatum disponatur unusquisque ad pestem et cetera aduersa, remoueamus a nobis peccatum et remouabitur pestis....**Et alibi dicitur quod remota causa remouetur effectus**....Cum igitur peccatum ut supra patuit sit causa pestis, ideo remoto peccato remouebitur ipsa pestilentia....O igitur peccatores si non uultis quod Deus mittat uobis pestilentiam, uel quod iam missam faciat cessare, **cessate a peccatis et cessabit pestilentia**.'

completely different. I quote it in the original Latin, to highlight the linguistic similarities: '*Sed sciendum est, quod ecclesiasticae prohibitiones proprias habent causas, quibus cessantibus cessant et ipsae.*'[338]

Ever after Gratian, the *cessante causa* topos was used fairly commonly in different contexts, most extensively by Innocent III in his letters and privileges. It also comes up in constitutions of the Fourth Lateran Council. In the 36th constitution it says: '*Cum cessante causa cesset et effectus, statuimus ut siue iudex ordinarius siue delegatus* [...].' More important is, however, constitution 22. It states that corporal sickness is sometimes caused by sin, and urges medical doctors to advice their patients to call doctors of the soul, so that once the spiritual disease is eliminated normal medical healing can be started. This advice is followed by the remark '*cum causa cessante cessat effectus.*'[339] Antonio García y García argues that this passage is modelled after Innocent III's *Commentarium in septem Psalmos poenitentiales*.[340] Thus the constitution 22 not only established for the times to come the connection between sin and physical disease, but it also presented a new useful topos for the catastrophe sermons.

It is very plausible that the authority of General Council constitutions was significant in popularising the *cessante causa cessat et effectus* topos. Nevertheless one has to take into consideration that it was already reasonably well known before the Fourth Lateran Council. To the present author's knowledge, the first writer to use this topos to describe the relation between sin and punishment was Petrus Comestor in his *Historia Scholastica*: '*Et sanavit paralyticum ante se demissum per tegulas, primo remittens peccata ejus, quae fuerant causa morbi, quia quod ob causam fit, cessante causa cessare debet effectus.*'[341] Given the popularity of the *Historia Scholastica* in preaching circles, it is quite possible that this passage was in fact the primordial source for the *cessante causa topos*. Be that as it may, together with the 22th Constitution of the Fourth Lateran Council it was destined to sink into the minds of many clerical readers in centuries to come.

Purgatory in this World

It would be nice and convenient to have a single clerically promoted explanation for natural disasters. Alas, such is not the case. Not all the members of the clergy were promoting the theory of Divine wrath as a cause for natural

---

338. D.61, c.8 § 2.
339. IV Lateran Council, constitutiones 22 and 36.
340. *Constitutiones Concilii quarti Lateranensis una cum Commentariis glossatorum.* Edidit Antonius García y García. Monumenta Iuris Canonici. Series A: Corpus Glossatorum. Vol. 2 (Città del Vaticano, 1981), p. 69, n. 3; Innocentius III, *Commentarius in septem psalmos poenitentialis.* PL 217, col. 990. 'Saluberrimum ergo est concilium, ut qui indiget corporali medela, Spiritualium prius exigat et accipiat medicinam, quatenus cessante causa, cesset et effectus. Corporalis autem infirmitas, etsi saepe, non tamen semper provenit ex peccato.'
341. Petrus Comestor, *Historia Scholastica* PL 198, c. 1567.

disasters. Some of them were proposing a completely different explanation. God was not punishing or chastising sinners with natural cataclysms; He was merely testing the virtuous and the chosen ones sending them temptations and tribulations before granting them the ultimate reward in the kingdom to come. There were yet others who posited both of these explanations or put forward a synthesis.

This problem can be put into a wider context by asking: Why does the omnipotent God allow the existence of evil. Why does He allow evil people to prosper and, on the other hand, allow good and virtuous people to face adversities and sorrow? Or indeed, is there not a conflict between the evil in the world and the goodness of an omnipotent and omnipresent God? That is the so-called problem of theodicy, which ultimately was presented and answered by philosopher Gottfried Wilhelm Leibniz (1646–1716) in his *Essais de Théodicée* in 1710.[342]

By that time the problem was to prove the existence of God. This was necessary because the apparent contradiction between the existence of evil in the world and the goodness of God was bound to lead to atheism and secular values. In the Middle Ages, however, the implications were different. The non-existence of God was not a real option. The problem of evil had to be solved with other means.

In patristic times there had been several attempts to solve the problem of theodicy. Augustine took the view that originally God created a perfect world. Yet, it was created out of nothing, hence it was mutable and corruptible. This is exactly what happened with the Fall. The originally perfect creation rebelled against God through Adam's transgression. This brought guilt and punishment upon the whole human race. Thus evil was the unavoidable consequence of the creation of good. This Augustinian-type theodicy dominated the collective imagination of Western Christendom and has provided background for many popular Christian answers to the problem of evil in medieval and modern times.

Another popular solution to the problem of theodicy in the Middle Ages was put forward by Bishop Irenaeus (c. 130–c. 202). In his thinking perfect goodness is possible only by fighting temptations, or by the participation in evil. Thus, evil was seen as a necessary and unavoidable preparation for obtaining good.[343]

Both of these two main streams of theodicy are traceable in medieval explanations of natural disasters. The Augustinian theodicy and the concept of the Fall that is essential to it lies behind the view that natural disasters are God's punishment for sinners. The Irenaean theodicy corresponds to the idea

---

342. Wolfgang Breidert, Einleitung. In *Die Erschütterung der vollkommenen Welt. Die Wirkung des Erdbebens von Lissabon im Spiegel europäischer Zeitgenossen.* Herausgegeben von Wolfgang Breidert (Darmstadt, 1994), p. 3.
343. William Peterson, William Hasker, Bruce Reichenbach and David Basinger, *Reason & Religious Belief. An Introduction to the Philosophy of Religion* (New York – Oxford, 1991), pp. 107–108; Stewart Sutherland, *Evil and Theology*, in Companion Encyclopedia of Theology. Edited by Peter Byrne and Leslie Houlden (London - New York, 1995), pp. 473–474.

that natural disasters were only tribulations that were necessary for obtaining greater good, that is, the eventual salvation.

Let us now look at some examples that present the idea of natural disasters as preparation for the eventual reward in the kingdom to come. Nicolas de Gorran wrote in his third sermon *Ad impetrandam serenitatem*:

> *'Thirdly He* [i.e. God] *is restaurator of joy as it says: "and after tears and weeping thou pourest in joyfulness." Like a doctor He gives the joy of sanity after the bitterness of medicine. Luke vi: "Blessed are ye that weep now; for you shall laugh." John xvi: "Your sorrow shall be turned into joy." Luke xxii: "You are those who have continued* [with me in my temptations]*."'*[344]

This is the last passage of the sermon in question, its final words. Looking at the sermon as a whole, we notice that for Nicolas the primary cause of natural disasters (in this particular case heavy rains) was the sinfulness of people, which induced God's punishment. Nevertheless his sermon is a little different from the sources and explanations met in the previous chapter. One might say that on the whole it has a softer tone towards the sinners.

Many sources mentioned earlier have emphasised Divine wrath. They propose penance as the only possible means of surviving natural disasters. Nicolas, however, seems to emphasise the merciful nature of God. After the rain there will always be sunshine. People just need to bite the bullet and believe in God's mercy and the arrival of a brighter future after the temporal tribulation. The call for penance and amending one's life is not cast aside altogether, but it has retreated into the background, whereas the greater emphasis is on the virtue of patience.

Another example is provided by one of the few surviving sermons of the Friar Preacher Pierre de la Palud. It is on the theme *Tempus tribulationis est*, and Jean Dunbabin has dated it to the summer of 1316. At that time the harvest was completely blighted by heavy and continuous rains. Furthermore, the previous year's harvest had not been particularly good either. All this leads to an acute lack of victuals, and to famine. Once again we are given the common idea of flooding as a punishment for sins, but Pierre was not satisfied with only one explanation. He also informed his audience that they should interpret the dire situation as a means of eventual salvation: *'Through many tribulations we must enter into the kingdom of God.'* Pierre exhorts his readers to think about the difference between wild animals and domestic animals. If people have the stamina to stay patient under God's scourging, they just might in the end become domesticated to His will, and thus gain access to paradise.[345]

---

344. Nicolas de Gorran OP, *Sermones de communi sanctorum*. Sermo tertius ad impetrandam serenitatem. UUB MS C 18, f. 60v. 'Tercio leticie restaurator ibi "et post lacrimationem et fletum exaltationem infundis." Sicut medicus post amaritudinem medicine dat iocunditatem sanitatis. Luc. vi: "Beati qui nunc fletis quia ridebitis." Io. xvi: "Tristitia uestra uertetur in gaudium." Luc. xxii: "Uos estis qui permansistis."'
345. Jean Dunbabin, *The Hound of God. Pierre de la Palud and the Fourteeenth-Century Church* (Oxford, 1991), p. 54–55.

It is significant that Pierre introduced the "punishment of God" theme as an explanation for the floods, and then added that it was not only Divine punishment, but also a means of salvation for those who remained strong in the faith and did not complain against God. This seems to be the general picture when one reads extensive numbers of contemporary sources.

Without doubt the punishment explanation was generally more emphasised than the more comforting option of referring to tribulations before the eternal reward. Even if we look into the examples presented above we may notice that the tribulation model is in most cases presented only in connection with the punishment topos.

Yet this scheme changes very much when we leave aside natural disasters for a moment and do focus on another group of texts, that is, those concerned with other tribulations sent by God to test the righteous. Good examples are texts dealing with poverty and non-epidemic diseases, such as leprosy. Here we find that the general tone of preachers and other writers was totally comforting. It is nearly impossible to find the idea of poverty or disease as God's punishment for sins of the individual in question. Nearly all the homiletic writers took the view that poverty and sickness were only tribulations sent by God to those whom He really loves.

Here it is not necessary to present too many examples of such sermons and other moral theological writings; few cases will suffice. If we look into the four sermons to the poor and the burdened (*Ad pauperes et afflictos*) by the Franciscan Guibert de Tournai, we find that the central message of these sermons is to stay patient and not to envy others.[346] Recompense will eventually follow in heaven, so there is no need to be worried about the tribulations and misfortunes in this world. Guibert quoted Saint Augustine:

> '*Where the eternal salary is given, the tribulations that in this world seemed long, appear to be short and easy to bear. And this is the reason why tribulations ought to be endured, be they sent by the Lord or imposed as a penance, since those who have suffered small afflictions will receive much good, those who have suffered in small things, be it in the form of insults or being despoiled of goods, or bodily anguish, will receive many good things, namely grace in the present life, glory in the future.*'[347]

The general tone of Guibert de Tournai's sermons was by no means exceptional. Other preachers and writers of moral theological treatises took the same position.[348]

---

346. Guibert de Tournai OFM, *Sermones ad status*. Ad pauperes et afflictos sermones quattuor. BN lat. 15943, ff. 100r–106v.
347. Guibert de Tournai OFM, *Sermones ad status*. Ad pauperes et afflictos. Sermo primus. BN lat. 15943, f. 100r. 'Ubi merces eterna retribuetur breue et leue uidebitur quod in tribulationibus seculi longum uidebatur et hoc est causa cur debent sustineri tribulationes siue a Domino mittantur, siue per penitentiam iniungantur quia "in paucis uexati in multis bene disponentur," "in paucis uexati" siue sit contumelia uerborum siue spoliatio rerum siue angustia corporum, "in multis bene disponentur." In presenti per gratiam, in futuro per gloriam.'
348. For further examples, see Jussi Hanska, *And the Rich Man died*, pp. 92–103.

Jacques de Lausanne wrote about the dangers in general in his *Sermo in periculis*. He made the commonplace comparison of human life to sea travel. He wrote that surely travelling in a stormy sea is dangerous, but if we survive a storm, we also reach our destination sooner because of the strong winds. Similarly, temporary dangers and afflctions, if they are not strong enough to make us lose faith, strengthen our faith and help us to reach the ultimate rewards in heaven. In fact, the whole sermon concentrates on the positive effects of earthly tribulations. Tribulations are nothing else but Divine mercy for the sinners. God sends them to correct the evil and to put the just to the test. Jacques did not mention earthly tribulations as a punishment for sins one single time.

From the perspective of the modern point of view there seems to be a problem when natural disasters at the same time are seen as a purgatory in this world and as a punishment for sinners. It seems that these two ideas are simply contradictory and, what is even more important, they are mutually exclusive. Medieval authors, however, did not seem to think along these lines. In the sources the idea that one thing was at the same time a punishment for some, a trial for others, and a sign of sanctity for yet others did not seem unreasonable. Let us look more carefully at the words of Jacques de Lausanne: '*All this comes from Divine providence, so that God can show His mercy by correcting the evildoers and punishing them, and with these very same* (et per istas) *tribulations He can test the good.*'[349]

During the Late Middle Ages it became habitual to write more theoretically oriented sermons dealing with the idea of tribulation. One of them is *Sermo de tribulationibus patienter tollerandis* by Bernardino Tomitano da Feltre.[350] Bernardino made a great effort to show that tribulations are in fact positive for man's spiritual well being. He introduced to his audience an extensive collection of biblical quotations that seem to support this idea, ending with Hebrews 12:6 '*For whom the Lord loveth, he chastiseth.*' Bernardino rounded off his argument by asking the rhetorical question: '*Don't you see that God flogs his friends?*'

Bernardino's attitude was not exceptional. There are numerous other sources that emphasise that God is punishing those He loves; others are not worthy of the trouble. Bernardino also gave his own contribution to the theme of "purgatory in this world". First he stated that tribulations are in fact God's medicine to sick men, that is, sinners. Then he compared God to a judge and wrote that one of the most important functions of judges is to punish minor crimes so that the offenders will not fall into more serious ones, thinking they can go unpunished. Similarly, God punishes sinners in

---

349. Jacques de Lausanne OP, *Sermones de communi sanctorum*. Sermo in periculis. BAV. MS Vat.lat. 1250 II, f. 154v. '…quia sicut Deus in principio creauit celum et terram, sic omnia regit et ad proprios fines perducit et immo quidquid in nobis accidit, siue tempestas, siue defectus bonorum temporalium, siue quodcumque malum, totum est ex prouidentia diuina ut misericordiam suam ostendet malos corrigendo et puniendo et per istas tribulationes probet bonos.'
350.   See Appendix 1.

this world for their minor sins, so that He can avoid punishing them in the world to come.[351]

The idea of natural disasters as smaller punishments for sinners, to keep them from sinning more and falling victim to the ultimate punishments in hell, was already used by Eudes de Châteauroux in his *Sermo exhortatorius propter terremotum*. Eudes wrote:

> '*Lighter punishments are a preliminary sign of the heavier ones that will follow unless people will amend themselves. Just like a man who will first strike his ass with a twig to make it hurry, will later use a stick if it still refuses to move. Similarly a servant is first struck with a rod to educate him, and if he will not be corrected, only then will he be beaten with the cane, as the Lord says in Psalm: "And I will visit their iniquities with a rod: and their sins with stripes." Similarly in another Psalm the rod is put before the staff: "Thy rod and thy staff." For the punishments God sends us are nothing else but preludes of major and graver ones that will follow unless we correct our selves through penance.*'[352]

Eudes, however, did not give any more comfort to the sinners than the possibility of penance and avoidance of further punishments. He did not perceive natural disasters as useful tribulations for the righteous. For him they were merely a means of frightening the sinners into repentance. In this he was different from Bernardino Tomitano Feltre and other writers of the Later Middle Ages, who did put more emphasis on the positive sides of natural disasters. This more positive attitude is reflected in different genres of writing.

Jean-Claude Schmitt writes in his essay about healing in the Middle Ages that the sick took the role of the pauper who obtains his salvation by suffering just like Christ. According to Schmitt, illness was an ambiguous thing. It was a sign of sin, meaning that it was a just punishment and an incitement to conversion for the individual, or to the community in case of epidemics. At the same time, however, the illness was also a sign of virtue and of God's love. God tempts those whom He loves.[353] The analysis of Schmitt is very similar to the hypothesis proposed here with regard to natural disasters. This is only natural, since it is somewhat artificial to separate illness from natural disasters. Even individual illnesses were seen as *tribulationes*, not to mention epidemics. Therefore perceptions towards diseases were very similar to those of natural disasters. For medieval man, both were simply tribulations sent by God, or at least allowed to happen by Him.

---

351. *Sermoni del beato Bernardino Tomitano da Feltre*. Tomo II, p. 273. 'Nonne vides quod Deus flagellat amicos suos?'
352. Eudes de Châteauroux, *Sermones*. Sermo exhortatorius propter terremotum qui media nocte factus est Uiterbi et in multis locis. Pisa Cateriniana MS 21, f. 149r. For the Latin text see Appendix 2,C.
353. Jean-Claude Schmitt, 'Religione e guarigione nell'Occidente medievale', pp. 291–293.

The French Franciscan theologian Bertrand de Tour analysed the problem of physical punishments in his Rogation Day sermon. Bertrand observed that physical punishments are sometimes, though not always inflicted on us by God. There are numerous reasons for this. Sometimes, pains are inflicted on a man to purge his sins. Such was the case with Mary, the sister of Moses, who was struck with leprosy because she murmured against God. Sometimes they are inflicted on us to remove our pride, as was the case with Saint Paul in 2 Corinthians 12. Sometimes punishments are inflicted on people to test their patience, as was the case with Job. Sometimes they are inflicted so that the glory of God could be made manifest. Such was the case of the man born blind in the Gospel of John (John 9:1–7). Sometimes they are inflicted on people to give them a foretaste of the punishments of hell, as was the case with Antiochus and Herod.[354]

These various explanations soon became a topos in the genre of catastrophe sermons. This can be proven by comparing Bernard de Tours' sermon with the late fifteenth-century sermon entitled *Pestilentie signis, causis et remediis* by the Franciscan Bernardino da Busti. Bernardino wrote that some people think that God has forsaken them when they are tempted. This is not the truth: God does not always hate those he tempts. In fact, most often He sends tribulations and illness to people so that they will have greater merit come the day of judgement.

There are many reasons to tempt the just. Sometimes He sends them tribulations to increase their merits, like in the case of Job. Sometimes the just are tempted so that their patience can serve as an example to others, as in the case of Tobias, who became blind so that others could merit from his exemplary patience (Tobias 2:12). Sometimes the just are tempted to guard their virtue, so that they will stay modest and avoid the sin of pride, as in the case of Saint Paul, who was given a sting to his flesh by an angel of Satan to humiliate him (2 Corinthians 12:7). Sometimes they are punished to correct their sins, such as Mary, the sister of Aaron, who was struck with leprosy (Numbers 13:10–15). Sometimes they are simply tormented so that the glory of God could be manifest through them, as in the case of the man who was born blind (John 9:3). Bernardino did not forget the evildoers either. He wrote that sometimes the tribulations in this world were used to give the damned some taste of future punishments, as in the case of Herod (The Acts 12:23) and Antiochus (2 Machabees 9:6–11).[355]

---

354. Bertrand de Turre, *Sermones de tempore de epistolis*. In rogationibus, sermo primus. BAV. Vat.lat. 1242, f. 226r. 'Pene enim corporales aliquando infliguntur a Deo, aliquando ad peccati purgationem, ad hoc enim fuit inflicta lepra Marie sorori Moysi Num. xiio, aliquando ad superbie compressionem, ad hoc enim fuit datus stimulus Paulo ii Cor. xiio, aliquando ad patientie probationem sicut in Job, aliquando ad dei glorie manifestationem sicut in ceco nato Jo. ixo, aliquando ad pene eterne inchoationem, sicut in Antiocho et Herode.'
355. Bernardino da Busti OFM, *Rosarium sermonum* (venezia, 1498). Sermo de pestilentie signis, causis et remediis, f. 256r. 'Sunt quidam qui statim ut a Deo flagellantur putant se ab Ipso derelictos uerba pro themate nostro assumpta singuli dicentes qui tamen

Even though Bernardino da Busti is not quoting Bernard de Tours, the parallels are striking. It would seem that Bernardino drew his examples from Bernard or, what is more likely, from the common tradition that may or may not have started with Bernard de Tours' model sermons. Both preachers presented biblical persons as exemplary figures. In relation to our argument the most important figures are those who exemplified humility and patience before tribulations. Bernard de Tours and his imitators mention Job and Paul the Apostle. There was a third figure, not included in this catalogue of exemplary figures, who was often presented in similar contexts, that is, King David.

An example of David's exemplary role is a passage from the twelfth-century *vita* of saint Venantius Fortunatus. The passage starts with putting forward the idea of earthly tribulations as spiritual benefits. The writer exhorted his readers to pray that God does not exclude them from His inheritance, but rather corrects them with the tribulations of His mercy. Thereafter he compared his audiences to the above-mentioned champions of patience Saint Paul, David and Job. About David he wrote: '*Also Prophet David prayed that he would be corrected with tribulations: "Prove me," he said, "Lord and try me: burn my reins and my heart.*"'[356]

Out of these three model figures of suffering and patient saints, Job seems to have been most widely used. He was an archetype of the good and suffering Christian and of the rewards that were waiting in the end, if one only managed to keep his patience in the midst of tribulations. The role of Job as a promoter of patience can be seen in numerous sources. Hugues de Saint-Cher wrote in his commentary on Job:

> '*The book of Job is written so that we can imitate his patience, and think about the final result of patience, and having reflected upon that let us go on being patient, for it has been written: "Through many tribulations we must enter into the kingdom of God."*'[357]

---

sepe falluntur quia non semper Deus fagellat hominem quia eum non amet, imo sepe ei tribulationes inmittit et infirmitates ut habeant maius meritum, uel aliis multis de causis quas ponit magister de sententias 4o di. 15o capitulo primo. Aliquando enim mittit ut merita augeantur flagellato patienter tolleranti, ut Job libri eius primo capitulo, uel per patientiam eius detur exemplum aliis, sicut Thobie ut dicitur libri eius secundo capitulo, uel ad custodia uirtutum, ut in humilitate persistat ut Paulo Secundo Cor. 12o, uel ad corrigenda peccata ut Marie lepra Numeri 12o, uel ad gloriam Dei ut ceco nato Johannis nono, uel ad initium pene ut Herodi Actuum 12o Antiocho mundi Macha. 9o quatenus hic uideatur quod in inferno sequatur.'

356. AA.SS.Junii: II. *De sancto Fortunato*, p. 111. 'Ne, ergo nos, dilectissimi, ab hereditate sua Pater coelestis excludat; optemus, ut nos per flagella suae pietatis emendatos efficiat, mentis nostrae duritiam comprimat, carnis nostrae lascivias severitatis suae mucrone trucidet, quod magis mirere, eo clariores per laborum exercitia reddat. Numquidnam nos, dilectissimi, Paulo Apostolo meliores? Numquid Davide Rege mitissimo sanctiores? Numquid Job probatissimo justiores?....Propheta quoque David, ut flagellis corrigetur orabat: "Proba," inquit, "Domine, et tenta me: ure renes meos et cor meum."'

357. Hugues de Saint-Cher OP, *Postilla in librum Job*. In Ugonis de Sancto Charo

Job was not only an example of patience to people suffering from natural disasters or other unforeseen punishments of God. As has been proven by Nicole Bériou, he was also a model to follow for the lepers as well as for the sick and the poor in general.[358] The spiritual meaning of Job is crystallised in the above-quoted Venantius Fortunatus' *Vita*:

> '*Blessed Job is praised by the Divine voice. The fact that there is no one like him in this world is proven by the highest confirmation: His sons were taken away from him, his fortune was despoiled, and he was stripped of his high dignities. Furthermore, he was struck by disease, and was covered with open wounds from his feet to the top of his head. All this was done so that the faithful may understand that in this world we always have to cry: for what here is sown with tears, will there be reaped with joy; and who now cry after their losses, will in future collect with joy the fruits of their labour.*'[359]

The strength of Job's character lies in the fact that his sufferings, as described in the Bible and even more so as described by the theologians and preachers, were worse than anything normal people were likely to meet. It was easy to argue that if Job could handle all that and remain patient, then everyone else should be able to imitate him in the face of their lesser sufferings.

The above-quoted sermons of Bertrand de Tours and Bernardino da Busti presented tribulations in this life both as punishments for the sinners and as edification for the just in many different ways. The examples they used, however, did not comprise natural disasters and they were mostly discussing the matter on an individual level. They were dealing with personal tribulations, which happened to one individual only, not to a whole town or community. Therefore they did not make the point that the same disaster say an earthquake, at the same time could have been interpreted to be a punishment for some and a trial for the higher reward of others.

What needs to be verified is that different interpretations proposed by medieval writers were not necessarily mutually contradictory or exclusive. It is not so difficult to make this point with recourse to the implicit message

---

Opera Omnia. Tomus I (Köln, 1621), f. 395v. 'Scriptus est igitur liber Job, ut eius patientiam imitemur, ac finem patientiae consideremus, consideratumque per patientiam consequamur. Sic enim scriptum est: "Per multas tribulationes oportet nos intrare in Regnum Dei."'

358. Nicole Bériou, 'Les lepreaux sous le regard des predicateurs d'apres les collections de sermons ad status du XIIIe siècle', in N. Bériou et F-O. Touati, *Voluntate Dei leprosus. Les lepreaux entre conversion et exclusion aux XIIème et XIIIème siècles* (Spoleto, 1991), p. 76; Jussi Hanska, And the Rich Man died, pp. 93–94.

359. AA.SS.Junii: II. *De sancto Fortunato*, p. 111. 'Beatus Job divina voce laudatur, et quod ei similis in terra non sit, superna assertatione probatur: et tamen filiis orbatur, possessionibus spoliatur, a dignitatibus sublimatus dejicitur, [pessimo] insuper morbo percutitur, et a planta pedis usque ad verticem vulnus aperitur; ut profecto fideles intelligant, in hoc mundo semper esse plorandum: quia, qui hic in lacrymis seminant, illic in gaudio metent; et qui hic euntes deflent, in futuro cum exaltatione laborum suorum manipulos colligent.'

of the sources, but explicit reasoning to such direction is rare. Bernardino da Busti has divided his argumentation on the temporary setbacks in this world into two sermons. The first one is the above-mentioned sermon on *Pestilentie signis, causis et remediis* which, despite its name, does not limit itself to discussing the plague, but deals with all kinds of temporary tribulations. The main argument of this sermon is that such tribulations are mostly to be interpreted as signs of God's anger, even though, as we have seen, he points out that other interpretations were possible.

His second sermon titled *De tribulationibus et aduersitatibus patienter portandis* drives home the message that tribulations were not only punishment for the sinners, but at the same time God's means of testing the patience of the elect and purifying them further. Bernardino wrote:

> *'As the sun, working naturally, with similar ways has different effects because of the different propensities of matter, so also the tribulations have different effects on different people according to their various qualities. For the evildoers who are beyond any correction, the tribulations bring eternal damnation, and are for them in some way the beginning of hell. [...] For the good the adversities produce salvation and great utility.'*[360]

If we take a liberty to interpret what Bernardino is saying, we can infer that a natural disaster, say a plague epidemic could be cast by God everywhere at any time, and it would still produce the various desired effects in the population. The sinners beyond correction would be punished, the correctable ones would learn and mend their ways, and the just would be tempted and become even better. It would not be a catastrophe if some of the just would die for surely they would only benefit from being taken away from this world. After all, they are in the greatest possible state of perfection, and thus bound to be saved.

Bernardino actually does elaborate on the possibility of the just being killed by the plague. He wrote that some of the good religious die during the epidemics so that the divine justice is concealed from the sinners who are not worthy of knowing about it.[361] This explanation does not convince the modern reader, who is left wondering whether the just were happy to die just to conceal the Divine plan from the evildoers. However, Bernardino's explanations show how difficult a problem it was to explain why the good also had to suffer.

---

360. Bernardinus da Busti OFM, *Rosarium sermonum* (Venezia, 1498). Sermo de tribulationibus et adversitatibus patienter portandis, f. 241v. 'Sicut sol agens naturale licet uniformiter se habeat, propter diuersas materie dispositiones uarios effectus producit, sic tribulatio propter uarias homines qualitates diuersimodi operatur in eis. Circa malos enim incorrigibiles operatur eternam damnationem, et eis est principium quadammodo inferni.[...] Iustis proficit ad salutem et magnam utilitatem aduersitas.'
361. Bernardino da Busti OFM, *Rosarium sermonum* (venezia, 1498). Sermo de pestilentie signis, causis et remediis, f. 259r. 'Si autem queritur quare moriuntur peste boni religiosi qui non sunt superbi, respondeo quod fecit hac Deus ad occultandum sua iudicia, peccatores enim non merentur intelligere quod ea pestis ueniat propter eorum superbias et delicta et sic Deus colligit et rapit bonos esca malorum.'

What exactly were the good effects brought about by the tribulations for the just? According to Bernardino, tribulations liberate the just from the temptations of the flesh, they make them better people, and most of all; purify them from their minor sins.[362] The last argument could be called *purgatory on this world topos*. Ever since Saint Augustine of Hippo, who thought that the penitential process was essentially a matter of this world, this purgatory topos was repeated frequently.[363] Bernardino wrote:

> '*If we all are sinners, then we are necessarily obliged to do penance of our sins. [...] The fact is that no one can obtain the joy of everlasting life before he has gone through some punishment. Therefore it is necessary that our sins be purified through punishment, for God is just and He wants justice to be done, as David says in Psalm 10: "The Lord is just and hath loved the justice." Justice wants crimes to be punished. [...] If this purification does not take place in this world, it necessarily takes place in the other. [...] Since the purification in the other world is much harsher than the one in the present, it is better for us that we are purified from our sins here. However, this cannot happen without the help of afflictions and tribulations.*'[364]

This topos can be encountered in numerous late medieval moralistic tractates and sermons.

The late-fifteenth century preacher Paul Wann had obviously come across the problem of the suffering of the good, and felt obliged to comment on it in his sermon *In Dominica infra octavam ascensionis*. According to the publisher's introduction, this sermon was preached to a live audience, before it was included in a model sermon collection. Paul wrote that there are three reasons why tribulations do us good: they forgive us our guilt, or at least diminish the punishments; they distribute the grace of God, and help us to acquire glory in Heaven. When dealing in a more detailed manner with the first of these reasons, he repeats all the standard arguments in favour of the purgatory in this world.[365]

---

362. Bernardinus da Busti OFM, *Rosarium sermonum* (Venezia, 1498). Sermo de tribulationibus et adversitatibus patienter portandis, f. 241v.
363. On Saint Augustine see Jacques Le Goff, *The Birth of Purgatory* (Aldershot, 1990), p. 70.
364. Bernardinus da Busti OFM, *Rosarium sermonum* (Venezia, 1498). Sermo de tribulationibus et adversitatibus patienter portandis, f. 242v. 'Si ergo omnes sumus peccatores, sequitur quod sumus obligati ad faciendum penitentiam ipsorum peccatorum. [...] Quod nullus potest habere gaudium uite eterne donec alicui pene obligatus est. Necesse est ergo peccata nostra per punitionem purgari, quia Deus iustus est uult iustitiam exerceri dicente Dauid Ps. 10o: "Iustus Dominus est et iustitias dilexit." Iustitia autem uult delicta puniri. [...] Si autem ista purgatorio non fiat in hoc mundo, necesse est ut fiat in alio. [...] Cum autem purgationes alterius seculi sint asperiores quam presentis, melius est quod hic purgemur de omnibus peccatis nostris. Hec autem purgatio non potest fieri nisi mediante affllictione et tribulatione.'
365. Paul Wann, *Sermones de tempore* (Hagenau, 1491). Dominica infra octauam ascensionis. Sermo 46, f. D5r.

The concept that tribulations were in the end good for those who suffered them produced numerous writings from preachers and moral theologians; writings that emphasised the need for patience and the sinfulness of complaining. The peasants were stereotypically suspected and blamed for not understanding their own benefit and for 'murmuring' against God. Johannes von Freiburg instructed priests who took confessions of *rusticos et agricolas* to ask their penitents whether they had been impatient in front of God's punishments and spells of bad fortune.[366] Equally impressive is the *exemplum* story presented in the anonymous Franciscan *Speculum laicorum*:

> *'There was a certain peasant in Kent. When he had sowed his fields, a serious drought occurred and he murmured gravely against God. He had his servants to carry water to the fields and irrigate them. On the following night God sent universal rain which richly irrigated all the other fields of the said country; but not a single drop of water fell on his field. Later on the others collected rich harvest, but his fields, dry as they were, caught fire and were burned down.'*[367]

Thus we see that all through the Later Middle Ages people were told that tribulations are good for the just, and they ought to be suffered with patience. Everyone had his cross to carry and the optimal ways of behaviour were encouraged with positive exemplary figures, such as Job. The negative behaviour was named sin and had to be rooted out by preachers and confessors.

Pastoral Care and Spiritual Healing

It has been established that the preachers and theologians taught that natural disasters were either caused by the sinfulness of men or they were meant to purge the elected so that they would be worthy for the greater rewards in the other world. It remains to be asked what was the impact of such teaching on the surviving catastrophe victims?

Putting the blame of the disaster on the victims themselves and emphasising that it took place because of their sins certainly caused guilty feelings in them. According to the psychologist Gabriele Taylor guilt is a legal concept. A person is guilty if he breaks a law, which may be of human or divine origin, real or imaginary. As a consequence of this action he has put himself into a position where he is liable for punishment, or where given repentan-

---

366. Johannes von Freiburg, *Confessionale*. British Library MS Add. 19581, f. 192r. 'Item si in flagellis Dei et infortuniis impatiens fuit uel contra Dei mordiate locutus fuit.' Johannes' book was one of the most succesful confessors manuals during the whole Middle Ages. There are hundreds of surviving manuscripts.
367. *Le Speculum laicorum. Edition d'une collection d'exempla composée en Angleterre à la fin du XIIIe siècle.* Par J. Th. Welter (Paris, 1914), pp. 79–80.

ce, he may be forgiven.[368] These ideas can be used to explain the attitudes and mentalities of medieval man in front of a natural disaster. They were feeling guilty for the loss of lives and damage done. Thus the phenomenon that psychologists describe as survivor guilt was transformed to idea that the catastrophe took place because of sinful actions, that is, because of a crime against the Divine law.

In addition to those who were suffering from genuine survivor guilt there were others who were ready to believe that they were feeling guilt once it was said to them often enough by the authoritative members of the Church. In short, some people (as there still are in our modern society) were weak enough to be manipulated into feeling guilty. Such cases of getting carried away by the religious preaching and teaching are not rare even in our days. Some people are more open to suggestion than others.

This is not to say that priests and friars were knowingly manipulating the people, they were merely teaching them the ideas they held to be true on the basis of their own religious conviction. It is generally known, that such a religious message is received more eagerly in some times and areas than in others. These specific situations are known as revivals. Times of distress caused by natural disasters were of course potential times of revivals. The flagellant movements are proof of this.

The role of the Church in the process of understanding and coping with natural disasters seems to have been rather ambiguous. It seems likely that on one hand churchmen caused or manipulated people to feel collective guilt. At the same time however, they offered a solution for the problems of those who were feeling guilty. It is quite likely that accepting guilt, confessing one's sins, and doing penance probably helped the victims to deal with their guilty feelings and traumas.

In some post-medieval cases it seems that the churchmen were deliberatively using this chance of alleviating the burden of the survivors with absolution as a psychological tool. A massive earthquake struck Umbria and other central Italian regions in 1703. As a consequence of this cataclysm the people of the region were in a state of shock. Pope Clement XI was quick to realise this. He claimed that the earthquake was due to the sins of the people and in order to feel safe again people had to reconcile themselves with God. As a vehicle of this reconciliation a massive collective penance was needed. Clement chose to help the victims and ease their feelings of guilt by conceding them a plenary indulgence only shortly after the disaster.[369]

One is tempted to assume that Clement was thinking more about the mental well being of the people than about the redemption of their sins. No doubt the plenary indulgence helped the people that had assumed the opinion that this

---

368. Gabriele Taylor, *Pride, Shame, and Guilt. Emotions of self-assesment* (Oxford, 1985), p. 85.
369. Silvia Grassi Fiorentino,' "Nella sera della Domenica...". Il terremoto del 1703 in Umbria', pp. 146–147.

earthquake was punishment of their sins, to get along. Clement not only had given the people a rational explanation for their miseries, but also guaranteed them that there would not be another earthquake, at least not in the immediate future, since their sins had been washed away with the plenary indulgence.

According to Gabriele Taylor a person suffering from guilt can act in three ways. He can make repayment as best as he can, or continue sinning and harden himself against the mental problems brought along by guilt, or continue to suffer from guilt with possibly serious consequences to himself.[370] The remedy offered by the Church, that is, the penitential process including contrition, confession and satisfaction was probably the closest thing to modern psychiatric treatment a person suffering from guilt could have had in the Middle Ages. It offered him a chance of making amendment and thus the possibility of healing the mental symptoms caused by natural disasters. He was guilty and reminded of that too, but at the same time he was also told that there was a means of washing away the guilt and obtaining forgiveness, that is, confession, absolution and penance.

If we look into the penitential process more closely we find that all its parts had possible sanitary effects on the survivors. The first element is contrition, that is, a strong sense of guilt that allowed the survivors to emphasise their feelings and thus to unload the pressure inside them. It was not only possible to express one's feelings in the state of contrition, but it was also the expected reaction. The sinner was supposed to feel miserable and be tormented over his sins. One of the most often described signs of true contrition were tears. Thus the social expectations of contrition allowed people to express openly the feelings and anguish they were suffering.

We could speculate even further on the therapeutic role of the medieval church in natural disasters. When Emile Durkheim was writing his classic study on suicide, he found out that whatever the proportion of Catholics and Protestants in the total population, and wherever this comparison could be made in the case of suicide, Protestants were found to kill themselves much more often than Catholics.[371] The interpretations of Durkheim have been questioned, but one can hardly do away with his statistical material, which proves convincingly his basic argument about the rarity of suicides among the Catholics.

Durkheim observed that both Protestantism and Catholicism condemn suicide. The difference in suicide practises originates from the spirit of free inquiry typical to Protestantism. He concluded that the higher suicide rates in protestant communities result from protestant churches being less strongly integrated than the Catholic Church. One might very well question whether this explanation really is adequate, or whether there is more to it. Could it be the case that the very act of confessing one's sins and getting absolution from them made it much easier for Catholics to live with their personal inadequacies and feelings of guilt?

---

370. Gabriele Taylor, *Pride, Shame, and Guilt*, p. 93.
371. Emile Durkheim, *Suicide. A Study in Sociology* (London, 1975), pp. 73 and 157.

One has to be careful not to make too much out of Durkheim's study, which is based on relatively modern source material. The Catholic Church at Durkheim's time was not the same as the Catholic Church of the Middle Ages. Furthermore, his conclusions are out dated. Nevertheless, Durkheim's statistics, which as such are still valid material, seem to indicate that Catholics were better able to support the pressures of life than Protestants. If the confession system and its therapeutic effects can explain this, there is no reason why the same system would not have been equally therapeutic and effective in the Middle Ages.

However, not all historians of natural disasters have taken the view that the Church had an altogether mentally positive, or therapeutic effect for the survivors. T.D. Kendrick, who studied the history of the Lisbon earthquake in 1775, describes what he calls *'frantic preaching and exhortations'*. They were very similar to those catastrophe sermons we have analysed above. The main cause of the disaster was interpreted to be the deliberate chastisement by God of a sinful people.[372] Having described the contents and style of these sermons and exhortations he writes:

> *'Again and again we ask ourselves how much ordinary people listened to and were affected by these exhortations during the months following the earthquake, and at what pace and in what stages the mood of helpless surrender to fear changed to a recognition that it was a proper duty for a man to show proper courage and try to take possession of, and repair, his ruined environment [...] it is, however, quite certain that the continued sermonizing and reproach did have a seriously disturbing effect on the people and was a positive hindrance to recovery.'*[373]

Thus Kendrick took the completely opposite view. According to him, the preaching of penance and repentance did not help the people to live through the aftermath of disaster, but rather undermined their attempts at reconstruction and recovery. This is also the opinion of Daniel Defoe in his novel *A Journal of the Plague Year*. The book is about the plague epidemic in London in 1665. Defoe put the following words into the mouth of his main character, an imaginary merchant who survived through the epidemic:

> *'Neither can I acquit those ministers that in their sermons rather sank than lifted up the hearts of their hearers. Many of them no doubt did it for the strengthening the resolution of the people, and especially for quickening them to repentance, but it certainly answered not their end, at least not in proportion to the injury it did another way.'*[374]

Before dismissing this passage as a piece of literature one should remember that Defoe's novel allegedly was based on stories told to him by an older relative who actually lived through the London plague epidemic of 1665.

---

372. T.D. Kendrick, *The Lisbon Earthquake*, pp. 78–79.
373. T.D. Kendrick, *The Lisbon Earthquake*, p. 87.
374. Daniel Defoe, *A Journal of the Plague Year* (London, 1957), p. 28.

Perhaps people at the end of the seventeenth century had already began to question whether it was wise to preach the wrath of God, punishment and repentance in connection of natural disasters. If this is the case, we can raise the question, whether such opinions were already voiced in the Middle Ages.

Were the catastrophe sermons or more generally, the ecclesiastical activities in connection with natural disasters help or a hindrance to the psychological healing of the survivors? This is an extremely difficult question to answer. Surprisingly, the role of religion and confession is one thing that has been overlooked in the history of psychology. Not one of the standard manuals on catastrophe psychology mentions the role of religion and its possible therapeutic effects. Perhaps this is the reason why religion has traditionally been perceived as an antithesis of psychology.

C.G. Jung was an interesting exception to this rule. He dealt with religion, and more importantly, with confession in many of his writings. Jung condemned Sigmund Freud and those who followed his line of psychology by declaring that they were practising psychology without *psyche*. By this he meant that they did not take into account the human soul and its needs.

Jung saw the problem of modern times as being the fact that people lacked meaning for their lives. People suffering from the neurosis caused by this lack of meaning were not cured by medicines; they needed to be spoken to. Jung discussed this spiritual healing in a lecture he held before the Alsatian Pastoral Conference at Strasbourg in May 1932:

> *'For instance, a suitable explanation or a comforting word to the patient can have something like a healing effect which may even influence the glandular secretions. The doctor's words, to be sure, are "only" vibrations in the air, yet their special quality is due to a particular psychic state in the doctor. His words are effective only in so far as they convey a meaning or have significance. It is this that makes them work. But "meaning" is something mental or spiritual. Call it a fiction if you like. Nevertheless this fiction enables us to influence the course of the disease far more effectively than we could with chemical preparations.'*[375]

He continued:

> *'With this realization the doctor sets foot on territory which he enters with the greatest caution. He is now confronted with the necessity of conveying to his patient the healing fiction, the meaning that quickens – for it is this that the sick person longs for, over and above everything that reason and science can give him. He is looking for something that will take possession of him and give meaning and form to the confusion of his neurotic soul.'*[376]

Given the context in which Jung gave his lecture it is clear that the 'something' that *'will take possession of him and give meaning and form to the confusion of his neurotic soul'*, was indeed religion. Thus one can say that

---

375. C.G. Jung, 'Psychotherapists or the Clergy', in *Psychology and Religion: West and East. The Collected Works of C.G. Jung* II (London & Henley, 1977), p. 330.
376. C.G. Jung, 'Psychotherapists or the Clergy', p. 311.

for Jung religious belief indeed had healing power, and loosing religion was dangerous. For Jung the most important performance of healing was confession as it was practised in the Catholic Church. He wrote:

> *'There can be no doubt that the psychoanalytical unveiling of the unconscious has a great effect. Equally, there can be no doubt of the tremendous effect of Catholic confession, especially when it is not just passive hearing, but an active intervention. In view of this, it is truly astonishing that the Protestant Churches have not long since made an effort to revive the institution of confession as the epitome of the pastoral bond between the shepherd and his flock.'*[377]

When writing *not just passive hearing*, Jung compared the question and answer-method of confession to psychoanalysis. He was thinking about the Catholic sacrament of confession in the early twentieth century, but the essentials of the confession had been the same from the Fourth Lateran Council of 1215 and the new idea of confession and penance introduced by it. The priest was supposed to help the penitent whenever he felt that his 'patient' was not telling everything he should, be that because of shame, bad memory or whatever. In fact the detailed questioning after the free confession from the part of the sinner was an obligatory part of the confession. The confessors went through a series of additional questions, which were often arranged according to different categories of sins, such as seven capital sins and the sins against the Decalogue. All this was necessary because the confession had to be complete. Otherwise the absolution did not guarantee liberation from purgatory or even hell.[378]

Jung took the view that there are areas in human experience where a priest simply has more credibility than the doctor, therefore *'an intelligent psychotherapist would be glad if their endeavours were supported and supplemented by the work of the clergy.'*[379] If we draw together Jung's ideas of religion and confession we notice that he accepted the idea that man needs some coherent system with which he can explain the world and give meaning to his life.

A lack of such a system leads to different neurosis and mental problems. Many of the problems of his age were indeed due to the loss of belief and traditional values. Jung therefore reasoned that the Church could be beneficial to the mental health of the people, and that priests, especially catholic ones with their centuries-old tradition of confession, could have a positive effect on patients suffering from such neurosis. For Jung, catholic confession was supporting or even supplementing psychotherapy. The implications of such

---

377. C.G. Jung, 'Psychoanalysis and the Cure of Souls', in *Psychology and Religion: West and East. The Collected Works of C.G. Jung* II (London & Henley, 1977), pp. 350–351.
378. Thomas N. Tentler, 'The Summa for Confessors as an Instrument of Social Control', in *The Pursuit of Holiness in Late Medieval and Renaissance Religion*. Edited by Charles Trinkaus and Heiko A. Oberman (Leiden, 1974), pp. 114–117.
379. C.G. Jung, 'Psychoanalysis and the Cure of Souls', p. 354.

thinking for the study of medieval catastrophe history are evident. The teaching of the Church and especially the confession was a precursor to modern psychotherapy, or other modern forms of mental therapy; it was producing similar effects in people who were traumatised by their experiences during disasters.

On the basis of what is said in this chapter we may conclude that ecclesiastical activities, most of all sermons, processions and penitential rites (especially confession), were probably at the same time useful and harmful for the survivors. They may well have partly increased the fear and angst of people, and they may also have distracted their attention from reasonable practical activities, such as rebuilding and helping other victims. However, it is not very likely that practical activities were in reality neglected because of the spiritual ones. They were not mutually exclusive but complementary. Furthermore, one is tempted to believe that the rational explanation provided by the Church and the chance of washing one's guilt away brought more comfort than angst and fear. If one is to believe in Jung's ideas, it is also obvious that the pastoral care provided by the Church did indeed bring similar results as different help organisations and psychoanalysts achieve in connection with modern disasters.

Presenting the causes of natural disasters in such a mechanical and rational form as the medieval preachers and moral theologians did, removed all gratuity and arbitrariness from the natural disasters. The input of the catastrophe sermons to the process of coping with such disasters was to give a logical reason for what had happened. This made catastrophes more tolerable for the survivors.

Having heard and understood catastrophe sermons and liturgy, the people were equipped with a knowledge concerning the reasons for the occasional occurrence of natural disasters. Even more importantly, they were equipped with the knowledge of how to prevent such disasters from happening, or at least, from happening again. Even if all spiritual precautions failed and a catastrophe took place, they always had a means of making sense of it. Either they themselves or other members of the community had failed by sinning or neglecting to do penance.

Finally, the liturgical ceremonies and other concrete activities that the Church performed itself and made the people to perform were of a therapeutic nature. Perhaps the processions and collective prayers were not as sound as rebuilding from an economic point of view, but at least these were activities that lifted the populace out of apathy and despair. Therefore one is inclined to think that the general effect of the *religion panique* was positive.

5 Epilogue: The Extended Middle Ages

The Italian writer Giovanni Guareschi wrote in his post world war II short story collection *Mondo Piccolo "Don Camillo"*:

> '*Each year, during the festival of the village, people carried the crucifix of the high altar in procession, and when the procession arrived at the bank of the river, the waters were blessed so that the river would not become mad, but rather behave itself like a gentleman.*'[380]

The imaginary village of Don Camillo was by no means the only place where processions with crucifixes and saint's relics were performed in the late 1940's. Giovanni Guareschi tells his readers that the village in question does not lie in any particular place, it is somewhere along the banks of the river Po. It does not exist in reality, but yet it is more real than the real world. It captures the spiritual essence of '*Il grande fiume*'. In the post world war II period it was and still is in many remote and agrarian parts of Europe important to make sure that rivers will not go mad, but behave themselves like gentlemen. The habit of blessing rivers and other natural elements to assure their good behaviour is one of the things that have survived from the Middle Ages to the present day.[381]

However, the blessing of waters carried out in the imaginary village of Don Camillo and countless others similar villages all over the catholic world, has become a local feast where people drink, dance and have a good time. It

---

380. Giovanni Guareschi, *Mondo piccolo Don Camillo* (Milano, 1994; first published in 1944), p. 178. 'Tutti gli anni, per la sagra del paese, si portava in processione il Cristo crocifisso dell'altare, e il corteo arrivava fin sull'argine e c'era la benedizione delle acque, perché il fiume non facesse mattate e si comportasse da galantuomo.'
381. A good example being the *Rituale Romanum* a priest's handbook for the Catholic Church. For this book I took a look at the 1925 edition authorised by Pius XI. It still included processions *ad petendam pluviam, ad repellendam tempestatem, tempore penuriae et famis*, and *tempore mortalitatis et pestis*. These are still included in the never editions of the Rituale; *Rituale Romanum* Pauli V pontificis maximi jussu editum aliorumque pontificum cura recognitum atque auctoritate Sanctissimi Domini Pii Papae XI (Turonibus, 1925), pp. 356–364.

has become a carefully cherished relic of past times rather than a religious rite intended to give real protection to the villagers. In this chapter we try to find out when the medieval attitudes and rites in connection with natural disasters and their threat gave way to the so-called modern rational worldview.

It is clear that this did not happen overnight when the so-called Middle Ages came to an end, which, of course, is still very much open to debate. There is no consensus among historians when the early modern period actually began. Historians of different subjects and from different countries have presented numerous, from their perspectives all perfectly logical, timelines for this transition. Jacques Le Goff put one of the most interesting forward:

> *'The long period relevant to our history—for us both as professionals and as men living in the flux of history—seems to me to be the long stretch of the Middle Ages beginning in the second or third century and perishing slowly under the blows of the Industrial Revolution—Revolutions—from the nineteenth century to the present day. The history of this period is the history of pre-industrial society.'*[382]
> (Jacques Le Goff)

What exactly does Jacques Le Goff mean when he says that the Middle Ages continued right up until our modern time? Even if there had been differences in opinion about just when the Middle Ages ended, no one had claimed that they continued beyond the first decades of the sixteenth century. What Le Goff did was to forget all the, let us say, external signs, such as artistic styles, the growing use of vernacular languages, the reformation, the invention of print, the discovery of the new world and so on. He chose simply to concentrate on the mentalities and the thought processes of ordinary people in their everyday life.

Le Goff's message can also be inverted. It has been argued that the process of slow change that finally led to the birth of modern western mentality and the vanishing of medieval mentality had started well before any proposed end of the Middle Ages. It was not the reformation or the natural scientists of renaissance that first started to question the efficacy of the rites and magic performed by the church. Various heretical sects had openly challenged them during the High and Late Middle Ages. The most well known cases were the Wycliff and Lollard agitations.[383] One needs to remember though that it was not the divine origin of natural disasters that was questioned, but only the effectiveness of the ceremonies, prayers, and relics. The attack against the very foundations of the ecclesiastical explanations for natural disasters does belong to the history of modern period, not to the Middle Ages.

Even if we accept that the Renaissance and afterwards the Enlightenment did introduce some technological, artistic, philosophical and scientific novelties that make these periods appear as turning points in history, we may

---

382. Jacques Le Goff, *Time, Work, & Culture in the Middle Ages* (Chicago, 1980), p. x.
383. Adoph Franz, *Die kirchlichen Benediktionen im Mittelalter*, vol 2, pp. 616–623.

argue that the life of ordinary man did not change dramatically. His basic attitudes to himself and to the surrounding world remained very much the same as they had been before. Religious beliefs remained virtually unaltered. Even when we look at the Reformation we see that, in the end, the continuity of tradition, not the novelties are most significant. A catholic person entering a Lutheran church in Finland, Sweden or Norway would recognise instantly most parts of the liturgy and beliefs he encounters. It is a familiarity produced by a common heritage. Therefore it is not surprising that the medieval attitudes towards natural disasters and the means of preventing and surviving them changed very slowly during the first two centuries of what we are accustomed to call modern age.

However, the closer we get to the modern age the more obvious it becomes that there was a change in attitudes towards nature and its biblical interpretations. According to Norman Cohn, the process of scientific study and the secularisation of nature took hold in the latter half of the seventeenth century, after which '*the Christian religion was gradually ceasing to be what it had been for a thousand years: the core of the western culture.... Above all, science was becoming an autonomous activity, with its own criteria of truth. A new conception of nature as a machine, governed by impersonal laws, was spreading abroad.*' Nevertheless, as Cohn says, the belief in Divine providence not only survived but also fflourished in the middle of this fundamental change. The tension between religion and natural science had not yet reached the level of outright confflict. On the contrary, most scientists tried to reconcile science with religion; in fact, many of the leading natural scientists were deeply religious themselves.[384]

Amos Funkenstein expresses this same opinion in different words, when he stresses that sixteenth and seventeenth centuries were the lflourishing period of secular theology. By this he means that during these centuries numerous lay philosophers and scientists dealt with theological questions in their scientific writing. It needs to be emphasised that their books were also destined to be read by laymen. This tendency was most common in protestant areas, but not altogether absent in the catholic regions either. This secular theology meant breaking the barrier between theology and natural philosophy that was typical for medieval universities. It made it possible for anyone to study theological questions, and in Protestant regions even made it virtuous activity to study nature. The natural world was perceived as God's temple refflecting the ingenuity of its creator. Alas, thorough study of nature unearthed questions that proved to be dangerous for religious conviction, and hence the secular theologians of the seventeenth century, even if they were not generally hostile to religion, prepared the way for the next generation of scientists whose posture was often anti-theological, anti-religious or even atheistic.[385]

---

384. Norman Cohn, *Noah's Flood*, p. 47.
385. Amos Funkenstein, *Theology and Scientific Imagination from the Middle Ages to the Seventeenth Century* (Princeton, 1986), pp. 3–9.

What these, and other historians of science often fail to acknowledge is that the most advanced or most secular views of nature were in many cases accepted only by the learned elites. For example Funkenstein's book which deals with the most interesting ideas turns out to be less useful from the point of view of this study, since it concentrates on the opinions of front row theologians and natural philosophers. The ordinary people and their religious views have too often been neglected, perhaps because they generally chose to hold on to the old religious beliefs and ignored innovative new ideas.

This chapter deals with the mental history of natural disasters in the post Tridentine Catholic Church as well as in reformed parts of Europe. The Council of Trent (1545–1563) has been interpreted as the turning point in the history of the Catholic Church. It was the beginning of the Counter Reformation. Nevertheless, this chapter aims to prove that traditional or medieval conventions and ways of thinking were not abandoned overnight. The scientific or, as some people prefer to put it, rational understanding of nature replaced the magico-religious understanding of nature extremely slowly.

Post-Tridentine Catholicism

Perhaps the most famous example of the continuity of medieval customs are the plague processions organised by Carlo Borromeo the bishop of Milan during 1576 and 1577. He led processions with relics through the city of Milan, dedicated a new chapel to Saint Roch, had the church of saint Sebastian restored and amplified, and made the citizens take a solemn vow in front of the martyrs of Milan. He also took care that there were continuous praying sessions in Milanese churches, collective pilgrimages to the seven churches of Rome and other penitential activities. In 1579 he approved new episcopal constitutions on the organisation of processions. They were taken from well-known models, such as processions of Mamertus of Vienne and Gregory the Great.[386] The measures taken by Carlo Borromeo turned out to be successful and later, in 1610, he was canonised – at least at that time his actions against the plague still did find papal approval.

A.N. Galpern has studied the religious beliefs of people in sixteenth-century Champagne. His book includes numerous examples of the continuity of medieval means of protection against the threat posed by nature. During a severe drought in 1556, the peasants of the surrounding countryside marched village by village to the cathedral of Troyes, in the hope that local saints, whose relics were stored in the cathedral, would intercede with God for rain. In 1573, in Provins, the people of two parishes, lead by the Dominicans and the Franciscans organised a procession to the churches of the town of Nogent-sur-Seine and to the village church Chalautre-la-Grande. The processions

---

386. Heinrich Dormeier, 'Il culto dei santi a Milano in balia della peste (1576–1577)', pp. 233–235.

carried the head of Saint Ayoul and other relics. According to a witness '*At both places they were honourably and devoutly received by the priest and the people.*' In 1579, the residents of Tours were so frightened by an earthquake that they decided to make amendment for their sinful lives and organised a procession in which more than three hundred men and women marched barefoot during the winter time. The summer of 1583 brought an epidemic of the plague. From July to October thousands of people in northern Champagne and elsewhere were adorned with a white habit, to go in procession to the Cathedral of Reims. During these processions hardly anyone was left in the villages to guard the livestock.[387]

The most interesting event described in Galpern's book took place in Courlon-sur-Yonne in 1579. The parishioners wanted their *curé* to organise a procession to a neighbouring church or chapel, to pray to God to preserve the fruits of the earth. It was a year of spring frosts. The priest agreed to have a procession, but only to a place that was closer by than the one proposed by the parishioners. When the procession came to the place where the roads parted an argument started between the priest and the parishioners. The outcome was that several parishioners threw the priest into the river Yonne, where he nearly drowned. The procession proceeded according to the wish of the parishioners.[388] This story proves that even if the members of clergy were not so enthusiastic about processions and comparable ceremonies of protective magic, their flocks were not easily alienated from the age-old customs. Furthermore, there were a good number of country priests who opposed fundamental changes to customary ways.

Numerous similar examples can be found for early modern Italy. A striking example of the role of Our Lady in the search for protection against natural disasters is the story of *La Madonna di Constantinopoli*. One can deduce from the name of this cult that it originated from the east. It gained huge popularity in Southern Italy during the sixteenth century. Her images were believed to be powerful protectors against natural disasters. One of the most famous copies was *La Madonna di Constantinopoli* in Naples. Her protection was sought during the plague epidemic of 1575 and her cult was officially recognised in connection with the famine of 1596–1603. The Virgin also showed her favour by protecting the Neapolitans during the eruption of Vesuvius in 1631 and the plague of 1656.[389]

Sources from the sixteenth century onwards describe, not only the traditional forms of cult and liturgy for protection against natural disasters, they also include passages that allow us to see that change was on its way. In the middle of stories of catastrophe preaching, processions and other penitential activities one finds traces of modern scientific thinking.

---

387. A.N. Galpern, *The Religions of the People in Sixteenth-Century Champagne* (Cambridge, Massachusetts and London, 1976), pp. 48, 85, and 184–185.
388. A.N. Galpern, *The Religions of the People in Sixteenth-Century Champagne*, p. 86.
389. Michele Bassi, 'La Panaya Odighitria e la Madonna di Constantinopoli', *Arte Cristiana* 772 (1996), pp. 3–8.

Epilogue: The Extended Middle Ages

On 17 November 1570 an earthquake struck the town of Ferrara. The damage was quite extensive and the people were terrified. The contemporary chronicler Ippolito de Roberti says that they were so scared that they looked as if they had been dug up from their graves. Fear of further earthquakes forced people to sleep out in the open. However, the first shock was soon over and on 22 November they started to react. A procession was organised, guided by bishop Rossetti. The relics of the patron saints Giorgio and Maurelio were carried and growing numbers of people participated. During the following days, preachers, and in particular Dominican friars, took advantage of what had happened and gave people a religious interpretation. This interpretation followed the already familiar pattern of sin and divine wrath. There was, as the historian Emanuela Guidoboni rather cynically notes, almost a race in exhorting people to public acts of penance, and indeed, such acts followed. Many people started to wear grey clothes, walk barefooted, drag themselves on their knees and whip themselves in streets. Despite these penitential acts new earthquakes followed and yet new penitential processions.[390]

Here we have all the typical medieval explanations and reactions in front of a natural disaster in the 1570's, at a time that many historians are inclined to assign to the early modern period. Everything was just as it had been during the Middle Ages, except for one interesting detail. A certain nobleman named Lucio Maggio had personally travelled to Ferrara to see whether the damage was as bad as he had been told. He had been unwilling to believe this, since Ferrara was considered to be a relatively safe area according to the natural philosophers of the age.[391]

There are two interesting and non-medieval details in his action. First of all, one may notice that he came to the affected area on purpose to verify whether what was rumoured was true. By doing so he put himself at risk just for the sake of scientific curiosity. This seems to reflect what we are accustomed to know as renaissance mentality. For medieval man such behaviour would usually have appeared as vain curiosity and, what is even worse, it would have been perceived as tempting God by putting oneself in danger. God's punishment was meant for inhabitants of Ferrara, not for Lucio Maggio.

Another definitely anti-medieval feature in this story is Lucio's unwillingness to accept information that was against the latest scientific knowledge. It is true that already medieval writers and commentators had accepted the idea that in some areas earthquakes are more common than in others. As we have seen before, Thomas Aquinas mentioned Sicily while commenting on Aristotle's *Meteorologics*. And Matthew Paris took pains to inform his readers that earthquakes are not very common in England, as the terrain is not cavernous. However, both Thomas and Matthew very willingly accepted that despite these geographical limitations God was omnipotent, and as such He

---

390. Emanuela Guidoboni, 'Riti di calamite: terremoti a Ferrara nel 1570–1574', pp. 112–120.

was able to produce an earthquake anywhere if He so wanted. The learned renaissance nobleman Lucio Maggio chose instead to believe the opinions of natural philosophers rather than to accept the idea of God's omnipotence. We may conclude that despite the traditional and 'medieval' behaviour of the masses, things were changing in the 1570's.

It is obvious that this change started from above, that is, from the ranks of the clergy, and the clergy alone, not from ordinary believers. Already in the Late Middle Ages there are signs of doubt concerning the efficacy of different rites of protection. Some more educated members of the clergy took the position that the Church ought to be stricter about ceremonies that came closer to magic than religion. Furthermore, the violence and uncontrollability of some processions and penitential movements born during the plague epidemics made the Church reconsider some forms of liturgy and lay participation in them. Hubert Meurier, a canon of Reims wrote in 1584 a book on processions in which he noted that it was not the clergy that in most cases exhorted the people to these forms of devotion, but that the people forced the clergy to organise them.[392] We cannot be sure whether Canon Meurier's opinion can be generalised, but considering the episode of the priest thrown into the river in Courlon-sur-Yonne, there may very well be some truth in it.

No major changes in mentality can be found in the seventeenth-century sources. Jean Delumeau tells us that the people of the small French village of Broc turned to their bishop and demanded that he should excommunicate the hordes of ladybirds that were threatening their fields. In fact, a religious procession was organised from the village to a rural chapel dedicated to Saint Roch. There the exorcism took place, and after that the procession returned. Delumeau also presents other examples, less banal from the modern point of view. His point is that protective liturgical rites remained very popular among ordinary Christians. A process of modernisation and developing theological thinking made the Church less and less willing to organise such rites, but they were difficult to abandon because of popular resistance. The people did not want to risk loosing Divine protection by neglecting customary rites.[393] One also has to keep in mind that the average parish priest did not usually posses innovative thinking or sophisticated theological training. Therefore he was more likely to defend old customs than abandon them.

Much easier to suppress and stop were the unofficial rites and ceremonies which resembled magic more than prayer. Already during the last decades of the fifteenth century the church began to take a more uncompromising attitude towards superstitious methods of weather control. Primary targets were carrying the sacrament in weather processions, reading the incipits of the four Gospels to the four corners of the world, and the exorcism of storms.[394]

---

391. Emanuela Guidoboni, 'Riti di calamite: terremoti a Ferrara nel 1570–1574', pp. 108–109.
392. Jean Delumeau, *Rassurer et proteger*, p. 111.
393. Jean Delumeau, *Rassurer et proteger*, pp. 79–80 and 90–91.
394. Adoph Franz, *Die kirchlichen Benediktionen im Mittelalter*, vol 2, pp. 109–123.

The synodal statutes of Passau from the year 1470 provide an example of this attempt of reform. Bishop Udalric wrote that in his diocese the Christian faith was corrupted, as people performed odd ceremonies in the hope of good weather. He mentions the carrying of Christ's body through the fields and the reading of Gospel incipits. The bishop strictly forbids any such practises in the future, although he recommends other, official rites of protection to be carried out by the church.[395]

The custom of suppressing unorthodox means of weather control was continued by the post-tridentine synods. The 1610 synod of Augsburg prohibited all prayers and ceremonies against storms, except those that were especially accepted by the *Sacerdotale* book reformed by the bishop himself. Similar prohibitions and instructions are seen in other synodal statutes of the counter-reformation period.[396] It is important to remember, however, that the very existence of these synodal statutes proves that such forbidden and 'superstitious' ceremonies continued to be performed by parish priests. We do not exactly know how common they were in the seventeenth century, but obviously common enough to demand episcopal and synodal action.

The Italian marquis Marcello Bonito wrote a study on the history of earthquakes from the creation up to his own time in 1691. A violent earthquake, that, on 5 June 1688 had nearly destroyed the whole city of Naples inspired him. It is revealing that his description of the reactions and activities of Neapolitans in front of the disaster is very familiar when compared to medieval sources. He wrote:

> '*With their minds taken over by terror, conquered by the fear of imminent and evident danger of death, some people shouted for the protection of the most holy Virgin Mary and all the saints of the heavenly court, others cried out the most sweet name of our most beloved redemptor and saviour Jesus Christ with tears in their eyes, yet others turned towards the holy and indivisible Trinity with acute remorse over their errors and true acts of contrition, relying totally on its immediate and boundless mercy.*'[397]

Even though Bonito gave a good number of scientific explanations for earthquakes, the most important cause for him seemed to be Divine will.

---

395. Synodus Pataviensis 1470, statuta synodalia, in *Concilia Germaniae*. Ed. J.F. Schannat & J. Hartzheim, tomus V, ab anno 1400 ad 1500 (Coloniae, 1763), pp. 486–487. 'Dudum in nostra diocesi inolevit corruptela fortassis primo ex fidelium devotione, quod nonnullis temporibus almum Corpus Christi per campos et segetes ad diversa loca, etiam ad ignem deportatur...; in pluribus etiam locis leguntur quatuor evangelia ad quatuor mundi partes cum suis ceremoniis contra fulgura et tornitrua.'
396. Adoph Franz, *Die kirchlichen Benediktionen im Mittelalter*, vol 2, pp. 641–649.
397. Marcello Bonito, *Terra tremante*, p. 2. 'L'anime angustiate, e trafitte dall' imminente, ed evidente pericolo di morte, altre acclamando con sospiri il Patrimonio della Vergine Sanctissima Maria con tutti gli altri Santi delle Celeste Corte: altre con lagrime implorando il dolcissimo nome del nostro amantissimo Christo Gesù, Redentor e Salvator nostro: altre con vivo pentimento de' lor'errori, ed atti di verace contrittione invocando la santissima, ed individua Trinità, nell' imminenza sua Pietà, in tutto se stesse.'

All in this world is vanity. With earthquakes God in his supreme goodness wants to make people understand this truth and live accordingly.[398] What can be said of Marcello Bonito's traditional ways of thinking is even truer with regard to the people of Naples. We see once again all the signs of the medieval *peccatis exigentibus hominum* topos.

This is equally true with regard to the reactions of the people of Umbria, who were struck by a violent earthquake in 1703. Those who scribbled down their feelings in the aftermath of the disaster invoked biblical images from Psalms 56 and 76, as well as apocalyptic descriptions from the opening of the sixth seal (Apocalypse 7:12): '*And I saw, when he had opened the sixth seal; and, behold, there was a great earthquake, and the sun became black as sackcloth of hair; and the whole moon became as blood.*' These apocalyptic visions were as might be expected connected to concepts of collective guilt and sinfulness. Even in Rome, which was far away from the epicentre, people started to organise penitential processions walking barefooted, wearing sackcloth, dropping ashes upon themselves, and wearing chains on their feet and human skulls in their hands.[399]

Even the reactions of the clergy amounted to the same old traditional explanations and solutions. Pope Clement XI himself explained that the earthquake was brought upon the people by their own sins. Having put the blame on sinners, the pope also gave them spiritual medication to help them to survive the situation. Immediately after the earthquake he gave plenary indulgence to all the people of the affected area. This was a means of reconciling the people with God.[400]

Putting aside all the medieval features of this case we nevertheless notice again some more modern details. We know, for instance, that this earthquake, just like the one in Naples in 1688, produced masses of scientific writings concerning earthquakes as natural phenomenon. A case in point is *Breve discorso meteorologico de' terremoti* by Lucantonio Choras.[401]

The most disastrous earthquake during the early modern period was the Lisbon earthquake of 1775, which practically destroyed the whole city and caused enormous loss of life. Furthermore, the Lisbon earthquake was documented much better than other, earlier examples thanks to the new means of information distribution: newspapers. Be it the mortality rate or the fact that it was the first media catastrophe of the early modern time; the Lisbon earthquake has also been studied in considerable detail. The English historian T.D. Kendrick provides the best study. His book includes the standard themes of wild-eyed preachers frantically exhorting their flocks to do penance and catastrophe processions. The general conclusion drawn from Kendrick's book seems to be that even in 1770's earthquakes were still interpreted as signs

---

398 Marcello Bonito, *Terra tremante*, p. 3. 'Dio per sua somma bontà ci facci capire, e praticar questa verità.'
399. Silvia Grassi Fiorentino, '"Nella sera della Domenica...". Il terremoto del 1703 in Umbria', pp. 146–149.
400. Silvia Grassi Fiorentino, '"Nella sera della Domenica...". Il terremoto del 1703 in Umbria', pp. 146–149.
401. Silvia Grassi Fiorentino, '"Nella sera della Domenica...". Il terremoto del 1703 in Umbria,' pp. 143–144.

of Divine Wrath – at least for the unlearned majority of the population.[402]

The fact that a more scientific attitude or worldview was slowly emerging does not mean that the traditional means of dealing with natural disasters were at the same time in decline – on the contrary. If we look at hagiographic sources, we find plenty of evidence that old protective cults were gaining new popularity and that many new saints specialised in protecting people against natural disasters were canonised. An example of such a new protector saint is Carlo Borromeo of Milan. His reputation of holiness was first and foremost based on his activities during the plague epidemics. It is no co-incidence that he is shown leading a penitential plague procession in the altar painting of the Roman church San Carlo ai Cattinari. Furthermore, several existing saints who did not have a specific reputation as protectors against natural disasters were suddenly honoured as protectors. Hagiographic writers industriously produced evidence of miracles and created an historical background for these new devotions.

An example is provided in the case of Madonna della Lettera in Messina, Sicily. Without any doubt, the cult of Our Lady was extremely popular in Messina around 1640. People thought that the Virgin had saved their city from the worst during the earthquake of 1638. The Jesuit Placido Samperi described the popularity of the cult, writing that there hardly was a family that did not have at home a picture of the Virgin. Father Samperi therefore wrote his *Iconologia della Gloriosa Vergine Madre di Dio* (1640) which states that the Holy Virgin not only protected Messina in 1638, but also during the earthquakes of 369, 1171, 1456, 1493, 1498, 1509 and 1566.[403]

Owen Chadwick tells us that old protective rites against storms, that is, the carrying of the holy sacrament in procession, and reading the incipits of the four gospels to the four points of the compass were still approved by the catholic diocese of Bamberg and Würzburg in the 1770s. Chadwick also provides further similar examples of the surviving magico-religious mentality from the different parts of the late eighteenth-century catholic Europe. He also documents several cases where natural disasters were thought to have been caused by the sins of the people. For example, when Vesuvius erupted in 1794, a penitential procession was organised by the cardinal archbishop of Naples.[404]

We may conclude our excursion into post-Tridentine Catholicism with the words of Sara Cabibbo who has studied the cults of Sicilian saints in relation to earthquakes from sixteenth to the late eighteenth century. She writes:

> '*The documentation used to analyse the relationship between saints and the earthquakes that took place on the island during the arch of three centuries reveals the irritating repeating of a devotional model, always the same despite the passing of time.*'

---

402. T.D. Kendrick, *The Lisbon Earthquake*, passim.
403. Sara Cabibbo, *Il paradiso del Magnifico Regno*, pp. 87–88.
404. Owen Chadwick, *The Popes and the European Revolution* (Oxford, 1981), pp. 3–7, 11–14.

What was included in this devotional model? Invoking the help of a local patron saint or protector, giving thanks for a miraculous survival, attacking the sins that brought on the Divine punishment in the first place, performing correctional prayers, asking forgiveness, and doing penance in the form of processions, and finally organising votive masses and pilgrimages under the guidance of ecclesiastical authorities and confraternities. Hence we see, and indeed so does Cabibbo, an obvious continuity from the times of the early church and the Middle Ages.[405]

One naturally must take into account that religious life in the Italian *Mezzogiorno* during the early Modern period and after might have been more traditional or, if one likes, more medieval than in other parts of Europe. Nevertheless, Cabibbo's 'irritating pattern' that keeps coming up in the sources refflects rather well the religious mentalities of post-Tridentine Catholic Europe.

Protestant Revolution?

It is understandable that the traditional rites and means of protection against natural disasters held their place in the catholic parts of Europe. However it is worthwhile to look whether this is also true for the protestant parts of Europe. In this context, Jean Delumeau has made interesting remarks about the hostile reaction of common believers in protestant countries to the abolition or repression of the age-old means of protecting the crops and the people against all sorts of catastrophes.[406]

This question becomes even more pressing if one takes into account the tradition of historical studies in protestant countries. It has been a convention to emphasise that the reformation was an historical or even a revolutionary turning point. In practise this has meant that protestant church historians have focused their attention on the changes brought by the reformation. This has been done at the expense of continuity, which, especially in the Scandinavian countries and in England, was in reality very strong. Very few things changed overnight with the reformation. This seems also to be true with regard to the religious and mental attitudes in front of natural disasters. Only a few historians have seriously studied the survival and development of a 'catholic' means of protection against the threats posed by nature. It is no co-incidence that one of the most important historians in this field, Jean Delumeau, is himself a catholic.[407]

There were two major issues that contributed to the survival of traditional religion with all its semi-magic ceremonies and protective rites. The first one is the general popular resistance to too drastic changes. The second one is

---

405. Sara Cabibbo, *Il paradiso del Magnifico Regno*, p. 82.
406. Jean Delumeau, *Rassurer et protéger*, p. 399.
407. The most thorough studies are Eamon Duffy's *The Stripping of the Altars*, Keith Thomas', *Religion and the Decline of Magic* and Jean Delumeau's, *Rassurer et protéger*, especially pages 399–448.

the fact that the reformers were not heralds of a scientific and rational way of thinking. They were as much as the Catholics subscribing to the traditional magico-religious worldview.

Popular resistance

There is no doubt that the protestant reformation brought about considerable changes in liturgy. A case in point is England where, during the decades immediately following the break with Rome, the catholic tradition was in many parts respected, but some interesting changes were nevertheless made. The most important of them concerned the religious processions that were practically abolished. In the 1530's the candle processions around the churchyard in Windsor, which were organised to obtain protection against the plague, were forbidden and declared to be superstitious. Similarly, in the city of London there had been a procession against epidemic disease in 1528, and again in 1543, but the latter one is the last known case of aldermen asking a ritual act of collective contrition from the bishop.[408]

The Royal Injunctions of 1547 put an official end to the religious processions traditionally held at times of specific need. Curiously enough this step was taken for the same reasons as those mentioned in catholic parts of Europe: the general disorder that such processions generated among the people and their superstitious nature. The prayer was considered to be equally effective if it was offered within the church building. Hence the *processiones causa necessitatis* came to halt.

However, abolishing penitential processions altogether did not succeed. Due to the resistance of the believers one procession had to be retained that is, the processions during the Rogation Days. Under the Anglican procedure the Rogation Day processions underwent some alterations. They were still performed on one of the old Rogation Days, that is, Monday, Tuesday or Wednesday of Ascension week, but only on one day instead of all three. The procession was carried out by perambulating the parish boundaries. At convenient places the curate was to admonish the people of the need to give thanks for the fruits of the earth. The traditional psalms and litanies were sung, but no banners were carried, nor did the procession stop at wayside crosses.[409]

As Keith Thomas emphasises, despite these few changes and weighing down of the liturgical pomp, the perambulation remained recognisable for those who were used to old Catholic processions, and so did the magical powers connected to them in popular thinking. Many people attributed mechanical efficacy to the ceremony. Furthermore, there is evidence that the clergy hung on to the old customs. They were reluctant to leave behind the banners and had difficulty in renouncing the habit of reading prayers in the places where the crosses had once stood.[410]

---

408. Paul Slack, *The Impact of Plague in Tudor and Stuart England*, p. 37.
409. Keith Thomas, *Religion & the Decline of Magic*, pp. 62–63.
410. Keith Thomas, *Religion & the Decline of Magic*, pp. 63–64.

Similarly, the most rigorous reformers threatened public Masses and prayers for obtaining the protection of the saints. In 1534 William Marshall, one of the assistants of Thomas Cromwell issued an English *Primer*. It was meant to replace the books of *Horae* and other devotional books meant for the lay audience. Marshall took the view that catholic Latin primers included far too many superstitious elements and decided to leave them out from the English edition. One of the omitted parts was the Litany of the Saints, which as we have seen, was one of the most important liturgical texts used in connection with seeking protection against natural disasters. The fact that Marshall's *Primer* reflected the King's religious policy and was published with a claim to a royal patent for six years did not stop a public outcry. The proposed changes were simply too dramatic and strong public response forced Marshall to publish a second edition one year later, this time including litanies and several other items omitted from the first edition.[411]

The popular resistance encountered by the English reformers was not something typically English. Similar attitudes were obvious in other protestant regions. In 1523 the peasants around Wittenberg were furious with the city-dwellers who had broken the old regulations concerning fasting during the Lent. The peasants took the view that such transgression of old religious norms had angered God and caused the river Elbe to rise and flood the fields.[412] It is worth pointing out that the city-dwellers had absorbed the new religion, but the peasants took traditional catholic attitude. This was the tendency everywhere. People living in the countryside and more remote places were slower to accept new ideas. This is not to say that the majority of the people living in cities were Protestants. On the light of the English evidence analysed by Eamon Duffy it seems that the traditionalists were in a majority everywhere long after the reformation.[413]

Even when the abolition of penitential masses and processions succeeded, the reformers were forced to offer something else for the faithful to calm down the opposition. In 1563 Archbishop Parker of Canterbury, Bishop Grindal of London and William Cecil wrote together a printed prayer form, which was intended to replace Old Catholic penitential processions and special masses and prayers. It was to be used in all churches on Wednesdays and Fridays and combined with a public fast, meditations and abstinence at home. There were seven sermons to be read from authorised homily books and then one more '*on the justice of God in punishing impenitent sinners.*' Such official prayers and days of public fasting were appointed in connection with every public epidemic from 1563 onwards.

It is easy to see that these new public prayers did not differ much from the penitential processions of catholic times. In fact, there were some doubts whether they departed too much from the prayer book. The only major difference was that they were to be carried out within the churches or in the

---

411. Eamon Duffy, *The Stripping of the Altars*, pp. 382–383.
412. Euan Cameron, *The European Reformation* (Oxford, 1992), p. 11.
413. Eamon Duffy, *The Stripping of the Altars*, pp. 377ff., especially pp. 478–503

privacy of homes instead of during public processions. Paul Slack therefore concludes that the reformation drove the religious responses to plague off the streets, but that they continued in churches and in homes.[414]

If one looks for specific prayers for protection against natural disasters, numerous examples of them can be found all over protestant Europe. Delumeau gives several examples, starting from the sixteenth century German *Betbüchlein* and ending with the English *Book of Common Prayer*. These prayer books include all the typical prayers against natural disasters. Some of them were connected to specific situations such as the Turkish invasion in 1566 or the plague of 1607, others were simply meant to be used in connection with some typical disaster such as an epidemic, a flood, and a drought.[415]

One could add examples from early Scandinavian Lutheran prayer books. For example, Michael Agricola's mid sixteenth-century prayer book (*Rukouskiria Bibliasta*) from the diocese of Turku in Finland includes most of the votive prayers that were included in the late medieval catholic *Missale Aboensis* from the same diocese. Agricola's prayerbook includes prayers for most of the saint's feasts and prayers for Rogation Days, and several prayers for votive masses, such as *pro tempestiva pluvia, ad petendam tempestivam pluviam, pro serenitate*, and *tempore pestilentie*. It even includes the litanies, although prayers for the intercession of saints have been removed from it. In fact, Agricola's prayer book was very traditionalistic when compared with the English Book of Common Prayer. The 1549 version of the Common Prayer book rejected most of the saints of the old *de sanctis* calendar. Only the great feasts of Christmas, Easter and Whitsun, and a few biblical saints' days were left.[416]

Moderate Reformers

Not all the reformers were militants like Thomas Cromwell or William Marshall. In fact most of the key figures in the history of the protestant reformation were rather lenient concerning the traditional protective cults and liturgical rites. Even if they did not necessarily accept them, they did not question the legitimacy of seeking protection from religious ceremonies and understood the social functions performed by such cults and ceremonies.

It is a well known and well advertised by numerous historians and biographers that Luther did not accept all the liturgical and ceremonial features of the Catholic Church. Indeed, it was the area where most superstitious beliefs and false doctrines attacked by him were to be found. Luther did not accept the

---

414. Paul Slack, *The Impact of Plague in Tudor and Stuart England*, pp. 37 and 228–229.
415. Jean Delumeau, *Rassurer et protéger*, pp. 430–439.
416. Michael Agricola, *Rukouskiria Bibliasta* (Stockholm, 1544, Facsimile edition: Porvoo, 1987), passim; *Missale Aboense secundum ordinem fratrum praedicatorum* (Lübeck, 1488, facsimile edition: Porvoo, 1988), passim; Eamon Duffy, *The Stripping of the Altars*, pp. 464–465.

protective power of saints, relics, specific masses, and other liturgical rituals. His specific targets were the use of holy water and salt, which, of course were the basic substances of all the ecclesiastical magic.[417] The views of Luther were radical indeed, but nevertheless, he did not question the divine origin of natural disasters, nor did he question the notion of Divine omnipotence and God's active control of nature. One might say that in reality Luther did not add anything new to the criticism raised by a number of other, earlier medieval dissidents. The difference was, of course, that Luther managed to get unforeseen support for his theological ideas, and consequently the church failed to silence or eliminate him.

It is also important to note that Luther was not opposed to all the traditional ceremonies, blessings and prayers. On the contrary, he did not accept excessively progressive priests either. Many ceremonies of the Catholic Church were to Luther, if not dear, then at least acceptable. He might have been indifferent towards them, for the only thing that really counted for Luther was the purity of faith. Many reformers were even less militant than Luther concerning the traditional popular religion. Philip Melancthon for example, was willing to accept the role of saints as intercessors as long as the prayers were addressed to saints in general, not to a particular saint.[418] The Convocation of the Church of England shared Melanchton's views about the saints in 1536 that reaffirmed the traditional reliance on the saints, but rejected the idea of the saints for specific needs or benefits.[419]

Thus the mainstream of the protestant reformation did not question the role of God behind natural disasters. The reformers sought to abandon some magico-religious catholic ceremonies, but accepted others. As we have seen, they also introduced some of their own.

The Waning of the Traditional Religion

On the basis of the evidence presented above, one can conclude that the reformation brought about only superficial changes in attitudes towards natural disasters and means of coping with them. The frameworks stayed the same. There still was not adequate scientific knowledge to allow people to know why disasters took place and how they could prevent them. The old magico-religious rites were merely stripped from some of their most distinctive Catholic features. It is possible that the reformers were willing to do more, but there was enough resistance to change to prevent them from undertaking more radical measures.

When we move beyond the period immediately following the reformation we notice that the development in the seventeenth and eighteenth centuries was very similar to the one in Catholic Europe described in the previous

---

417. Adoph Franz, *Die kirchlichen Benediktionen im Mittelalter*, vol 2, pp. 623–629.
418. Jean Delumeau, *Rassurer et protéger*, p. 411.
419. Eamon Duffy, *The Stripping of the Altars*, p. 393.

chapter. In connection with the plague epidemic of 1665, pamphlets that appeared took the traditional view that the plague was brought about by national sins, such as swearing, covetousness, women's dress and make-up and the prophanity of the Stuart Restoration Court. Looking at the measures taken, one notices that not only the attitudes exhibited an obvious continuity from medieval and early reformation customs. The plague of 1720 was fought with a national fast day (16 December) and with the obligatory sermons condemning the sinfulness of times. There is also some evidence that these official religious campaigns as well as countless local plague sermons had some effect on the population. There clearly was an increasing attendance in services and one might even speak of local revivals.[420]

Holland provides another example of this continuity of religious attitudes and responses to natural disasters. In 18 September 1692 there was a moderate earthquake in Holland (roughly six on Richter's scale). This earthquake, as was common, led to a good deal of different pamphlets and other writings explaining the causes of disaster to be published. Several of these reproduced the age-old explanation of God's wrath. For example Georg Bernhard Petri te Zaandam, a Lutheran preacher, wrote that it was the omnipotent God that caused this earthquake to happen because of the sins of people. He did briefly explore what natural philosophers had to say about the causes of earthquakes, but moved swiftly on to theological explanations. Another anonymous writer wrote a pamphlet titled *Christelijke aanmerkingen op de zware aardbevinge* and proposed apocalyptic explanations very similar to those medieval ones we have analysed above. Not surprisingly he even quoted Luke 21:11 to support his argument.[421]

There were also those who explained the earthquake in terms of natural philosophy. Standard ideas taken from Aristotle's *Meteorologica* were proposed along with other writers of classical antiquity. There were also some new ideas, for example theories of Italian Girolamo Cardano who had proposed in his book *De subtilitate* in 1550 that earthquakes were caused by underground explosions, were also accepted by some Dutch writers. These scientific theories were, as in the Middle Ages, often presented together with religious explanations. These two ways of explaining natural disasters were co-existing rather than conflicting.[422]

However, as in the case of Catholic Europe, there are also signs of religion loosing its hold. In connection with the 1665 plague epidemic mainline theologians chose to see God as a less interventionist being. Hardly anyone seriously denied that God was able to interfere if He was willing, but He was, nevertheless, relegated to the background. The intellectual debate centred on the possible natural causes of an epidemic and its treatment. It was accepted that epidemics worked according to natural laws laid down by God in creation, but it was believed that He did not personally interfere, say by selecting who

---

420. Paul Slack, *The Impact of Plague in Tudor and Stuart England*, pp. 247–248, 286–287, and 328.
421. Rienk Vermij, 'Natuurgeweld geduid', *Feit & fictie* 3 (Groningen, 1996), pp. 50–54.
422. Rienk Vermij, 'Natuurgeweld geduid', pp. 56 and 59–61.

were to be killed and who were to survive. The time of religious miracles was over. Attention was concentrated on the so-called secondary causes of the plague, or what we would call natural causes.[423]

This mechanical cosmology, where God is only given the role of a craftsman who has designed the mechanical universe, but who has then left it to run according its own course originates from Descartes' famous writing *Principia philosophiae* in 1644.[424] It is, however, essential to understand that only some members of the learned elite accepted Descartes' ideas. The great majority of the population hung on to the old Christian doctrine of the interventionist God. This is apparent even in connection with reasonably modern events such as the cholera epidemic of 1832.

The Asiatic cholera was by no means the most dangerous disease in nineteenth-century Europe. More people were killed by tuberculosis. Cholera was, however, the most terrifying disease to struck Europe after the plague. Its incubation time was very short and once the disease struck, the victim's conditions weakened very fast and the outcome was ugly enough to frighten people. There were violent spasms of vomiting, diarrhoea, and painful muscular cramps before the final collapse of the system and death. The threat posed by cholera was not permanent, and therefore not psychologically manageable. Its impact was unpredictable, its causes unknown or disputed. It affected every layer of the population, although some groups more than others. All these facts contributed to the general terror and fear caused by the cholera epidemics that broke out in Europe in the beginning of the 1830's.[425]

What then were the religious responses to this epidemic, which caused a horror that, can only be compared to the earlier outbreaks of plague? In England the evangelicals, that is, members of the various protestant congregations (Methodists, Congregational, the Secession churches of Scotland, Baptists, and Anglican church) explained the epidemic with recourse to the old idea of interventionist and vengeful God of the Old Testament. It might be added that when the epidemic reached the United States, its causes were explained as in England. These views did find some echo in the opinions of the English people. In 1832 there were many local religious revivals, especially in the countryside. Furthermore, the government organised an official day of fasting, prayer and humiliation on 21 March 1832. Presumably, it was intended to appease the wrath of God and thus restore the good health of the nation. The success of this national repentance day was considerable; the churches were full all over the country. The government and the doctors had failed, and the nation looked back to more traditional means of protection and security.[426]

---

423. Paul Slack, *The Impact of Plague in Tudor and Stuart England*, pp. 247–248.
424. Norman Cohn, *Noah's Flood*, pp. 58–59.
425. R.J. Morris, *Cholera 1832. The Social Response to an Epidemic*, pp. 14–16; Richard J. Evans, Death in Hamburg. *Society and Politics in the Cholera Years 1830–1910* (Oxford, 1987), pp. 228–229.
426. R.J. Morris, *Cholera 1832. The Social Response to an Epidemic*, pp. 131–132 and 147–148; Charles E. Rosenberg, *The Cholera Years. The United States in 1832, 1849 and 1866* (Chicago, 1962), pp. 40–54.

Old cholera cemetery in the outskirts of Turku in South-West Finland is a testimo-ny of for the univeral nature of the 1830–32 cholera epidemic. (Photo: Pekka Tolonen).

The success was, however, not as total as it would have been few centuries before. Parts of the population were not impressed with the doctrine of an interventionist God. The Unitarians dismissed the national fasting and prayer day as '*the tribute of political expediency to sectarian cant*'. The opinion of the scientists was that even though God undeniably existed and had created the world, it was functioning according to the natural laws provided by this creation. Thus the epidemic was not directly caused or manipulated by God. Even though science did not accept the idea of an interventionist God, it was still another generation before Darwin and Huxley brought science and religion into direct conflict. There were yet others who did not want to accept religion as any kind of explanation for the epidemic. The working-class radical papers were very hostile towards ecclesiastical ways of disaster management. They took all the liberties to ridicule fasts and prayers and claimed that God was nothing more than a ruling class agent and hence to be ignored.[427]

427. R.J. Morris, *Cholera 1832. The Social Response to an Epidemic*, pp. 130, and 148–149.

In England, the religious explanations seem to have been accepted more readily in countryside than in urban centres. It is remarkable that Richard J. Evans nearly neglects the role of religion in his book about the cholera epidemics in Hamburg. A good example is the passage where he discusses the contemporary opinions on the causes of the 1830–1832 epidemics. He gives plenty of space to both leading medical theories, that is, the contagionist theory and the miasmatist theory. Then he moves onto a third major theory, which he calls a moral or psychological one. It ascribed infection to the moral weakness of the victims. This theory, however, is not religious, but speaks simply of the living habits and attitudes of the victims. It was moralising but not in terms of the Christian religion. It emphasised hygiene, mental courage and soberness. The victims were often labelled as drunkards.[428]

In other places, cholera epidemics did cause rioting and general unrest among the population. However, the mob did not point its finger to alleged sins, religious minorities, or even to the blasphemous doctrines of heretics. In fact, God and theology were completely ignored when the mob was seeking causes for the lethal epidemics. Some rioters accused the ruling classes of an attempt to poison the poor, while others attacked the public authorities in general and in particular members of the medical profession because of their incompetence.[429] All this implies that by the early 1830's the role of Christian religion as a protector against natural disasters and as an explanatory force was loosing ground to more secular explanations and theories. The long Middle Ages were finally reaching their end.

---

428. Richard J. Evans, *Death in Hamburg*, pp. 231–237.
429. Richard J. Evans, 'Epidemics and Revolutions: cholera in the nineteenth-century Europe', in *Epidemics and Ideas. Essays on the Historical Perception of Pestilence*. Ed. Terence Ranger & Paul Slack (Cambridge, 1992), pp. 158–163.

Conclusions

Medieval man was highly dependent on nature and its benevolence. Just one bad year could seriously endanger his existence, and two in a row certainly meant famine, epidemics and a rising death toll. In addition to bad years and climatic problems his survival was threatened by different natural disasters. Universal epidemics such as the infamous *Black Death* are well known to historians. Their impact on mentality, demography and the economy has been easy to perceive and appreciate.

Not all natural disasters affected the whole of Europe and made such a definite impact on the history of mankind. Some natural disasters had very limited economic and demographic effects. They did not have a serious impact on the mentality of the European people as a whole, nor were they seen as turning points in history. These disasters, whether they were earthquakes, floods, droughts, volcanic eruptions, heavy rains or storms, had only a local impact. Such disasters have left much fewer sources, and historians, with the exception of local historians and dilettantes with antiquarian interests, have neglected them. Only during the last few years have things begun to change, not in the least thanks to the French *nouvelle histoire*.

In many cases traces of local disasters reveal themselves only in some apparently insignificant detail. There might be an inscription on a wall showing the water level during the floods of this or that year. There may be a note in a guidebook of some small parish church telling that the *campanile* was rebuilt after the earthquake of 1296.

We register such details without giving them too much attention. However that particular flood could have destroyed the bridges, drowned a significant number of people and left others homeless. It could have swept away the seed from the fields causing hard times in the up-coming winter. The earthquake might have killed half of the parish population and destroyed the houses of most families living in the town. Even local disasters caused serious problems because there was no strong central government willing to help the victims. If help was available, the bad infrastructure and logistics made it difficult to distribute relief.

Each of these hypothetical examples might have been the worst disaster ever from the point of view of the local population. For the victims, these local disasters were more serious than the *Black Death*, which they might never have heard of. Yet after five or six hundred years these catastrophes are marked only by the inscription on a wall, or perhaps a small entry in a local chronicle, whereas the *Black Death* is central in our studies of the late medieval mentality.

Such local natural disasters occurred, and indeed still do occur, fairly often. There was not a generation that did not experience some kind of natural disaster. Most likely such disasters did happen not only once, but several times. The frequency and potential loss of lives caused by even small-scale disasters hence had a long-term effect on the mentality and activities of the people. They had to be prepared to deal with such disasters.

In this book, the measures taken by people confronted by natural disasters have been divided into three categories: preventive measures, ad hoc measures during the crisis, and measures taken afterwards to resume the normal course of life. There was not much medieval man could do to stop natural disasters. The level of natural science and engineering was not up to it. In most cases the true causes of natural disasters were unknown even to the most educated. This meant that people could not anticipate such events and could do even less to stop them. Such impotence in the face of a real threat made them turn to magical or religious solutions.

There was a long magic-religious tradition to protect oneself against the hazards of a hostile nature. This tradition included the rites of an organised religion, performed by professional priests, such as different rites of the state religion in Rome, as well as rites originating from animistic pagan cults. When the early Christian church was creating its own preventive rites for confronting nature and natural disasters, it incorporated and assimilated some of the rites from pagan cults.

The Christian Church assumed the basic philosophy that nature was controlled by higher beings, and thus could only be controlled with their help. This was not essentially different from the views expressed by the Church's pagan predecessors. The only difference was that God, Jesus, the Holy Virgin and the Saints replaced the pantheon of Roman Gods and Germanic deities, not to mention local animistic deities. It is still very much an open question whether the Church was continuing the old pagan rites under a new Christian disguise or interpretation, or whether it introduced a new religion incorporating some old exterior forms to make it easier for people to accept it. Be that as it may, it is obvious that by the time of the Later Middle Ages the whole of Europe was thoroughly christianised and so were the means of dealing with natural disasters in a magic-religious manner.

Preventive measures consisted of official protective rites and personal means of protection. There were two kinds of important official rites. First of all, there were the Rogation Day Litanies and processions. The major litanies performed on saint Mark's Day (25 April) originated from the Roman *Robigalia* feast. The minor Litanies originated from the penitential processions held by Mamertus, bishop of Vienne around the year 470. Both these litanies were celebrated to ask Divine protection for the crops and the members of the community.

The second level of official protective rites consisted of local protective cults. The Church taught that the saints were to be respected and that their intervention on behalf of a community or an individual person could persuade God to look favourably on them. On a practical level the saints were often seen as small deities from whom protection and all kinds of favours could be obtained. Realms, towns, churches, communities, confraternities, and even individual persons had their patron saints whom they revered and who were expected to keep up their side of the bargain, and protect their worshippers.

In addition to these collective protective measures backed up by the Church authorities people did their best to obtain personal protection. Frequently the means of getting personal protection came very near or transgressed in a variety of ways the border dividing accepted Christian religion from superstition. All kinds of religious items were used to obtain protection. People carried on their bodies amulets, prayers written on small pieces of parchment, or even holy water and pieces of the Host stolen from the churches. Undoubtedly, especially in the more remote areas, protection was also sought from surviving pagan rituals.

Alas, the protection of the saints, prayers, personal amulets and lucky charms often failed and the people had to face an actual disaster situation. The measures taken during imminent danger can be divided into collective and individual reactions. Which reaction had preference was often determined by the very nature of the disaster. Some sudden and violent natural disasters, earthquakes for example, did not leave room for organised rites, but demanded immediate action. Slowly developing situations such as droughts or floods left more room for collective activities and rites.

The collective measures to deal with natural disasters remained very similar throughout the Middle Ages. Small details and liturgical particles changed in different times and according to local practices, but the basic pattern remained the same. The standard method to deal with disasters was the performance of *letanias causa necessitatis*. In most cases these consisted of three elements: penitential processions, catastrophe sermons, and votive masses.

Processions were held according to the model provided by the Rogation Day processions. They started from a church, and in most cases ended in the same church. In between, the procession visited one or more stations (often station churches). The participants carried crucifix, reliquaries of available saints and symbolic banners. Members of the clergy, both secular and regular, organised according to their rank, formed the head of the procession. Behind the clergy followed the ordinary parishioners as the procession moved on. Litany of the saints and penitential psalms were sung. The participants were required to wear penitential clothing and sometimes they also performed other penitential activities such as self-flagellation. If there was enough time, the participants also prepared themselves for the procession by fasting, by giving alms, and the performance of other acts of charity.

Customarily sermons were delivered during these processions. There seems to have been no strict timing for them. Sometimes they were preached before the procession started (indeed sometimes it was the sermon that inspired the whole procession), sometimes they were preached in station churches or other stations where the procession halted temporarily, and sometimes they were preached when the procession had reached its final destination.

Only a few strictly speaking catastrophe sermons have survived to the present. This does not mean that catastrophe sermons were a rarity since it was possible to use model sermons for Rogation Days. They were very similar to actual catastrophe sermons. Counting these possible catastrophe sermons there are literally hundreds of surviving sermons, and most of them model sermons. Therefore it is clear that such sermons were always available and judging from the evidence concerning processions, it is obvious that sermons were considered to be an essential part of them. It was the sermon that informed the participants about what had happened and what they should do to amend the situation.

The procession itself was a part of the catastrophe liturgy and in most cases the procession incorporated a mass or was followed by it. Many liturgical manuscripts contain numerous votive masses and votive prayers, which could be incorporated to a standard mass turning it into a votive one. The belief was strong that prayers and masses, when properly carried out, could appease God and thus bring the catastrophe to an end. One cannot emphasise too much that all these three elements, that is processions, sermons and votive masses, were essential parts of the disaster liturgy. Sometimes, they were performed separately, but this was often because there was no time or possibility to organise the liturgy in its complete form.

All these collective means of dealing with natural disasters were organised from above. Sometimes, the initiative came from the ecclesiastical authorities, sometimes from the lay authorities. In principle, it was the bishop who decided, but in practise the consent and co-operation of different participants was needed. If the relics were carried in procession, permission had to be asked from the owner, which very often, as in the case of the relics of saint Geneviève in Paris, was some important monastic house. All these administrative operations took time, and sometimes even more time was taken to assure that the procession took place at the right moment, for example to make it co-inside with the feast day of some important patron saint.

In many cases there was no time to wait for the official collective rites, and therefore individual solutions needed to be found. One of them was to take flight. Especially in cases of earthquakes the sources often inform us that people simply moved out of their towns and villages and slept out in the fields until the situation was cleared.

If one chose not to escape there were various other means of protection. If there was time, one could amend one's ways and commit oneself to penitential activities according to the scheme of contrition – confession – satisfaction. If there was no time for such long-term activities, a few other possibilities remained. Some people put their trust in personal prayers such as the *Pater noster*, the *Ave Maria*, or the reading of the litany of saints. Some people crossed themselves, for it was believed that the sign of the cross gave protection against demons. One could also seek the protection of consecrated buildings. Numerous sources describe the death of large numbers of people because they had sought protection in the churches during an earthquake.

The most conventional means to seek personal protection was invoking the help of a particular saint. This was done normally by making a *votum*, that is, an oath to do something in exchange if the saint was to save him or her. Typical promises were entering a religion or doing a pilgrimage. The problem with such *vota* is that they are very rarely documented in connection with natural disasters. Miracle collections of saints contain thousands of examples concerning a *votum* and subsequent miracle, but these include practically no references to natural disasters.

This, however, does not imply that saints were not invoked during natural disasters, as they were invoked in connection with sickness or accident. Common sense tells us that the protection of saints must have been sought. To support this assumption, we can rely on some fragmentary evidence in hagiographic sources, and on the archives of the *Penitenzieria Apostolica* housed in the Vatican archives. The latter include some cases where persons were seeking absolution from breaking such a *votum*, because they had not kept their part of the bargain.

When the immediate danger was over, people were left to count their losses and to wonder about what exactly had happened. They had to pull themselves together and get on with their lives. In order to do so, they had to understand what had happened. This need to know was often manifested in texts written afterwards to explain the disaster. Sometimes the urge to know was strong enough to take official action in this matter. Giovanni Villani's chronicle tells that after the floods of 1333 the magistrates of Florence asked learned men and theologians to explain the reason for the disaster. As said before, there was no sufficient scientific knowledge during that time to explain natural disasters adequately. There were only the explanations of natural philosophers, astrologists and theologians.

The scientific explanations of natural philosophers were in most cases not based on experimental science or on personal observation, but were taken from the books of Aristotle or from medieval encyclopaedic writers such as Isidore of Seville, Thomas de Cantimpre, Bartholomeus Anglicus, and most of all Vincent de Beauvais. The explanations offered by these authorities were not easily understandable for common people, nor did they give them much comfort or security for the future. Astrologers said that the constellations of the planets were causing natural disasters, and indeed, everything else in the world. If one knew them well enough and could read them correctly, one could foretell the future and understand everything. Astrological explanations were no doubt easier to understand than the complicated ideas of natural philosophers. Nevertheless, they were still beyond the everyday mental world of the population. What was even worse, they did not offer any security for the future, or consolation for the victims.

Even if these explanations were fairly popular among the learned, the one accepted by the population at large was without doubt the explanation given by the Church. The central idea in religious explanations of natural disasters was that they were brought on by divine intervention. God was omnipotent. As such He was naturally able to control nature and all natural phenomena. If God was the cause of disaster, there was some reason why it happened and therefore there were means to make sure it would not happen again. This explanation went down very well with the masses because it operated on an understandable level and furthermore, because it seemed to offer them a change of doing something about it.

Here it is important to emphasise that these three basic explanations of natural disasters were not mutually exclusive. It was not impossible to believe that vapours breaking violently from underground caverns caused earthquakes, and still hold to the general opinion that God was controlling this process. Many took the view coined by Thomas Aquinas that there were indeed natural laws that guided nature under normal circumstances. God, however, was capable and sometimes also willing to work against these natural laws. They were not binding Him, and how could they. After all He had created nature and had power to control it as it pleased Him. The same person who believed in Aristotle's explanation of earthquakes and that God had the final word in the matter might very well admit that there must be something in astrology too. That is exactly how Villani understood the causes of the floods of 1333 in Florence.

If we look into the religious explanations of natural disasters we find out that, despite the common basic idea of God as ultimate reason, there were major differences in emphasis. Some religious writers gave macro-level explanations, which connected natural disasters to the idea that history was reaching its eschatological culmination, that is, the final days, the coming of Antichrist or the Second Advent and the final judgement. There was no consensus about what would actually happen and in what order, but one thing was common in the analysis of apocalyptic writers: natural disasters were signs heralding these last days.

This apocalyptic emphasis was particularly strong in the thirteenth century, when the exegetical writings of Joachim of Fiore on the Apocalypses and other eschatological parts of the Bible were most popular. Another peak in apocalyptic explanations occurred at the time immediately following the Black Death. Eschatological thinking was not limited to learned Churchmen writing for other learned Churchmen, but actually penetrated the whole of Christianity. An example of the impact of an apocalyptic worldview at a lower level was the flagellant movements. Their outbreaks seem to have followed some kind of natural disaster or particularly hard times.

Despite the popularity of apocalyptic explanations, most medieval writers chose to explain natural disasters as individual events, not in connection with eschatological history. These authors maintained that disasters were either caused by God himself or at least allowed to happen by Him. In the latter case the explanation was often that the actual events were caused by demons with permission of God. Why did God allow such natural disasters to happen? The most common view in the sources is that He wanted to punish the people for their sins. Many catastrophe sermons use the topos that presents sin as a cause (*causa*) and disaster as an effect (*effectus*), and then urge their audiences to mend their ways. For when the cause is removed, so is the *effect (cessante causa cessat et effectus)*.

The logical connection between sin and natural disasters was commonly accepted. Eudes de Châteauroux even wrote in his sermon that if man wants to know the signs from which he can know in advance when natural disasters are bound to strike, he should observe the sinfulness around him. Eudes' idea was that when sinfulness reaches a certain level, disasters would be imminent.

The fact that not only sinners and evil men were killed by natural disasters led Christian writers to consider the so-called problem of theodicy. Why is there suffering in the world if God is loving and omnipotent, as He is said to be by the Church. This problem was acutely sensed, although it in most cases dealt with in a more limited fashion, such as by asking why the innocent and the righteous get killed in natural disasters. Numerous writings were dedicated to this question. In case of natural disasters these writings took the attitude that suffering, while it undoubtedly was punishment for the wicked and as such completely justifiable, it was at the same time something else. For those who had already shown their value and needed no more to prove themselves, death through disaster was a quick way out of this world. For the essentially good but not quite saintly it was a means of being elevated to the next level of moral perfection. A disaster was a trial that made better people out of those who survived it without deserting and without despairing.

For those who had done something sinful, that is, for nearly everyone, a natural disaster was a warning. God in his mercy wanted to show these people their faults and allow them to mend their ways so that they would not be punished with eternal damnation. The suffering in this world was also a kind of inner worldly purgatory. It purged people from their minor sins and thus saved them from much harder suffering in the purgatory proper. This again was merciful since, as medieval writers were keen to emphasise, no suffering in this world was comparable to the torments of even a smallest time in purgatory.

This 'positive' attitude, which saw natural disasters and the suffering brought along with them as signs of divine mercy rather than wrath, can be compared to the contemporary writings about poverty and illness. The reasoning is similar. Poverty and illness too were seen both as signs of punishment and as signs of divine favour. The same archetypical heroes, Job especially, were marched forward to serve as role models in both cases. The message was clear. The dead were either duly punished for their sins or taken away for greater rewards, whereas the living were expected to patiently make the best out of the situation, do penance and turn the catastrophe to their own victory in the long run.

The event of catastrophe is the moment when the sources normally pick up the story and also leave it behind. Only rarely do we read what actually happened when the situation was over and how the people who survived continued their lives. Catastrophe psychology is a branch of modern scientific psychological research. While most of the theories of modern catastrophe psychology are impossible to test with medieval sources, there are some ideas that perhaps help us better to understand how medieval catastrophe victims managed to go on with their lives after the catastrophe was over.

The need to find guilty persons manifested itself, for example, in psychotic witch-hunts for scapegoats in connection with epidemics and other major disasters. Since it was not a question of man-made disasters where it is easy to point the finger at someone, and since there was no scientifically relevant information about the causes of natural disasters, it is no wonder that the role of scapegoats was given to outsiders. Those who were not members of the community and bound by its rules were always looked upon with suspicion, and in exceptional circumstances they were always potential victims. This happened to the Jews, Heretics, Witches and other social outcasts.

The Church, however, normally did not encourage believers to find culprits from outside. It tried to place the burden on the communities themselves. This brings us to another well-documented symptom of modern catastrophe victims: survivor guilt. The cry for penance was without doubt partly caused by the guilt felt by preachers themselves. Most certainly it did feed the same feeling in their congregations. The sense of guilt of the survivors who already might have been wondering why they had survived instead of their friends and relatives, was given more fuel by the preachers, who told it was their very sins that had caused the disaster.

Already some early modern writers had their doubts on the usefulness of such sermons and their religious education. Modern historians have followed their reticence. They have pointed out that instead of accusing themselves and dedicating their energy to penitential activities, people would have been better off by putting all their effort into rebuilding their houses or whatever repair was needed.

Yet, there is another side to this matter. One could argue that the preachers and confessors were actually performing the role that psychiatrists and counsellors have in today's catastrophes. Preachers were helping people to reconstruct and to understand what had happened, which is one of the necessary steps on the road to healing. The fact that the explanation for the event from the point of view of modern science was completely wrong does not matter. It might have been wrong; nevertheless it was coherent, seemingly logical and understandable. That was what counted for the victims. For them a false explanation was as good as a right one: they just needed an explanation.

If the Church was adding to the survivor guilt with its preaching about sin as a cause of the disaster, it also did its part in relieving the sense of guilt. The Church offered ceremonies and activities through which one could symbolically purify oneself from guilt. Furthermore, there was the actual sacrament of penance. Even if a person believed he was guilty of a disaster, he was offered forgiveness through the sacrament of penance. This must have provided considerable mental relief to a surviving disaster victim. He was told that he was indeed guilty, but that his guilt, unlike that felt by modern day catastrophe survivors, could be washed away by confessing and mending one's ways. On the whole, it is quite likely that the activities of the Church in and after catastrophe situations did help people to pull themselves together and continue their lives.

The religious responses and attitudes in front of natural disasters were more or less the same throughout the Middle Ages. Nor does the *longue durée* of the history of medieval religious responses to natural disasters end with the Middle Ages. There were chronological and geographical differences, but on the whole, an early medieval observer, had he been able to see late Medieval or early modern catastrophe processions, would have found enough familiar elements to know what they were and what was their function.

Following the concept of the *long Moyen Age* coined by Jacques Le Goff, this book also studied the gradual change from predominantly religious attitudes and explanations of natural disasters to the dawn of modern natural science and the emerging scientific worldview. Judging from recent studies on the history of post-Tridentine Catholicism, the attitudes and means of dealing with natural disasters did not vanish. On the contrary, in some areas the aid of saints if anything, was invoked more fervently, and processions were organised long into the modern period. This was not changed by the renaissance or by the discovery of the New World.

The sources show some symptoms of modern thinking, such as an increasing will and ability to study nature with empirical methods. Personal observation started to remove recourse to classical authorities as a means of gaining knowledge of nature and its ways. Nevertheless, for a long time these faint voices of rational thinking were often drowned out by the sound of bare feet marching in processions and voices singing litanies. The most significant change in post-Tridentine Catholicism from the point of view of disaster management was that the Church took a stricter attitude towards superstitious deformations of protective cults and ceremonies.

One might expect that the situation would have been different in the protestant regions of Europe. However, the differences were not so significant when compared to the continuity. It is true that protective cults took a very different form in protestant countries where public penitential processions and the cult of saints were not accepted. However, these visible expressions of protective cults were replaced with public fasts and prayer days, not to mention the individual prayers. The Protestants were as convinced as the Catholics of the fact that natural disasters did not occur against the will of God. For a long time, the faith about the power of God to intercede even against the laws of nature was unbreakable.

However, very slowly both Catholics and Protestants alike embraced the idea that God did not necessarily exercise His control over nature, but that He simply had created the system that functioned according to its own rules. New findings in natural sciences started to shake the trust in the fundamental and absolute truth of the Bible. Paradoxically, these findings were often done when the learned tried to find evidence that would support biblical truths. Early geologists seeking evidence of Noah's flood were forced to accept that the earth was many, many times older than was calculated on the basis of the Bible.

Finally this led to a situation where the majority condemned religious attitudes towards natural disasters as superstitious. It is impossible to give any exact dates on just when the old medieval, religious, irrational, or pre-modern worldview (how one chooses to call it is very much a matter of one's own beliefs) was replaced with a modern and scientific one. This change took place gradually during the course of centuries, and in different times in different regions of Europe. The Middle Ages were dying slowly as Jacques Le Goff put it. By the time of the early-nineteenth century the final victory of the scientific worldview was undeniable. It is true that many people still saw the 1832 cholera epidemic as a punishment of God. However, the majority thought differently. Scientists rejected the idea of Divine intervention, and even the uneducated masses had alternative explanations, offered to them by working class radical newspapers.

In line with the great medieval epidemics, the masses took to the streets and started rioting. This time, however, they were not after religious dissidents and outsiders whose activities had brought on Divine punishment. They did not suspect the Jews of poisoning the wells, or the demons. They were rioting against the public authorities whom they suspected of trying to solve social problems by poisoning the poor. By the beginning of the 1830's the old, predominantly religious, ways of explaining natural disasters had become a prerogative of the decreasing ranks of fundamentalist Christians, and this continues to be the situation today.

APPENDIX 1
TENTATIVE CATALOGUE OF SURVIVING MEDIEVAL CATASTROPHE SERMON

This Appendix includes all the medieval catastrophe sermons known to the author of this book. It needs to be emphasised that this catalogue is certainly not complete. It is extremely likely that there are some catastrophe sermons in Schneyer's *Repertorium* that have not been indicated here, and it is even more likely that there are others, not included in Schneyer's *Repertorium*, hence the title *Tentative Catalogue*. There are thirty sermons altogether from thirteen different preachers. These are divided as follows:

According to the number of sermons:

Dominican	17
Franciscan	6
Secular clergy	4
Unknown	3

According to the preachers:

Dominican	7
Franciscan	3
Secular clergy	1
Unknown	2

The proportion of mendicant preachers, especially that of Dominicans, is very high – as it is generally with medieval sermons one might add. The dating of the surviving catastrophe sermons is in many cases very vague, but without guessing too much one can propose division between different centuries of the Later Middle Ages:

According to sermons:

Thirteenth century	15
Fourteenth century	6
Fifteenth century	9

This implies that catastrophe sermons were indeed a continuous practise all through the Middle Ages. The relatively large number of thirteenth-century sermons is explained by the fact that both Eudes de Châteauroux and Nicolas de Gorran wrote many sermons, four and eight respectively. If we look into this division according to preachers, it looks more even.

According to preachers:

Thirteenth century	4
Fourteenth century	4
Fifteenth century	5

The geographical distribution of the preachers is the following:

France	6
Switzerland	1
Italy	5
Sweden	1

Appendix 1

The pre-eminence of France and Italy in this respect is no surprise considering what is known of the medieval sermons in general.

The following information is given under each entry:

—   The name of the preacher.
—   Biographical information on him, taken from Schneyer's *Repertorium* unless otherwise indicated.
—   The number of the sermon, and it's title in italics.
—   The manuscript or edition used.

A. The volume of Schneyer's *Repertorium*, page number, and the number of the sermon in question.
B. Thema and the Incipit of the sermon.
C. Dating and locating of the sermon.

Anonymous priest from Toulouse

The identification as a priest from Toulouse was done by Maier in the catalogue Burghesiana collection.

1. *Sermo pro pluvia*
BAV. MS Burghes. 138, ff. 232r–233r.

A. IX, p. 752, no.
B. Dimitte peccata eorum et da pluviam super terram (3. Kings 8:36) – Legitur in hoc capitulo quod Salomon perfecto…
C. The manuscript has been dated to the early fourteenth century. Beyond that it is difficult to say anything about the dating of the sermon.

2. *Pro serenitate uel sanitate*
BAV. MS Burghes. 138, ff. 233r–234v.

A. IX, p. 752, no.
B. Petite et accipietis (St John 16:24) – Quando aliquis est in necessitate positus non potest ad aliquam recurrere melius quam ad bonum patrem…
C. See above.

Eudes de Châteauroux

Born late twelfth century, studied in Paris, master of theology 1228, canon of Paris 1234, chancellor of the university 1238, cardinal of Tusculum 1244, died in 1273.[1]

1. *In processione facta propter inundationem aquarum*
Arras bibliothéque municipal MS 137 (olim 876), ff. 78v–80r.

---

1. For further biographical information see Fortunato Iozzelli, *Odo da Châteauroux. Politica e religione nei sermoni inediti*. Deputazione abruzzese di storia di patria. Studi e testi fasc. 14 (Padova, 1994), pp. 23–25; A. Charansonnet, 'L'évolution de la prédication du cardinal Eudes de Châteauroux (1190?–1273): une approche statistique,' in *De l'homélie au sermon. Histoire de la Prédication médiévale*. Édités par Jacquelin e Hamesse et Xavier Hermand (Louvain-La-Neuve, 1993), pp. 105–107.

A. Iv, p. 464, no. 862.
B. Quomodo convertit aquas inundationem in siccitatem et siccata est terra aquarum (Ecclesiasticus 39:29) – Hoc sex vicibus legimus factum esse. Primo in principio mundi…
C. Alexis Charansonnet places this sermon to the first edition of Eudes' sermons that was prepared before the year 1261.[2] One can speculate more with the possible dating of this particular sermon. As its title tells us, it was preached in connection with flood procession. We also learn from the sermon that the place was without any doubt Paris, for the sermon ends with following prayer: '*Let us then pray God that He will make flood of our sins to halt as well as the flooding of waters for the praise and glory of His holy name and the glorious Virgin, His mother and also the glorious virgin Genevieve and other saints whose bodies have been carried here. Amen* '[3] It is extremely unlikely that the relics of saint Genevieve would have been carried in procession in any other place. From biographical information we know that Eudes accompanied Saint Louis to crusade in 1248 and did not return to France. Thus we are looking for a year when flood processions were organised and that falls between the start of Eudes' studies in Paris and the year 1248. According to a manuscript listing all the processions where the relics of Saint Genevieve where used there were four possibilities: in 1206 there was a procession because of a flood, in 1233 for the same reason, and in 1240 and again in 1242 because of continous hard rains.[4] The date of 1206 can be counted out because it is far too early. Of the three other dates the year 1233 would suit best, because the procession was at that time organised because of a flood, however, one cannot exclude the possibility that the sermon was delivered either in 1240 or 1242 because flooding and heavy continuous rains are very similar reasons, and they were often connected. Further more, there is always a possibility that there was a procession not mentioned in the list. Summa summarum, the sermon was most likely delivered in Paris in 1233, 1240 or 1242.

2. *Propter timorem terremotus*
Arras bibliothéque municipal MS 137 (olim 876), ff. 88r–v.

A. IV, p. 464, no. 862.
B. Commota est et contremuit terra (Psalms 17:8) – Dicit Job V°: *Nihil fit in terra sine causa et de humo non orietur dolor*…
C. As in the case of the previous sermon Alexis Charansonnet takes the view that it belonged to a collection of Eudes' sermons edited before 1261. Without any internal evidence that would allow us to know anything about the place or time in question, it is impossible to place it in connection with some known earthquake.

2. A. Charansonnet, 'L'évolution de la prédication du cardinal Eudes de Châteauroux,' p. 114.
3. Arras bibliothéque municipal MS 137, f. 80r. 'Rogemus ergo Dominum ut inundationem peccatorum faciat cessare et etiam inundationem aquarum ad laudem et gloriam sui sancti nominis et gloriose uirginis matris sue nec non et gloriose uirginis Genouefe et aliorum sanctorum quorum hic corpora sunt allata. Amen.'
4. P. Ferret, *L'abbaye de sainte-Geneviève et la congregation de France*, pp. 309–310 and 354. Ferret's source is an ancient manuscript B.S.G. MS Fr. 21 containing a text titled *Historie de Sainte Geneviève et de son Église royale et apostolique*. I have not been able to identify this manuscript from the modern catalogues of Parisian libraries.

3. *Sermo exhortatorius propter terremotum qui media nocte factus est Viterbii et in multis aliis locis*
Pisa Catariniana MS 21, ff. 147v–149v.

A.   IV, p. 482, no. 1071.
B.   Catharacte de excelsis aperte sunt (Isaias 24:18) – Hanc comminationem fecit Dominus per Ysayam prophetam et complebitur...
C.   This sermon was preached in Viterbo sometime between 1267 and 1270. Eudes writes in a prologue for the edition of his sermons: "Item apud Viterbium anno Domini 1269, tempore vacantis ecclesie, composui sermones LXXXVI, quorum primus incipit: *Sobrii estote et vigilate*, ultimus vero: *Hunc humiliat et hunc exaltat*. This description fits perfectly to the sermon collection of Catariniana MS 21. However, Alexis Charansonnet has demonstrated that the manuscript contains sermons that most certainly were not preached in 1269. The datable sermons in this manuscript fall between the mentioned years 1267 and 1270.[5]

4. *Sermo quando timetur de terremotu*
Pisa Catariniana MS 21, ff. 149v–151v.

A.   IV, p. 482, no. 1072.
B.   Clamor meus veniet ad aures eius (Psalm 101:2) – Possumus dicere quod psalmus qui incipit: *Diligam te Domine*...
C.   See above number three. This sermon was probably delivered few days later than the *Sermo exhortatorius propter terremotum qui media nocte factus est Viterbii et in multis aliis locis* that has a very urgent feeling about it and the earthquake is discussed as something that just happened. This sermon refers to the earthquake as a *casus qui nuper accidit* which seems to imply that at least a few days had passed the two sermons.

Guy d'Evreaux OP

Flourished c. 1290–1293, his sermons are on the Paris pecia list of 1304.

Guy's Summa includes a part that gives prothemata for the sermons on different subjects. Five of them are titled *In omni necessitate sive pro pluvia, sive pro aliis negotiis*. However, save the exception of one sermon, these do not give the impression that they were meant to be catastrophe sermons. The one exception is included here.

In omni necessitate, sive pro pluvia, sive pro aliis negotiis
BAV. MS Vat.lat. 1252, f. 271v–272r.

A.   II, p. 362, no. 616.
B.   Dominus noster modicum iratus est sed reconciliabitur servis suis (2. Machabees 7:33) – Videmus in mundo quod servi aliquando forefaciant ergo dominum et quando vident eum...

5.   The whole prologue is edited in A. Charansonnet, 'L'évolution de la prédication du cardinal Eudes de Châteauroux,' pp. 141–142. For the dating of the manuscript and the earthquake sermons see Alexis Charansonnet, *L'université, l'Eglise et l'Etat dans les sermons du cardinal Eudes de Châteauroux (1190?–1273)*. Unpublished Doctoral Thesis (Lyon, 2001), Annexe 2 Essai de datation des sermons contenus dans le manuscrit de Pise, Bibliotheque Cateriniana 21, especially pages 640–645 and 657.

C. See above biographical information.

Nicolas de Gorran OP

Born c. 1210 in Le Mans, prior of Saint Jacques in Paris from 1276, died in 1295.

1. *Ad impetrandam serenitatem, sermo primus*[6]
UUB. MS C 18, f. 60r.

A. IV, p. 319, no. 964.
B. Adduxit spiritum super terram et immutate sunt aque (Genesis 8:1) – Anti quitus propter diluvium peccatorum factum est diluvium aquarum...
C. This sermon belongs to Nicolas' huge sermon collection known in printed versions as *Fundamentum aureum*. Alas, it cannot be dated very accurately. I have used an early manuscript (Uppsala Universitets Bibliotek C 18) which was once owned by Swedish prelate Laurentius Olavi de Vaxald. '*Iste est librum fratrum predicatorum conventus siktunensis quem dedit eis reuerendus pater dominus Laurencius Olaui decanus upsaliensis qui eciam postea in ordine professus obiit anno domini $M^o ccc^o xxxii$ tercia kalendas marcij*' Laurentius Olavi had studied in Paris in 1280's. It is likely that he brought the manuscript, which is definitely of French origin, with him when he returned to Sweden.[7] If this is so, Nicolas' sermon collection was in circulation before 1290.

2. *Ad impetrandam serenitatem, sermo secundus*
UUB. MS C 18, f. 60r.

A. IV, p. 319, no. 965.
B. Iunge currum tuum et descende ne preoccupet te pluvia (3. Kings 18:44) – Verbum est Helye ad Acab et potest esse verbum ad Ecclesiam...
C. See above no. 1.

3. *Ad impetrandam serenitatem, sermo tertius*
UUB. MS C 18, f. 60r–v.

A. IV, p. 319, no. 966.
B. Non delectaris in perditionibus nostris quia post tempestatem tranquillum facis et post lacrimationem et fletum exaltationem infundis (Tobias 3:22) – Tria incommoda molestant hominem in hac vita, scilicet, culpa commissa, pena immissa, leticia amissa...
C. See above no. 1.

4. *Ad impetrandam serenitatem, sermo quartus*
UUB. MS C 18, f. 60v.

A. IV, p. 319, no. 967.
B. Oravit Elias ut non plueret (James 5:17) – Helyas qui nobis proponitur in exemplum fuit fervens in devotione quia oravit...

---

6. J.B. Schneyer does not give titles to Nicolas' sermons. They are taken from the Uppsala manuscript C 18.
7. Margarete Andersson-Schmitt und Monica Hedlund, *Mittelalterliche Handschriften der Universitätsbibliothek Uppsala. Katalog über die C-Sammlung. Band 1. Handschriften C I–IV, 1–50*. Acta Bibliothecae R. Universitatis Upsaliensis Vol. XXVI:1 (Uppsala, 1988), p. 197.

Appendix 1

C. See above no. 1.

5. *Ad impetrandam pluviam, sermo primus*
UUB. MS C 18, f. 60v. and 74r. (the manuscript has been opened and then put together again in wrong order).

A. IV, p. 319, no. 968.
B. Si clausum fuerit celum et non pluerit propter peccata homini (3. Kings 8:35) – Numquam est dedecus culpe sine decore iustitie nec décor iustitie sine amore misericordie...
C. See above no. 1.

6. *Ad impetrandam pluviam, sermo secundus*
UUB. MS C 18, f. 74r.

A. IV, p. 319, no. 969.
B. Da pluviam super terram quam dedisti populo tuo in possessionem (3. Kings 8:36) – Quia omne bonum est ab uno et summo bono Deo, ideo ei debemus preces effundere...
C. See above no. 1.

7. *Ad impetrandam pluviam, sermo tertius*
UUB. MS C 18, f. 74r–v.

A. IV, p. 319, no. 970.
B. Petite pluviam a Domino (Zacharias 10:1) – In supplicationibus sive petitionibus petitum debet esse possibile, utile, desiderabile ut sic possit haberi...
C. See above no. 1.

8. *Ad impetrandam pluviam, sermo quartus*
UUB. MS. C 18, f. 74v.

A. IV, p. 319, no. 971.
B. Oravit Elias et celum dedit pluviam (James 5:18) – Tria sunt que movent hominem ad operandum, exemplum imitandum, ...
C. See above no. 1.

Jacques de Lausanne OP

Studied in Paris 1303, licenciate in theology 1317, provincial of France 1318, died 1322.

1. *Ad impetrandam pluviam*[8]
BAV MS Vat.lat. 1250 II, ff. 152r–v.

A. III, p. 75, no. 258.
B. Oravit et celum dedit pluviam (James 5:18) – Naturaliter pluvia non descendit super terram nisi nubes in celum...
C. See the biographical details above.

---

8. J.B. Schneyer does not give the title of this sermon. The title is taken from the BAV. MS Vat. lat. 1250 II, f. 152r.

2. *Sermo in periculis*
BAV MS Vat.lat. 1250 II, f. 153v–154v.

A.   III, p. 117, no. 759.
B.   Esther regina confugit ad Dominum pavens periculum (Esther. 14:1) – Secundum scripturas fuerunt aliqui philosophi ita excellentis ingenii et habuerunt intellectum ita elevatum...
C.   See the biographical details above.

3. *De pluvia vel pro alio tribulatione*[9]
BAV. MS Vat.lat. 1261, f. 162r–163r.

A.   III, p. 117, no. 760.
B.   Nunc clamemus ad celum (1. Machabees 4:10) – Archus quantumque fortis et ad sagittandum paratus non percutit nisi illum qui est oppositus sagittandi...
C.   See the biographical details above.

Giovanni Regina da Napoli OP

1315–1317 Master of theology in Paris, 1317 lector in Naples.

In processione pro pluvia impetranda
Napoli Biblioteca Nazionale MS VIII.Aa.11, ff. 70r–71r.

A.   III, p. 612, no. 106.
B.   Oravit et celum dedit pluviam (James 5:18) – Omnes ad presens sumus congregati ad rogandum Deum, quod det nobis pluviam pro quo facta est processio et cantata missa...
C.   Since the only existing manuscript is in the Biblioteca Nazionale of Naples and clearly of Italian origin, it is highly plausible that the sermon was delivered in Naples after 1317.

Arnoldus Royardus OFM

Lector in Toulouse; archbishop of Salerno 1321–1330, bishop of Sarlat 1330–1334.

Sermo ad postulandum pluviam
Toulouse MS 329, f. 156v.

A.   I, p. 356, no. 5.
B.   Da pluviam terrae (2. Paral. 6:27) – Ad munus divinae gratiae procurandae
tria   nos debent inducere sicut innuitur in his verbis...
C.   See above Arnoldus' personal information.

---

9.   J.B. Schneyer does not give the title of this sermon, but it is given in the manuscript.

Appendix 1

Guillelmus de Sequavilla OP

c. 1330 Rouen

[Sermo ad impetrandam serenitatem]

A. II, p. 596, no. 103.
B. Oravit, ut non plueret super terram (James 5:17) – Advocatus videns quod libellus conclusit coram aliquo judice in aliqua causa quando habet similem coram eodem judice...
C. See Guillelmus' personal information

Anonymous Swedish

The writer was quite likely a Brigittine monk since the only existing manuscript belonged to the library of Vadstena monastery. Furthermore the writer quotes saint Bridget's *Revelationes* and to the *Legenda sancte Birgitte* by Birgerius Gregorii.

The manuscript gives no title for the sermon, it merely states on the margin *Item sermo*. UUB. C. 226, ff. 101v–103r.

A. –
B. Quis dubitat quod cessante causa cesset et eius effectus – Igitur, si cessarent homines peccare, cessaret et Deus regnum perlagare...[10]
C. The writer refers to Bridget as beata and tells that she is already dead. He also quotes her legend as well as the *Revelationes*. Considering all this the sermon must have been written after 1391 (the year of saint Bridget's canonization), more ikely in the early fifteenth century.[11] The manuscript itself is dated to the fifteenth century Sweden. Thus the sermon was written down sometime in the fifteenth century.

Leonardus de Utino OP

Master of the students in Bologna 1424, *lector sententiarum* in Bologna 1426, Prior of the convent of Utino 1459, died 1469.[12]

De iudicio pestilentie et de causis eius
Sermones floridi de tempore (Lugdunensis 1496).

A. –

---

10. The *thema* is not taken from the Bible, but borrowed from the Canons of the fourth Lateran Council or from any number of other texts where it exists often in slightly modified form. It is possible that there may have been originally a biblical *thema* which have been dropped out by the copist. This is, however unlikely since the sermon is not built around any logical division. It merely states how the things are and what ought to be done about it without any rhetorical finesses.
11. Anonymous, *Sermo*. UUB C 226, f. 102v. 'Et multum orauit pro ipsa, quando fuit peregrina in hoc seculo, nequam ut attestatur in sua Legenda.'
12. *SOP* III, p. 80.

B.   Iudicium Dei abyssum multa (Psalm 35:7) – Ezechiel 14 capitulo dicit Dominus...

C.   In the last page of the printed edition one reads: *'Habes itaque lector optime sermones floridos quos composuit ac predicauit reuerendus Magister Leonardus de Utino sacre theologie doctor excellentissimus ac sacri ordinis predicatorum professor observantissimus quorum plurimos predicauit Florentie coram totam curiam romanam ibidem tunc temporis residente tempore sanctissimi domini Eugenii Pape quarti.'* In the beginning one reads: *'Sermones Floridi de dominicis et quibusdam festis fratris Leonardi de Utino sacre theologie doctoris ordinis predicatorum quos predicauit Florentie anno domini 1435 feliciter incipiunt.'* If this information is to be trusted our sermon was preached in Florence in attendance of the pope and the curia in 1435.

Gabriel Barletta OP

1. Sermo dei flagellis Dei
Sermones (Brixiae 1521)

A.   –
B.   Venit ira Dei in filios diffidentie (Ephesians 5:6) – Iam pluribus diebus laboraui, clamaui, miras ex parte Dei predixi...
C.   –

2. *De tribulationibus*
Sermones (Brixiae 1521)

A.   –
B.   Quos amo castigo (Apocalypse 3:19)
C.   –

Bernardino da Busti OFM (de obs.)

Joined the order c. 1475, died between 1513 and 1517.

1. Sabbato post quartam dominicam in quadragesima de pestilentie signis, causis et remediis
Rosarium sermonum (Venetiis 1498).

A.   –
B.   Dereliquit me Dominus (Isaias 49:14) – Sunt quidam qui statim cum a Deo flagellantur putant se ab ipso derelictos...
C.   –

2. *Feria quinta post quartam dominicam in quadragesima de tribulationibus et adversitatibus patienter portandis*
Rosarium sermonum (Venetiis 1498).

A.   –
B.   Anima eius in amaritudine est (4. Kings 4:27) – Sicut sol agens naturale licet uniformiter se habeat, propter diversas materias....
C.   –

Bernardino Tomitano da Feltre OFM (de obs.)

1. *Dominica III in quadragesima. De flagellis Dei et que sunt signa*
Sermoni del beato Bernardino Tomitano da Feltre. A cura di Padre Carlo Varischi da Milano. Tomus I (Milano 1964), pp. 273–285.

A. –
B. Nolite diligere mundum (1. John 2:16)
C. This sermon was preached to a live audience in Pavia in 1493.

2. *Sabbato post tertiam dominicam quadragesime. De tribulationibus patienter tollerandis*
Sermoni del beato Bernardino Tomitano da Feltre. A cura di Padre Carlo Varischi da Milano. Tomus I (Milano 1964), pp. 353–359.

A. –
B. Nolite diligere mundum (1. John 2:16)
C. This sermon was preached to a live audience in Pavia in 1493.

3. *Feria quinta post secundam dominicam post pasca in die sancti Marci. De peste.*
Sermoni del beato Bernardino Tomitano da Feltre. A cura di Padre Carlo Varischi da Milano. Tomus II (Milano 1964), pp. 265–273.

A. –
B. Rogate ergo Dominum (St Matthew 9:38)
D. This sermon was preached to a live audience in Pavia in 1493.

APPENDIX 2
ILLUSTRATIVE TEXTS. CATASTROPHE SERMONS OF CARDINAL EUDES DE CHÂTEAUROUX

These are transcriptions of the four catastrophe sermons of Cardinal Eudes de Châteauroux. Their dating and provenience has been discussed above in Appendix A. The spelling of the sermons has been retained in the form it is in the manuscript save the obvious errors that would change the meaning of the sentence. All the additions to the original text are presented within square brackets.

The biblical quotations, which according to the custom of Eudes, come mainly from the books of the Old Testament, are given in the footnotes. The same holds true for other sources.

A.

Sermo in processione facta propter inundationem aquarum.
Schneyer IV, p. 464, no. 862.
Arras Bibliothéque Municipal MS 137 (olim 876), ff. 78v–80r.

Quomodo conuertit aquas in siccitatem et siccata est terra [Ecclesiasticus 39:29]

Hoc sex uicibus legimus factum esse. Primo in principio mundi. Secundo post diluuium. Tertio quando filii Israelis transierunt Mare Rubrum. Quarto quando transierunt Jordanem. Quinto quando Helyas transiuit Iordanem. Sexto quando Helyzeus. Unde hic notandum primo quare sic Deus facit flumina inundare, secundo quomodo siccat.

Causa propter quam aqua totam terram operuerat a principio, uidetur Moyses assignare in principio Gen. quando dicit: *Terra autem erat inanis et uacua et tenebre erant super faciem abyssi et spiritus Domini ferebatur super aquas.*[1] Et preterea quia non erat firmamentum quod diuideret aquas ab aquis. Et uidetur Moyses respondere antipofore que posset ibi fieri. Quare ex quo deus terram fecerat permittebat eam ab aquis occupari, respondet: *Quia terra erat inanis*, id est infructuosa, *et uacua* habitatoribus, et ideo nullum dampnum erat nec etiam mirum si permittebat eam occupari ab aqua. Sic non est mirum de inundationibus que fiunt, immo plusquam mirum est quod dominus non inducit diluuium super terram quia inanis est et uacua, uere inanis quia infructuosa, mundus enim nullum fructum uel ualde parum facit. Hiis enim temporibus uidetur adimpleta prophetia Abacuch dicentis iii[o2]: *Ficus enim non florebit; et non erit germen in uineis, mentietur opus oliue et arua non afferent cibum, abscindetur de ouili pecus et non erit armentum in presepibus.*

Per hec quatuor genera hominum et quatuor genera bonorum operum designantur. Per ficum que dulcissimum fructum facit nec *potest deserere dulcedinem suam*, Iudicum ix[03] uiri contemplatiui. Et fructus contemplatiue et contemplationis in ficu est, id est flos et fructus. Sic est in contemplatione. Nota enim sic dicitur: *Patientia pauperum non peribit in fine.*[4] Quia licet actus patientie terminetur in hac uita, tamen fructus erit in eternum. Non sic erit de sapientia intellectu et ceteris uirtutibus contemplatiuis, quia sicut fructus [...][5]

1. Gen. 1:2.
2. Hab. 3:17.
3. Judg. 9:11.

(f. 79r.) non peribunt, sic nec actus. In illis enim uirtutibus que ex parte sunt essencialiter actus excidet sed non fructus. Sed in uirtutibus contemplatiuis idem est actus et fructus, id est, flos et fructus sicut est in caritate. Et ideo sicut caritas nunquam excidet, ita nec ille. Sed augebuntur et perficientur unde Prouerbum xxvii[o6]: *Qui seruat ficum comedet fructus eius.* Per ficum istam non tamen modo contemplatio designatur, immo clerici et religiosi. In ficu dum fructus ad maturitatem peruerniunt alii subcrescunt et ideo habundat in fructibus. Sic deberet esse in clericis et religiosis qui in bonis operibus deberent pre aliis habundare. Et dum unum faciunt, deberent aliud habere in proponito et uoluntate, ante etiam producit fructum quam folia que sunt ad modum palme humane, ut opera uerba precedant. Jhesus enim cepit facere et docere, Numeris xxiii[o7]: *Quis dinumerare possit puluerem Iacob et nosse numerum stirpis Israel?* Alia littera: *Quis inuestigauit semen Jacob et quis dinumerauit plebem Israelis?* Per Iacob contemplatiui qui luctantur cum angelo usque ad auroram que eis oritur in morte. Tunc fiunt Israelis et eis emarcessit omnis affectus carnalis.

Sed in quibusdam ficus ista sterilis est quia uerba habent non opera, et non sunt in eis malo granata coniuncta cum tintinnabulis. Hii sunt ficulnea de qua in Luca xiiii[o] et in Mattheo xxii.[o8] De hiis dicitur Joel i[o9]: *Ficum meam decorticauit nudans expoliauit eam et proiecit; albi facti sunt rami eiusdem.* Hii sunt clerici et quidam religiosi quos diabolus decorticauit qui etiam habitum clerici uel monachi nolunt deferre. Quis crederet quod arbor decorticata debet fructum facere uel etiam uiuere? Quis ergo habebit bonam opinionem de talibus? Nullus. O quantum fimi posuit Dominus circa radicem huius ficus et tamen fructificare non uult! De hiis enim dicit: *Ficus enim non florebit.*

Sequitur: *Et non erit germen in uineis.* De uinea uinum quod letificat cor hominis. Uinum enim in iocunditate creatum est. Per uinum opera iusticie que non tamen facientes letificant, sed etiam uidentes: *Letabitur enim iustus cum uiderit uindictam.*[10] et in fine Ysa.: *Erunt usque ad satietatem uisionis omni carni.*[11] Et in Prouerb. xxx[o12]: *Date siceram merentibus et uinum hiis qui amaro sunt animo. Bibant et obliuiscantur egestatis sue et doloris sui non reminiscantur amplius.* Ysayas. xxv[o] postquam locutus est de penis malorum dicit: *Faciet Dominus in monte hoc conuiuium pinguium.*[13]

Per uineam prelati et principes quorum officium est iusticiam exercere. Sed oportet ut uinea putetur et colatur, hoc est ut iniusticia resecetur et iniurie puniantur. Sed iam non est germen in uineis istis, quia ut dicit Ysa. xxv[o14]: *Quasi calore sub nube torrente propagines fortium emarcescere faciet.* Nubes torrens, id est, feruens et urens cupiditas est que iustitiam emarcescere facit et destruit. Joel Prima prima[15]: *Posuit uineam meam in desertum,* quando, scilicet, non putatur nec colitur. Sic quia principes et prelati non habent qui de eis faciant iusticiam, ideo iusticia derelicta ad iniurias extendunt manus suas. Et ideo non est germen in uineis istis.

4. Ps. 9:19.
5. Word illegible due to the bad quality of microfilm.
6. Prov. 27:18
7. Num. 23:10.
8. Luke 13:6–9 and Matt. 21:19–21.
9. Joel 1:7.
10. Ps. 57:11.
11. Isa. 66:24.
12. Prov. 31:6–7.
13. Isa. 25:6.
14. Isa. 25:10.
15. Joel 1:7.

Sequitur: *Mentietur opus oliue*. Per oliuam burgenses, qui si opera misericordie faciunt, ea uendunt, uel in peccato mortali ea faciunt. Et ideo mendax est huiusmodi opus.

Sequitur: *Et arua non afferent cibum*, id est, rustici. Aut quia sine pinguedine caritatis suntuel aut quia in aqua luxurie sunt immersi, aut quia salsugine odii sunt infecti [f. 79v.], aut quia nec seminati nec culti.

Quia ergo mundus sterilis est nec fert fructum, ideo non mirum si Deus permittit aquas inundare sicut a principio quando terra erat inanis et etiam uacua. Uere mundus uacuus a bonis personis unde deplorat Jeremias u⁰[16]: *Quomodo sedet sola ciuitas plena populo*. Sola a bonis, plena a malis! Amos u⁰[17]: *Urbs de qua egrediebantur mille, relinquentur in ea centum*. Item *tenebre erant super faciem abyssi*, eis enim sol iustitie non irradiat, non est firmamentum quod diuidat, id est, orationes et bona opera que obsistant ire Domini.

Item temporibus Noe diluuium mandauit. Et causa scribitur Genesis cui⁰[18]: *Ingressi sunt filii Dei ad filias hominum uidens autem Deus quod multa malitia esset in terra et cuncta cogitatio cordis intensa esset ad malum omni tempore penituit eo quod fecisset homines in terra, et precauens in futurum et talis dolore cordis intrinsecus: 'Delebo' inquit 'hominem'. Omnis quippe caro corruperat uiam suam*. Sic homines consuetudinibus malis inseparabiliter se coniungunt multiplicatur malitia. Cogitationes hominum intente sunt ad malum omni tempore. Tam clerici quam laici uias suas, id est, modus uiuendi currumpunt. Propter hoc Dominus adducit alluuiones et alias pestes que non sunt nisi comminationes, unde Psalmus[19]: *Annuntiauerunt celi iustitiam eius* pluuias emittendo fulgura et grandines. Et in Psalmo[20]: *Ueritas tua*, id est, iustitia *usque ad nubes* dum e nubibus uenti urentes et pestilentes producuntur. Ecclesiasticus xxxix⁰[21]: *Quomodo cathaclismus aridam inebriauit sic ira ipsius gentes que non exquisierunt hereditabit*.

Et sicut serui insurgunt contra aliquem qui domino suo iniuriam irrogauit et unus percutit eum ex una parte et alius ex alia, sic elementes insurgunt contra impios ad uindictam. Modo terra per terremotum, aqua per alluuiones, aer per ventos, ignis per fulgura. Sed quando Deus conuertit aquas in siccitatem sicut et a principio fecit, fit lux cognitionis qua cognoscimus quare Deus ita nos uerberet.

Secundo firmamentum per aquas inferiores penalitates nature, per superiores ultiones diuine. Penitentia est firmamentum que se opponit ne ultio diuina super nos effundatur. In hoc firmamento sunt septem opera misericordie quasi septem planete, et alia bona opera quasi stelle. Item legitur Genesis uiii⁰[22]: *Addixit Dominus spiritum super terram inminute sunt aque et clausi sunt fontes abyssy et catharacte celi et prohibite sunt pluuie de celo*. Et ibi preponitur *Recordatus est Dominus autem Noe cunctorumque animantium*. Propter paucos enim bonos Deus parcit malis, et si peccata nostra cessarent que sunt fontes abyssi, cessarent et pene que a Deo inferuntur, hoc, est clauderentur catharacte celi.

Siccata est terra in fundo Maris Rubri percussione uirge. Hec uirga beata uirgo que floruit

---

16. Lam. 1:1.
17. Amos 5:3.
18. Cf. Gen. 6:4–12.
19. Cf. Ps. 49:6.
20. Ps. 35:6.
21. Ecclus. 39:28.
22. Gen. 8:1–2.
23. There are four illegible words due to the poor quality of microfilm copy.

[——]²³ percussis fugit. Per hanc uirgam fiunt mirabilia. Hec est uirga Iesse. Si hanc haberemus in corde et in manu ei seruiendo, statim cessaret alluuio. Dicitur in uulgari: Ego teneo eum in manu mea, id est, in uoluntate mea. Si poneamus nos in uoluntate ipsius, et ipsa esset in uoluntate nostra.

Temporibus Iosue per asportationem arche. Stetit archa Iordanis.²⁴ Sic temporibus inundationum asportantur corpora sanctorum, unde nisi nolerint per peccata nostra, cessabit inundatio per meritis sanctorum quorum corpora tunc ablata. Legitur quarto Regum ii²⁵: *Tulitque Helyas pallium suum et inuoluit illud et percussit aquas (f. 80r.) que diuise sunt in utramque partem et transierunt ambo per siccum.* Infra eodem dicitur quod Helizeus pallio Helye, *quod ceciderat ei, percussit aquas et non sunt diuise. Et dixit: 'Ubi est Helye uerbum?' Etiam nunc percussitque aquas et diuise sunt huc atque illuc, et transiit Helyzeus.*²⁶ Quid hoc pallium Helye nisi caritas Christi? Ysayas lix°²⁷: *Coopertus est quasi pallio zeli.* Sed pallium istud inuolutum est. Non enim ex toto manifestauit Christus amorem suum erga nos, nisi inuolute et implicite. Hoc amore penas nobis debitas mitigat et aliquando amouet ex toto pallium Helysei. Amor est quo debemus eum diligere quod dereliquit nobis secundum quod dicitur prima [epistula] Iohannis iiii°²⁸: *In hoc est caritas; non quasi nos dilexerimus Deum, sed quoniam ipse primo dilexit nos.* Si habuerimus hoc duplex pallium, scilicet, ut Christus diligat nos et nos ipsum, tunc siccabitur in nobis diluuium peccatorum, diluuium etiam penarum.

Rogemus ergo Dominum ut inundationem peccatorum faciat cessare et etiam inundationem aquarum ad laudem et gloriam sui sancti nominis et gloriose uirginis matris sue, necnon et gloriose uirginis Genouefe et aliorum sanctorum quorum hic corpora sunt allata Amen.

B.

Sermo propter timorem terremotus

Schneyer IV, p. 464, no. 862.
Arras Bibliothéque municipal MS 137 (olim 876), ff. 88r–v.

Commota est et contremuit terra fundamenta montium conturbata sunt et commota sunt quoniam iratus est eis [Psalm 17:8]

Dicit Job u°²⁹: *Nihil fit in terra sine causa et de humo non orietur dolor*. Et in Thimeo: *Nichil fit cuius causa legitima non precesserit.*³⁰ Uere in terra nichil fit sine causa, nec pestilentis, nec fames, nec terremotus, sed fere omnia mala que accidunt peccata nostra incidunt super nos. Et uero dicit Dominus per Ysayam³¹: *Ue anime eorum quoniam*

---

24. Cf. Josh. 4:1–11.
25. 2 Kings 2:8.
26. 2 Kings 2:13–14.
27. Isa. 59:17.
28. 1 John 4:10.
29. Job 5:6.
30. Timaios 28a.
31. Isa. 3:9–11.

reddita sunt ei[s] mala. Dicite iusto quoniam bene quoniam fructum adinuentionum suarum comedet. Ue impio in malum; retributio enim manuum eius fiet ei. Deus enim iustus est et *reddet unicuique iuxta opera sua* ut dicit Psalmus[32] bonis bona, malis mala, unde Dominus precepit filiis Leui Deuteronomi xxvii° ut una pars filiorum israelis staret super montem Gazarim [pro Garizim] ad benedicendum populo et alia super montem Hebal ad maledicendum. Illi ad benedicendum facientibus precepta Domini, alii ad maledicendum transgressores.[33] Sic et Dominus in legis sene promittit multa bona bonis et comminatur multa mala malis.

Et sicut homines multis modis peccant, ita et Dominus eos multis modis punit ut *per que quis peccat per hec et puniatur* ut dicitur in libro Sapientie.[34] Et sicut legimus Dauid peccasse superbiendo de multitudine populi sui, sic et punitus est in dimunitione populi eiusdem per pestilentiam II Regum ultimo.[35] Et sicut Dauid peccauit polluendo uxorem Urie II Regum xi°[36], sic et punitus est in hoc quod Absalon polluit uxores eius II Regum xv.°[37] Sic et diues epulus qui nimis edendo et potando peccauerat, siti describitur estuare Lucas xvi.°[38] Et sicut egiptii merserant paruos filiorum Israeli in flumine, sic et bibere sanguinem sunt compulsi ut dicitur in libro Sapientie xi°[39]: *Pro fonte quidem sempiterni fluminis humanum sanguinem dedisti iniustis. Qui comminuerentur in traductione infantium occisorum.* Ideo comminatur Dominus per Ezechiel u°[40]: *In medio tui et* [f. 88v.] *tertia pars in gladio cadet in circuitu tuo, tertiam uero partem tuam in omnem uentum dispargam.*

Quia enim diuersi mode peccauerant ideo diuersis penis eis comminatur. Sic quia in multis delinquimus, in multis punimur. Et ideo pro eo, id est, pro Deo pugnat orbis terrarum aduersus insensatos. Quia enim sanitate abutimur, inducit Dominus pestilentias. Quia rerum habundantia abutimur, punimur fame. Quia pace, bello. Et quia cupidi sumus in augendo possessiones sicut dicit Ysayas u°[41]: *Ue qui coniungitis domum domo et agrum agro copulatis.* Ideo terremotus subuertit ciuitates et castra ut ad litteram domus eorum fiant sepulchra eorum in eternum.

Dicit Dominus per Ysayam xxiiii°[42]: *Concutientur fundamenta terre confractione confringetur terra et contritione conteretur terra commotione commouebitur terra, agitatione agitabitur terra.* Sicut enim ebrius angustiatur et prouocat uomitum ut sic alleuietur, sic terra quodammodo indignatur sustinere peccatores et eos uult expellere a se sicut equus indomitus sessorem uel etiam onager. Inducit etiam Dominus terremotum ut incutiatur timor hominibus. Dicitur in Psalmo[43]: *Qui respicit terram et facit eam tremere.* Tremit terra ut tremant homines, conteritur ut homines conterantur, aperit se ut homines

---

32. Ps. 61:13.
33. Cf. Deut. 27:11–13.
34. Wisd. of Sol. 11:17.
35. 2 Sam. 24.
36. 2. Sam. 11:1–4.
37. 2. Sam. 16:21–22.
38. Luke 16:24.
39. Wisd. of Sol. 11:7–8.
40. Ezek. 5:12. Eudes or the copist seems to have started the quotation from the middle. It runs in extenso: 'tertia tui pars peste morietur et fame consumetur in medio tui, et tertia pars gladio cadet in circuitu tuo, tertiam uero partem tuam in omnem ventum dispergam et gladium evaginabo post eos.
41. Isa. 5:8.
42. Isa. 24:18–20.
43. Ps. 103:32.
44. Ecclus. 1:16 or Ps. 110:10.

se aperiant per confessionem, ut homines incipiant sapientes esse quia *initium sapientie timor Domini*.[44] Ideo bene dicit Job: *Nichil in terra sine causa fit et de humo non egredietur dolor*, id est, ab homine qui ab humo dicitur. Propter hoc bene dicit Psalmus *Commota est et contremuit terra* etc. Ideo enim Dominus inducit terremotum et facit altera terribilia ad ostendendum quod iratus est nobis. Sed quid faciendum ad hec euitanda et maxime ad terremotum euitandum?

Docet Psalmus alibi: *Liguefacta est terra et omnes qui habitant in ea. Ego confirmaui columpnas eius.*[45] Terra que debet liquefieri cor nostrum est quod debet liquefieri calore ignis ire per zelum ut possimus dicere illud Psalmi: *Factum est cor meum tanquam cera liquescens in medio uentris mei.*[46] Et illud: *Et in meditatione mea exardescet ignis*[47], ut homo ira accendatur contra peccata sua. Dicitur Job xxuii°[48]: *Lapis calore solutus es uertitur*. Et hoc est quod dicit: *Liquefacta est terra et*, id est, *omnes qui habitant in ea*. Si irasceremur nobis ipsis, ira Dei cessaret et tunc confirmaret columpnas terre, id est, terram redderet stabilem et aptam habitationibus hominum et amoueret terremotus et alia nobis contraria. Rogemus ergo ut sic penitentiamus de peccatis ut reddamus nobis uultum Dei placabilem et serenum et cessemus a peccatis. Quia cessante causa cessabit et effectus. Hoc prestet nobis Dominus Ihesus Christus qui uiuit in secula seculorum. Amen.

C.

Sermo exhortatorius propter terremotum qui media nocte factus est Uiterbii et in multis locis.

Schneyer 4, p. 482, no. 1071.
Pisa Cateriniana 21, ff. 147v–149v.

Catharacte de exelsis aperte sunt et concutientur fundamenta terre confractione confringetur terra et contritione conteretur terra commotione commouebitur terra, agitatione agitabitur terra sicut ebrius [Isaias 24:18–20].

Hanc comminationem fecit Dominus per Ysayam prohetam et complebitur et consummabitur in fine mundi appropinquante magni iudicii die. Nichilominus iam multociens particulariter impleta est et timemus ne temporibus nostris peccatis nostris exigentibus in parte impleatur. Causam enim huius comminationis premittit propheta immediate ante predicta uerba dicens: *Secretum meum michi, secretum meum michi, ue michi. Preuaricatores preuaricati sunt et preuaricatione transgressorum preuaricati sunt formido et fouea et laqueus super te qui habitator es terre et erit qui fugerit a facie formidinis cadet in fouea, et qui se explicuerit de fouea tenebitur laqueo, quia catharacte de excelsis* etc. Quia enim multiplicate sunt transgressiones, ideo effunditur ira Dei super homines mittendo famem, pestilentiam, gladium, fulgura et tempestates, terremotus et

---

45. Ps. 74:4.
46. Ps. 21:15.
47. Ps. 38:4.
48. Job 28:2.

alia flagella adeo ut etiam bruta animalia ut leones, lupi et etiam insensibilia elementa uideantur insurgere contra insensatos in uindictam offensarum quibus miseri homines non cessant Dominum prouocare. Licet hoc occultum sit hominibus qui non attendunt quod talia proueniant ex ira Dei. Uerumptamen hoc reuelat Dominus amicis suis et reuelauit prophetis, unde Ysayas dicit: *Secretum meum michi, secretum meum michi*. Reuelatum enim erat ei, et si non aliis, quod Deus predictas penas effunderet super peccatores etiam in presenti, et multos maiores in futuro, et ideo bis dicit *secretum meum* [f. 148r.] *michi, secretum meum*, id est, secretum meum reuelatum est michi ad utilitatem et non aliis qui non credunt auditui meo, unde ipse dicit liii[049]: *Domine quis credidit auditui nostro*?

Sed uidens propheta multiplicationem peccatorum et per consequens penarum compatiens miseris peccatoribus dicit: *Ue michi*, et quare hoc dicat subiungit: *Preuaricatores preuaricati sunt* etc. per incultationem horum uerborum ostenditur multiplicatio peccatorum, et quia omne genus peccati comprehenditur sub quadruplicis legis preuaricatione, scilicet, legis naturalis, mosaice, euangelice et humane, ideo quater repetitur hic preuaricatio. Genera autem peccatorum que contra quatuor leges predictas committuntur exprimit cum subiungit: *formido et fouea et laqueus super te qui habitator es terre*.

Formido quo ad concupiscentiam oculorum que formidinem inducit. Cupidus enim timet amittere quod habet, timet ne possit habere quod non habet et concupiscit habere, et timet ne alius obtineat quod habere intendebat. Et appellatur timor iste formido quia uanus est, formidines enim appellantur larue uel expauentacula que ponuntur in satis ad terrendum aues ne rapiant seminata seu semina iactata et uane terrentur auicule ad hiis quia ledi non possunt ab ipsis, unde cupidis dicitur Job xv[o50]: *Sonitus terroris semper in auribus illius et cum pax sit ille semper insidias suspicatur.* et in Leuitico xxvi[o51] Dominus comminatur talibus: *Dabo pauorem in cordibus eorum in regionibus hostium terrebit eos sonitus folii uolantis et ita fugient quasi gladium.*

Per foueam intelligitur concupiscentia carnis in quam homo de facili labitur, sed difficultate ab ea eripitur, unde et de meretrice dicitur *fouea profunda meretrix*.[52]

Per laqueum superbia uite qua homo ambulat in magnis et in mirabilibus super se, de quo in Psalmus: *Cogitauerunt supplantare gressus meos absconderunt superbi laqueum michi*.[53] Et ad cumulum miserie peccatorum est quod dum credunt se expedire de uno genere peccatorum, incidunt in aliud, unde subiungit: *Et erit qui fugerit a facie formidinis cadet in foueam, et qui se explicuerit de fouea tenebitur a laqueo.* et cum pene peccatis respondeant in inferno, dampnati uolentes fugere penam alicuius peccati. Hoc est transire de una pena ad aliam iuxta illud Job xxiiii[o54]: *Transibunt a frigore niuium ad nimium calorem*. Incurrendo unam penam non propter hoc ab alia liberabuntur. Hoc est quod hic dicitur: *Qui fugerit a facie formidinis cadet in foueam*, tamen cadendo in foueam non eripietur a formidine, immo formido eam amplius terrebit, nec laqueo implicatus a fouea liberabitur.

Quia ergo cotidie multiplicantur peccata, ideo subiungit *quia catharacte de excelsis aperte sunt*. Catharacta est uia subterranea qua aqua sub terra discurrit, unde per translationem

---

49. Isa. 53:1.
50. Job 15:21.
51. Lev. 26:36.
52. Prov. 23:27.
53. Ps. 139:5–6.
54. Job 24:19.

in celo desuper catharacte dicuntur [f. 148v.] nubes uel discursus et meatus pluuiarum, uel tornitrua, uel fenestre nubium. Propter multiplicationem ergo peccatorum *catharacte de excelsis aperte sunt*, id est, fenestre et meatus per quas effunditur ira Dei sicut pluuia effunditur quando rumpuntur nubes et per hunc modum loquitur Ysayas et dicit lxiiii[55]: *Utinam disrumperes celos et descenderes a facie tua montes defluerent. Sicut exustio ignis tabescerent aque arderent igni.* Per similem modum imprecatur propheta cum dicit: *Effunde iram tuam in gentes que te non nouerunt et in regna que nomen tuum non inuocauerunt.*[56] Et alibi in Psalmus: *Effunde frameam*, id est, gladium *aduersus eos qui tribulant me*.[57] Stillat enim Deus iram suam quando paulatim et quasi guttatim immittit eam. Sed tunc dicitur eam effundere, quando eam habundanter emittit et quasi totaliter cum nichil de ea retinere uideatur. Quod tamen nunquam fecit, nec in effusione diluuii, nec in subuersione Pentapolis, quia multo maiorem penam meruerant quam tunc incurrerunt.[58] Propter ergo multiplicationem peccatorum et scelerum dicit Dominus: *Quia catharacte de excelsis aperte sunt*, id est, uie ire Domini aperte sunt ut super peccatores influat habundanter iuxta illud Psalmus: *Misit in eos iram indignationis sue.*[59] Indignationem et iram et tribulationem et inmissionem per angelos malos, quia angeli mali ministri sunt ire Dei super peccatores, sicut apostolus dicit de iudice temporali ad Ro. xiii[60]: *Dei enim minister est... uindex in iram ei qui male agit.* Et subiungit in Psalmus[61]: *Uiam fecit semite ire sue* ut libere, scilicet, possit currere ad modum fluuii. Sicut econtrario ad preces aliquorum bonorum uel quia homines ad penitentiam sunt conuersi, obturat semitam ire sue, uel ut omissio cesset, uel ut libere non discurrat, sicut legitur Gen. viii[62]: *Clausi sunt omnes fontes abyssi et catharacte celi et prohibite sunt pluuie de celo.*

Hoc fuit quando *recordatus est Deus Noe cunctorumque animantium et omnium iumentorum que erant cum eo in archa, et adduxit spiritum super terram et inminuite sunt aque*, hoc est quando Dominus recordatur peccatorum et ad misericordiam excitatur, sed quando penitere nolunt tunc catharacte de excelsis aperiuntur et concutiuntur fundamenta terre, id est, montes. Dicitur enim Psalmus: *Qui firmauit terram super stabilitatem suam et non inclinabitur in seculum seculi.*[63] Stabilitas terre est eius grauitas que fundat eam in medio elementorum quod est infimus locus. De montibus uero dicit Dei sapientia Prouerbium viii[64]: *Necdum montes graui mole constiterant.* Montes enim propter grauitatem molis sue impellunt terram ad locum infimum in quo stabilitur et fundatur, et ideo dominantur fundamenta terre, ut quod dicitur de Italiam? Uere possit dici de ea: *fundamenta eius in montibus.*[65] Hec fundamenta terre, id est, montes concutiuntur per terremotum propter uaporem inclusum cuius uiolentia scissure fiunt [f. 149r.] in terra ut euaporentur, et sic mouetur terra sicut uidemus in castaneis quando calore ignis generatur

---

55. Isa. 64:1–2.
56. Ps. 78:6.
57. Ps. 34:3.
58. Cf. Wisd. of Sol. 10:6.
59. Ps. 77:49.
60. Rom. 13:4. There seems to a fault by the copist. He has omitted part of the quotation. The full text is the following: 'Dei enim minister est tibi in bonum. Si autem male feceris time, non enim sine causa gladium portat. Dei enim minister est; vindex in iram ei qui malum agit.'
61. Ps. 77:50.
62. Gen. 8:2.
63. Cf. Ps. 135:6.
64. Prov. 8:25.
65. Ps. 86:1.
66. Deut. 32:22.

in eis, uapor concutiuntur et ui uaporis exiliunt de igne et disrumpuntur cortices eorum. Etiam uiolentia uaporis inclusi in interioribus partibus montium ignis generatur et sic quod legitur in cantico Deuteronomii[66]: *Fundamenta montium comburit*, id est, inferiores partes montium, et sic concutiuntur montes et mouentur et ardent usque ad inferni nouissima.

Et tunc sit quod subiungit Ysaias: *Confractione confringetur terra et contritione contereretur terra*. Inter confractionem et contritionem est differentia. Confringitur enim uas quando in duas uel plures partes magnas impulsu uel compulsione diuiditur. Contereretur uero quando in minutas partes diuiditur secundum quod alibi dicit Ysayas xxx[o67]: *Ueniet contritio eius et comminuetur sicut conteritur lagena figuli contritione perualida*. Et non inuenietur de fragmentis eius testa in qua portetur igniculus de incendio aut hauriatur parum aque de fouea.

Similiter differt agitatio a commotione. Agitatio enim addit ad commotionem frequentiam et uiolentiam. Tunc dicitur enim agitari aliquod corpus quando multotiens mouetur et cum uiolentia. Sic comminatur Dominus quod commotione commouebitur terra et non comminatio commouebitur immo agitatione agitabitur, id est, frequenter et uiolenter. Et nota ordinem. Primo ponit confractionem et postea contritionem. Similiter primo ponit commonitionem, postea ponit agitationem. Contritio enim uiolentior est confractione et agitatio commotione. Primo enim infert Deus leuiores penas ut uiolentiores caueamus et declinemus, sicut dicit Psalmus: *Dedisti eis significationem ut fugiant a facie arcus*.[68] Leuiora enim flagella signant quod grauiora subsequentur nisi homines se emendent. Sicut quis percutit uirga primo asinum suum ut festinet, postmodum baculo si noluerit festinare. Sic percutitur seruus primo uirga in quo eruditur, quod nisi se correxit postmodum baculo ferietur, unde signantur dicit Dominus in Psalmo: *Uisitabo in uirga iniquitates eorum et in uerberibus peccata eorum*.[69] Similiter alibi in Psalmo proponitur uirga et subiungitur baculus cum dicit: *uirga tua et baculus tuus*.[70]

Flagella enim et terrores quos Deus inmittit non sunt nisi quedam preludia maiorum et grauiorum fflagellorum que subsequntur nisi per penitentiam nos corrigamus. Sed uerificatur in quampluribus quod dicitur de diabolo. *Non fugabit eum uir sagittarius in stipulam uersi sunt ei lapides funde quasi stipulam estimabit malleum et deridebit uibrantem hastam*.[71] Sic lflagella Domini quasi stipulas contemptimus et reputamus quasi ludum paruorum qui consueuerunt facere hastiludum suum cum stipulis canaborum utentes eis probanos, id est, canabinis. Comminationes enim Domini factas perscriptos et que quotidie fiunt per predicatores et per ipsa que facit Dominus sicut per gladium, per pestilentias, per famem et sterilitatem [f. 149v.] per inundationes, per fulgura, per tempestates, per terremotus quasi ludum reputamus nec nos in aliquo emendamus. Sed fiet nobis sicut factum fuit diebus Noe et in diebus Loth quando superuenit interitus repentinus.

Sed nota quod dicitur: *Confractione confringetur terra* etc. et subiungit *sicut ebrius*. Ebrius enim grauatus crapula, prouocat nauseam et alleuiat se iuxta uerbum Ecclesiastici dicentis: *Si grauatus fueris in edendo multum surge, uome et refrigerabit te*.[72] Sic terra

---

67. Isa. 30:13–14.
68. Ps. 59:6.
69. Ps. 88:33.
70. Ps. 22:4.
71. Job 41:19–20.
72. Ecclus. 31:25.

sustinendo inimicos Dei, pascendo eos et uestiendo quasi grauata et indignata commouebit se et agitabit se et in se ipsa confringetur et contereretur ut eos abiciat a se. Sicut equs abicit sessorem qui eum grauat, et ebrius cibum et potum quibus grauatur per nauseam abicit a se, ideo post predicta subiungitur sicut ebrius. Similiter omnia elementa ad ultimum abicient a se et euoment peccatores, nec inuenient locum manendi inter elementa, nisi in infimo loco, in santina, scilicet inferni.

Emendemus ergo nos per penitentiam et mortem subitaneam preueniamus sani et uiui confitentes et facientes que in morte uel post mortem facere proponimus et sic morte subitanea non potuerimus preoccupari quod largiatur nobis sancta trinitas, unus Deus. Amen.

D.

Sermo quando timetur de terremotu

Schneyer IV, p. 482, no. 1072
Pisa Catariniana MS 21, ff. 149v–151v.

Secundo Regum xxii: *Clamor meus ueniet ad aures eius. Commota est et contremuit terra. Fundamenta montium concussa sunt et conquassata quoniam iratus est eis Deus. Ascendit fumus de naribus eius et ignis de ore eius uorabit carbones incensi sunt ab eo.* [2. Kings 22:7–9].

Possumus dicere quod Psalmus qui incipit: *Diligam te Domine fortitudo mea.*[73] Dauid repetit in secundo Regum xxii° et premittitur: Loqutus est autem Dauid Domino uerba carminis huius in die qua liberauit eum Dominus de manu inimicorum suorum et de manu Saulis et ait *Dominus petra mea* etc.[74] quibusdam uerbis tamen mutatis, et in ipso titulo psalmis, et in serie eiusdem Psalmi. Uel possumus dicere quod hic psalmus alius est a psalmo qui ponitur in libro psalmorum quamuis in multis conueniant, sicut tertiusdecimus psalmus qui incipit: *Dixit insipiens in corde suo*[75] alius est a quinquagesimo secundo psalmus qui similiter incipit. Similiter psalmus ille *paratum cor meum Deus paratum cor meum.*[76] Uidetur contineri secundum primam partem eiusdem psalmi in illo psalmo *Miserere mei Deus miserere mei quoniam in te confidit anima mea.*[77] Reliqua autem pars uidetur contineri in psalmus qui *incipit Deus repulisti nos* [78] paucis tamen uerbis mutatis.

Et in hoc instruimur quod non debemus erubescere repetere aliquando in scriptis nostris uel sermonibus que alibi scripsimus uel predicauimus. Nec laborare debemus ut semper noua utamus. Nec debemus erubescere scribere uel proponere uerba que alii scripserunt

---

73. Ps. 17:2.
74. 2 Sam. 22:1–2.
75. Ps. 13:1.
76. Ps. 107.
77. Ps. 56.
78. Ps. 59.
79. Jer. 1:9.

et proposuerunt, immo ea securius possimus et scribere et proponere aliorum uestigiis inherendo [f. 150r.] et tunc fiunt nostra, sunt bene et fideliter ea assumamus iuxta illud: *Et bene cum recitas incipit esse tuum.* Ieremias enim cuius os Dominus tetigerat et dixerat ad eum: *Ecce dedi uerba mea in ore tuo* non erubescit assumere eadem uerba que dixerat et scripserat.[79] Ysaias propheta ut apparet in omnibus, nec etiam uerba Abdie qui homo laicus erat, ut apparet, in onere Edon. Similiter facit et Ezechiel. Similiter beatus Iohannes qui scripsit Apocalipsim quam Dominus Ihesus Christus ei reuelauerat. Assumit non tamen modo sentencias sed etiam uerba que scripserant prophete et in eorum libris leguntur, ut apparet in illis uerbis *dicent montibus cadite super nos et collibus operite nos* que scribuntur Osee x.[80] sicut et decalamo apocalypsis xi° de quo scribitur Ezechiele xl°[81]. Similiter de quatuor animalibus in Apocalypsis iiii° de quibus scribitur Ezechiele primo.[82] Et ut in summa colligamus uidetur liber Apocalypsis esse quidam epilogus prophetarum Ueteris Testamenti.

Etiam ipse Saluator inchoauit predicationem suam a uerbis sui precursoris, scilicet, *penitentiam agite appropinquabit regnum celorum* Mt. iiii° et Mt iii.[83] Matheo iii° legitur quod Johannes dixit illa uerba, Matheo iiii° legitur quod Saluator cepit predicare et dicere *penitentiam agite* etc. Ipse etiam Saluator sermonem quem fecerat discipulis suis in monte sedens, postmodum descendens de monte et stans in loco campestri eundem sermonem per magne parte turbis repetiit ut daret nobis forma eadem repetendi cum uiderimus expedire. Sic apostolus aliqua que dixit in una epistola ut in prima ad Thimoteum repetit in epistola ad Tytum. Siue ergo ille psalmus qui continetur in Libro Psalmorum et ille qui scribitur in secundo Regum idem sit uel diuersus ea tamen que in eis continentur uera sunt et equalis auctoritatis.

Uerba autem que prelibauimus scripta sunt in secundo Regum et licet parum differat ab illis que scribuntur in Libro Psalmorum ea tamen assumimus quia proposito nostro magnum congruere uidentur. Illa tamen non relinquimus sed etiam ea assumemus prout uiderimus oportunum. Uerba ergo que prelibauimus ista sunt: *Clamor meus ueniet ad aures eius* etc., et ostenduntur nobis in hiis uerbis quatuor. Primo casus qui nuper accidit cum dicit: *Commota est et contremuit terra.* Secundo ostenditur causa propter quam accidit ibi: *quoniam iratus est eis Deus.* Tercio quod crescente ira Dei crescit et uindicta et augentur flagello ibi: *ascendit fumus.* Quarto quid in talibus casibus sit agendum ibi: *et clamor meus ueniet ad aures eius.*

Dicit itaque: *Commota est et contremuit terra.* Casus iste frequenter accidit sicut et alia flagella que Dominus immittit ut Dominum timeamus. Ideo enim terribiliter in fulguribus scilicet et tornitruis, in clangore tubarum et terremotu uenit Dominus daturus legem, ut terror illius esset in populo israelis, sicut scribitur Exodo xx°, ut illo terrore fierent memores mandatorum que Dominus eis dabat.[84] Fierent in qua memores ad faciendum ea, sicut doctor patientem terret [f. 150v.] cum eum erudit, ut terrore illo ea que tradit magister paruo parui memorie imprimantur. Sic Dominus mittit nobis terrores diuersorum generum ut timeamus Dominum et ut timentes que precipit faciamus, et ab hiis que prohibet abstineamus.

Multipliciter enim terret nos Dominus sicut in serie predicti psalmi continentur. Immittit

---

80. Apoc. 6:16; Hos. 19:8.
81. Apoc. 11:1; Ezek. 40:3–5.
82. Apoc. 4:6–8; Ezek.
83. Matt. 3:2; 4:17.
84. Cf. Exod. 20:18.
85. Ps. 17:5.

enim nobis infirmitates mortiferas unde dicit: *Circumdederunt me dolores mortis*, id est, dolores uehementes et ducentes ad mortem. Terret nos ponendo ante oculos nostros casum angelorum malorum unde subiungit: *Torrentes inquitatis conturbauerunt me*.[85] Torrentes enim proueniunt ex resolutione niuium. Sic angeli ardore concupiscentie male inflammantis amiserunt candorem innocentie, et facti sunt nobis torrentes turbulentissimi trahentes nos ad mare inferni impulsionibus suis et impetibus suis. Promittit nos ligari fumibus peccatorum quibus trahimur ad infernum, unde sequitur: *Dolores inferni circumdederunt me*.[86] Hebraica ueritas habet fumes inferni. Permittit nos preoccupari multiplicibus perplexitatibus. Hoc est quod dicit: *preoccupauerunt me laquei mortis*.[87] Propter ista terret nos terremotu, unde dicit: *Commota est*, et uiolentia uentorum et tempestatibus, unde subiungit: *Et ascendit super cherubin et uolauit*[88] quasi ut gem ad currendum angelos qui presiuit uentis ut eos soluant. Fulgum autem utitit pre fulgori in conspectu eius [...][89] tonabat de celo Dominus, mittit grandines, misit sagittas suas et dissipauit eos fulgura et consumpsit eos. Et apparuerunt effusiones maris et multa alia que in predictum psalmis serie continentur.

Hec facit Dominus ut terror eius et timor sit in nobis. Sed potest dicere cum propheta Malachia primo[90]: *Si ego Dominus ubi est timor meus*? Econtrario liberat nos a hiis periculis. Multiplicat beneficia ut pius pater. Sed potest dicere: Si ego pater, ubi est amor meus? Homines timentes eos, diligimus Deum non timemus cum dicat propheta Ysayas viii[o91]: *Ipse pauor uester et ipse terror uester*, et in euangelio: *Nolite timere eos qui occidunt corpus* etc.[92], et epistula Iohannis: *Fratres nolite diligere mundum nec ea que mundo sunt*.[93] Clamat Dominus in lege et in euangelio: *Diliges Dominum Deum tuum*,[94] et hoc est maximum et primum mandatum quia hoc mandatum debet tenere primum locum in corde nostro, sed iam nullum locum ibi habet.

Solliciti sunt inquirere philosophi et scolastici de causis terremotus et fulguram et tornitruum et per que signa prenosticari possint. Et dicunt quod causa terremotus uapor est inclusus in uisceribus terre. Et ponunt exemplum de musto, siue de uino nouo, quod tanta uis est feruoris eius, id est, uaporis feruidi quem in se habet, ut uasa quamuis grandia et noua, si sint eo repleta, absque spiramen illito disrumpat, sicut legitur in Iob Heliu posuisse exemplum de musto dicens: *An uenter meus quasi mustum absque spiraculo quia quod ligunculas nouas disrumpit*.[95] Sic uapor inclu[151r.]sus in uisceribus terre, terram disrumpit.

De tornitru dicit Philosophus quod est extinctio ignis in nube. Fulgur ergo est materia terrea eleuata ui uaporis ascendentis, et ibi ignita descendit ratione terre nature quam habet et discurrit quasi uagando huc et illuc et penetrat ratione ignee nature quia ignitum est. Unde postquam extinctum est non potest se mouere sicut nec lapis nec ferrum. Et ignis quo erat ignitum reuolat sursum iuxta illud: Supersosque colligit ignes.

---

86. Ps. 17:6.
87. Ps. 17:6.
88. Ps. 17:11.
89. Illegible word.
90. Mal. 1:6.
91. Isa. 8:13.
92. Matt. 10:28.
93. 1 John 2:15.
94. Deut. 6:5; Matt. 22:37; Mark 12:30; Luke 10:27.

Legitur Apocalypsis x°: Et cum clamasset dicit de angelo cuius *facies erat ut sol et pedes eius tanquam columpna ignis. Et cum clamasset loquta sunt septem tornitrua uoces suas. Et cum loquita fuissent septem tornitrua uoces suas ego scripturus eram et audiui uocem de celo dicentem signa que locuta sunt septem tornitrua noli ea scribere.*[96] Et uolunt quidam dicere quod Iohannes uolebat scribere causas tornitruorum et prenostica eorum, sed inhibuit ei hoc angelus. Quicquid autem sit de hoc, parum ad nos inquirere de causis fulgurum uel terremotus uel de signis prenosticantibus ea, cum hic habeamus expresse que sit causa terremotus cum dicit: *Commota est* etc. et subiungit: *quoniam iratus est eis Deus*. Hec est causa et fulgurum et terremotuum, causa scilicet efficiens, causa finalis, ut terreamur et Deum timeamus.

Signa prenostica sunt multiplicatio peccatorum et contemptus Dei et noua assecuratio que iram Dei accendunt unde subiungit: *Ascendit fumus de naribus eius et ignis de ore eius uorabit*, sicut signum est quod ira hominis accenditur quando ipse uehementior prorumpit de naribus eius. Quid autem faciendum sit ad euadendum ea et quod optimum remedium? Docet nos propheta cum promittit: *Clamor meus ueniet ad aures eius*. Hoc est efficax remedium, unde consuerunt homines clamare Kyrie eleison quando sentiunt terremotum, et est optima consuetudo. Et interpretatur Kyrie eleison Domine miserere. Qui hoc dicit se non excusat nec iudicium petit sed tamen misericordiam.

Et nota quod dicit *clamor meus*. Tunc oratio nostra clamor est quando ab amore procedit et ui amoris quasi natura ignea ad aures Dei uehitur et rapitur et nota quod dicit ad aures eius, non quia Deus aures habet sed ad ostendum quod immediate uenit ad Deum non ad angelos, uel apostolos, uel ad alios sanctos, quia nullus tamen uult quod preces nostre axaudiantur sicut ipse Deus. Et ideo mulier chananea non clamabat ad apostolos ut misererentur eius et filie sue sed ad ipsum dominum Ihesum.[97] Et nota quod in psalmus dicit *Clamor meus in conspectu eius introiuit in aures eius*.[98] Hic dicit ueniet ad aures eius, sed ideo dicit introiuit, quia ut dicit Dominus per Ysayam[99]: *Antequam clamauerunt ad me ego exaudiam eos* per preordinationem et in Psalmo[100]: *Preperationem cordis eorum audiuit auris tua*, quia ipsa preparatio deprecandi sine proponitum pro deprecationem a Domino reputatur quo ad effectum. Uidentes ergo karissimi, ea que in mundo accidunt terreamus Deum, timemus faciendo mandata ipsius, prohibitiones eius obseruando et ueniam et misericordiam ab eo in[f. 151v.]stanter petamus ut eam consequi mereamur. Amen.

95. Job 32:19.
96. Apoc. 10:1–4.

Bibliography

A. Manuscripts:

A.1. Archives:

Città del Vaticano, Archivio Segreto Vaticano: *Penitenzieria Apostolica*, vol. 7–10.

A. 2. Libraries:

Aldobrandinus de Toscanella, *Sermones de tempore*. Città del Vaticano, Biblioteca Apostolica Vaticana MS Ottob. lat. 557.
Anonymous, *Sermo*. Uppsala, Uppsala Universitets Bibliotek MS C 226.
Anonymous, *Sermo pro pluvia*. Città del Vaticano, Biblioteca Apostolica Vaticana MS vat. Borghes. 138.
Anonymous, *Sermo pro serenitate uel sanitate*. Città del Vaticano, Biblioteca Apostolica Vaticana MS Borghes. 138.
Bertrandus de Turre, *Sermones de tempore*. Città del Vaticano, Biblioteca Apostolica Vaticana MS Vat. lat. 1242.
Fredericus Pisanus Visconti, *Sermones*. Firenze, Biblioteca Laurenziana MS Plut. 33.sin.1.
Guibertus Tornacensis, *Sermones ad status*. Paris, Bibliothèque Nationel MS lat. 15943.
Guido Pisanus, *Descriptio terremoti*. Città del Vaticano, Biblioteca Apostolica Vaticana MS Vat.lat. 11564.
Inquisitio de fide, uita et moribus, fama et miraculis recolende memorie domini Thome de Cantilupo quondam episcopi dicte ecclesie Herefordensis et ea contingentibus. Città del Vaticano, Biblioteca Apostolica Vaticana MS Vat.lat. 4015.
Jacobus de Losanna, *Sermones de communi sanctorum*. Città del Vaticano, Biblioteca Apostolica Vaticana MS Vat.lat. 1250 II.
Jacobus de Losanna, *Sermones*. Città del Vaticano, Biblioteca Apostolica Vaticana MS Vat. lat. 1261.
Johannes Friburgensis, *Confessionale*. London, British Library MS Add. 19581.
Johannes Regina de Neapel, *Sermones varii*. Naples, Biblioteca Nazionale MS VIII.Aa.11.
Johannes Rigaldus, *Sermones*. Città del Vaticano, Biblioteca Apostolica Vaticana MS Vat. lat. 957.
Konrad Holtnicker, *Sermones de tempore*. Città del Vaticano, Biblioteca Apostolica Vaticana MS Vat. Borghes. 180.
Missa pro vitanda mortalitatem. London, British Library MS Addit. 40146.
Nicolas de Gorran, *Sermones de communi sanctorum et de occasionibus*. Uppsala, Uppsala Universitets Bibliotek MS C 18.
Nicolaus de Aquaevilla, *Sermones de sanctis*. Città del Vaticano, Biblioteca Apostolica Vaticana MS Vat. lat. 1251.
Odo de Castroradulphi, *Sermones*. Arras, Bibliotheque municipal MS 137.
Odo de Castroradulphi, *Sermones varii*. Pisa, Biblioteca Cateriniana MS 21.
Petrus de sancto Benedicto, *Sermones de tempore*. Città del Vaticano, Biblioteca Apostolica Vaticana MS Vat. lat. 1253.

B. Printed Sources

AA.SS. Juni 2. Romae et Parisiis, 1867.
Aegidius de Lectinis: *De essentia, motu et significatione cometarum*. In Latin Treatises on Comets Between 1238 and 1368 A.D. Edited by Lynn Thorndike. Chicago, 1950.
Bernardinus de Busti: *Rosarium sermonum*. Venezia, 1498.

S. Bernardino da Siena: *Le prediche volgari*. Publicate dal padre Ciro Cannarozzi O.F.M. Predicazione del 1425 in Siena, vol. secundo. Firenze, 1958.

Boccaccio, Giovanni: *The Decameron*. Translated by John Payne. New York: Modern Library, 1930.

Bonito, Marcello: *Terra tremante, overo continuatione de terremoti della creatione del Mondo fino al tempo presente*. Napoli, 1691.

The Chronicle of Bury St Edmunds 1212–1301. Edited with introduction, notes and translation by Antonia Gransden. London: Nelson, 1964.

Chronik des Franciskaner Lesemeisters Detmar. Herausgegeben von F.H. Grautoff. Erster Teil. Hamburg, 1829.

Concilia Germaniae. Tomus V ab anno 1400 ad 1500. Ed. J.F. Schannat & J. Hartzheim. Coloniae, 1763.

Constitutiones Concilii quarti Lateranensis una cum Commentariis glossatarum. Edidit Antonius García y García. Monumenta Iuris Canonici. Series A: Corpus Glossatorum. Vol. 2. Città del Vaticano, 1981.

Corpus benedictionum pontificalium. Ed. Dom Edmond Moeller. CCSL 162 B. Turnhout: Brepols, 1973.

Corpus Iuris Canonici. Editio Lipsiensis secunda post Aemilii Ludouici Richteri curas ad librorum manu scriptorum et editionis Romanae fidem recognouit et adnotatione critica instruxit Aemilius Friedberg. 2 volumes. Graz: Akademische Druck u. Verlagsanstalt, 1959.

Defoe, Daniel: *A Journal of the Plague Year*. London, 1957.

Diplomatarium Suecanum. Stockholm 1829ff.

Franciscus Pipinus Bononiensis: *Chronicon*. In L.A. L.A. Muratori, *Rerum Italicarum Scriptores* IX. Milano 1726.

Gregorius Magnus: *Epistolae Gregorii Magni, appendix ad sancti Gregorii epistolas III, charta quae relicta est de litania majore, in basilica Sancta Mariae*. PL 77.

Guillelmus Durandus: *Rationale divinorum officiorum*. Roma, 1477.

Honorius Augustodunensis: *Gemma animae*. PL 172.

Hugo de sancto Caro: *Postilla in librum Job*. In Ugonis de Sancto Charo Opera Omnia. Tomus I. Köln, 1621.

Innocentius III: *Commentarius in septem psalmos poenitentiales*. PL 217.

Isidorus Hispalensis: *De natura rerum*. PL 83.

Jacobus de Voragine: *Chronicon Genuense ab origine urbis usque ad annum 1297*. In L.A. Muratori, *Rerum Italicarum Scriptores* IX. Milano, 1726.

Iacobus de Voragine: *Legenda aurea*. Edizione critica a cura di Giovanni Paolo Maggioni. Tomo I. Firenze, 1998.

Iohannes Beleth: *Summa de ecclesiasticis officiis*. Edita ab Heriberto Douteil. CCCM 41A. Turnhout, 1975.

Johannes Herolt: *Sermones discipuli de tempore*. Strasbourg, 1494.

Johannes von Werden: *Dormi secure de tempore*. Augsburg, 1485.

–. *Dormi secure de sanctis*. Strasbourg, 1493.

Johannes abbas Victoriensis: *Liber certarum historiarum*. Ed. Fedorus Schneider. Tomus I. MGH. Scriptores Rerum Germanicarum 1. Hannover – Leipzig: Impensis bibliopolii Hahniani, 1909.

Johannes von Winterthur: *Chronica*. In Die Chronik Johannes von Winterthur. Herausgegeben von Friedrich Baethgen. MGH. Scriptores Rerum Germanicarum. Nova Series 3. Berlin: Weidmannsche Buchhandlung, 1924.

Journal d'un Bourgeois de Paris 1405–1449. Publié par Alexandre Tuetey. Paris, 1881.

Lecoy de la Marche, Anton: *Anecdotes historiques, légendes et apologues tirés du recueil inédit d'Étienne de Bourbon, dominicain du XIIIe siècle*. Paris, 1877.

Matthaeus Parisiensis: *Chronica Maiora*. Seven volumes. Rerum Britannicarum Medii Aevi Scriptores 57. London 1872–1884.

Meffreth: *Hortulus regine*. Sine loco, sine anno, BAV signum: Inc.Barberini.BBB.V.10.

Michael Agricola: *Rukouskiria Bibliasta*. Stockholm, 1544, Facsimile edition: Porvoo, 1987.

Missale Aboense secundum ordinem fratrum praedicatorum. Lübeck, 1488, facsimile edition: Porvoo, 1988.

Paulus Wann: *Sermones de tempore*. Hagenau, 1491.

Pelbartus de Themeswar: *Sermones Pomerii de tempore*. Hagenau, 1501.

Petrus Comestor: *Historia Scholastica*. PL 198.
Processionale ad usum insignis ac praeclarae ecclesiae Sarum. Ed. W.G. Henderson. Leeds, 1882.
Le rire du prédicateur. Ed. Albert Lecoy de la Marche. Présentation de Jacques Berlioz. Brepols, 1999.
Rituale Romanum. Pauli V pontificis maximi jussu editum aliorumque pontificum cura recognitum atque auctoritate Sanctissimi Domini Pii Papae XI. Tours, 1925.
Salimbene de Adam: *Cronica*. 2 vols. Ed. Giuseppe Scalia. CCCM 125 & 125A. Turnhout: Brepols, 1998–1999.
Sicardus Cremonensis: *Mitrale sive de officiis ecclesiasticis summa*. PL 213.
Le Speculum laicorum. Edition d'une collection d'exempla composée en Angleterre à la fin du XIIIe siècle. Par J. Th. Welter. Paris, 1914.
Thomas Aquinas: *In Aristotelis libros De caelo et mundo, De generatione et corruptione, Meteorologicorum expositio*. Cura et studio P. Fr. Raymundi M. Spiazzi O.P. Torino – Roma, 1952.
Thomas Cantimbratensis: *Liber de natura rerum*. Teil I, text. Berlin & New York: Walter de Gruyter, 1973.
Tomitanus de Feltre: *Sermoni del beato Tomitano da Feltre*. A cura di p. Carlo Varischi da Milano, 2 volumes. Milano, 1964.
The Westminster Chronicle 1381–1394. Edited and translated by L.C. Hector and Barbara F. Harvey. Oxford: Clarendon Press, 1982.
Villani, Giovanni: *Cronica*. 8 volumes. Firenze, 1823.
Vincentius Ferrer: *Sermones sancti Vincentii fratris ordinis predicatorum de tempore. Pars estivalis*. Nürnberg, 1492.
Vincentius Bellovacensis: *Speculum naturale*. Graz, 1964.

C. Literature

Abulafia, David: *Frederick II a Medieval Emperor*. London: Allen Lane, 1988.
Andersson-Schmitt, Margareta & Hedlund, Monica: *Mittelalterliche Handschriften der Universitätsbibliothek Uppsala. Katalog über die C-Sammlung*. Band 1. Handschriften C I–IV, 1–50. Acta Bibliothecae R. Universitatis Upsaliensis vol. XXVI:1. Uppsala, 1988.
d'Avray, David. L.: 'Method in the Study of Medieval Sermons",' in *Modern Questions about Medieval Sermons. Essays on Marriage, Death, History and Sanctity by Nicole Bériou and David L. d'Avray*, Biblioteca «Medioevo Latino» 11. Spoleto, 1994.
Bailey, Terence: *The Processions of Sarum and the Western Church*. Pontifical Intitute of Medieval Studies. Studies and Texts 21. Toronto, 1971.
Bassi, Michele: 'La Panaya Odighitria e la Madonna di Constantinopoli,' *Arte Cristiana* 772 (1996).
Bataillon, Louis-Jacques: 'Approaches to the Study of Medieval Sermons,' *Leeds Studies in English*, new series 11 (1977).
–. *La prédication au XIIIe siècle en France et Italie*. Aldershot: Variorum, 1993.
Batlle, Carmen: 'Destructions naturelles des villes de la Couronne d'Aragon au Bas Moyen Âge,' in *Stadtzerstörung und Wiederaufbau*. Band 1. *Zerstörung durch Erdbeben, Feuer und Wasser*. Hrsg. Martin Körner. Bern – Stuttgart – Wien, 1999.
Battenberg, Friedrich: *Das Europäische Zeitalter der Juden. Band I: Von den Anfängen bis 1650*. Darmstadt: Wissenschaftliche Buchgesellschaft, 1990.
Benedictow, Ole Jorgen: *Plague in the Late Medieval Nordic Countries. Epidemiological Studies*. Oslo, 1992.
Bériou, Nicole: ''Les lepreaux sous le regard des predicateurs d'apres les collections de sermons ad status du XIIIe siècle,' in N. Bériou et F-O. Touati, *Voluntate Dei leprosus. Les lepreaux entre conversion et exclusion aux XIIème et XIIIème siècles*. Spoleto: Centro Italiano di Studi Sull'Alto Medioevo, 1991.
Berlioz, Jacques. 'Les recits exemplaires, sources imprevues de l'histoire des catastrophes au Moyen-Age,' In *Sources travaux historiques* no. 33 (1993). Histoire des catastrophes naturelles. Paysages-enviroment.

–. *Catastrophes naturelles et calamités au Moyen Age*. Firenze: Sismel Edizioni del Galluzzo, 1998.

Biraben, Jean-Noël: *Les hommes et la peste en France et dans les pays européens et méditerranéens* (2 vols). Paris: Mouton 1975–1976.

–. "Temps de l'Apocalypse." In *Les malheurs des temps. Histoire des fléaux et des calamités en France*. Sous la direction de Jean Delumeu et Yves Lequin. Paris: Larousse, 1987.

–. 'Das Erdbeben von 1348. Ein historischer Beitrag zur Katastrophenforschung,' *Historische Zeitschrift* 233 (1981).

Bourin-Derruau, Monique: *Temps d'equilibres, temps de ruptures XIIIe siècle*. Nouvelle histoire de la France Médiévale 4. Paris: Seuil, 1990.

Breidert, Wolfgang: 'Einleitung,' in *Die Erschütterung der vollkommenen Welt. Die Wirkung des Erdbebens von Lissabon im Spiegel europäischer Zeitgenossen*. Herausgegeben von Wolfgang Breidert. Darmstadt, 1994.

Briffaud, Serge: 'Introduction,' In *Sources travaux historiques* no. 33 (1993). Histoire des catastrophes naturelles. Paysages-enviroment.

Brilioth, Yngve: *Svenska kyrkans historia. Andra bandet. Den senare medeltiden 1274–1521*. Stockholm: Svenska kyrkans diakonistyrelsen, 1941.

Cabibbo, Sara: *Il paradiso del Magnifico Regno. Agiograpfi, santi e culti nella Sicilia Spagnola*. Roma: Viella, 1996.

Cameron, Euan: *The European Reformation*. Oxford, 1992.

Cardini, Franco: *Magia, stregoneria, superstizioni nell'Occidente medievale*. Firenze, 1979.

–. *Minima medievalia*. Firenze: Arnaud, 1987.

Carpentier, Élisabeth: *Une ville devant la peste. Orvieto et la peste noire de 1348*. Bruxelles: De Boeck université, 1993 (second edition).

Casagrande, Carla. & Vecchio, Silvana: 'Cronache, morale, predicazione: Salimbene da Parma e Jacopo da Varagine,' *Studi Medievali*, ser. 3, no. 30 (1989).

Chadwick, Owen: *The Popes and the European Revolution*. Oxford, 1981.

Charansonnet, Alexis: 'L'évolution de la prédication du cardinal Eudes de Châteauroux (1190? – 1273): une approche statistique,' in *De l'homelie au sermon. Histoire de la prédication médiévale*. Édités par Jacqueline Hamesse et Xavier Hermand. Louvain-la-Neuve: Université catholique du Louvain, 1993.

–. *L'université, l'Eglise et l'Etat dans les sermons du cardinal Eudes de Châteauroux (1190?–1273)*. Unpublished Doctoral Thesis. Lyon, 2001.

Chiffoleau, Jacques: *La comptabilité de l'au-delà. Les hommes, la mort et la religion dans la région d'Avignon à la fin du Moyen Age (vers 1320 – vers 1480)*. Collection de l'Ecole Française de Rome 47. Rome, 1980.

–. 'Les processions parisiennes de 1412. Analyse d'un rituel flamboyant,' *Revue historique* 284 (1990).

Cipolla, Carlo: *Before the Industrial Revolution. European Society and Economy, 1000–1700*. London: Routledge and Kegan Paul, 1980.

–. *Miasmas and Disease. Public Health and the Environment in the Pre-Industrial Age*. New Haven: Yale University Press, 1992.

Cohn, Norman: *The Pursuit of Millenium*. London, 1957.

–. *Noah's Flood: the Genesis Story in Western Thought*. New Haven: Yale University Press, 1996

Coulet, Noël: 'Processions, espace urbain, communaute civique', *Cahiers de Fanjeaux* 17 (1982). Liturgie et musique (IXe–XIVe siècle).

–. 'Dévotions communales: Marseille entre Saint Victor, Saint Lazare et Saint Louis (XIIIe–XVe siècle)', in *La religion civique à l'époque médiévale et moderne (Chrétienté et islam)*. Sous la direction d'André Vauchez. Collection de l'École Francaise de Rome 213. Roma, 1995.

Daniel, Christopher: *Death and Burial in Medieval England 1066–1550*. London, 1999; 1st published 1997.

Delumeau, Jean: *La peur en Occident (XIVe–XVIIIe siècles). Une cité assiégée*. Paris: Fayard, 1978.

–. *Rassurer et proteger: le sentiment de sécurité dans l'Occident d'autrefois*. Paris: Fayard, 1989.

Dickson, Gary: 'The Flagellants of 1260 and the Crusades,' *Journal of Medieval History* vol. 15, no. 3. (1989).

Dohar, William J.: *The Black Death and Pastoral Leadership. The Diocese of Hereford in the Fourteenth Century*. Philadelphia: University of Philadelphia Press, 1995.
Dormeier, Heinrich: 'Il culto dei santi a Milano in balia della peste (1576–1577),' I in *Modelli di santità e modelli di comportamento*. A cura di Giulia Barone, Marina Caffiero e Francesco Scorza Barcellona. Torino, 1994.
Duffy, Eamon: *The Stripping of the Altars. Traditional Religion in England 1400–1580*. New Haven and London, 1992.
Dunbabin, Jean: *The Hound of God. Pierre de la Palud and the Fourteenth-Century Church*. Oxford: Clarendon Press, 1991.
Durkheim, Emile: *Suicide. A Study in Sociology*. London, 1975.
Eliade, Mircea: *The Myth of Eternal Return*. Princeton 1974.
Emerson, Richard Kenneth: *Antichrist in the Middle Ages. A Study of Medieval Apocalypticism, Art, and Literature*. Manchester: Manchester University Press, 1981.
Evans, Richard J.: *Death in Hamburg. Society and Politics in the Cholera Years 1830–1910*. Oxford: Clarendon Press, 1987.
–. 'Epidemics and Revolutions: cholera in the nineteenth-century Europe,' in *Epidemics and Ideas. Essays on the Historical Perception of Pestilence*. Ed. Terence Ranger & Paul Slack. Cambridge: Cambridge University Press, 1992.
Ferret, P.: *L'abbaye de sainte-Geneviève et la congregation de France*. Tome I. *L'abbaye de sainte-Geneviève*. Paris, 1883.
Ferzoco, George: 'The Schneyer Archive,' *Medieval Sermon Studies* 39 (1997).
Figliuolo, Bruno: *Il terremoto del 1456*. 2 vols. Edizioni Studi Storici Meridionali, 1998.
Finucane, Ronald C.: *Miracles and Pilgrims. Popular Beliefs in Medieval England*. New York: St Martin's Press, 1995.
Fiorentino, Silvia Grassi: '"Nella sera della Domenica…". Il terremoto del 1703 in Umbria: trauma e reintegrazione,' *Quaderni storici* 55 (1984).
Fossier, Robert: 'Le temps de la faim,' in *Les malheurs des temps. Histoire des fléaux et des calamités en France*. Sous la direction de Jean Delumeu et Yves Lequin. Paris: Larousse, 1987.
– & Neveaux, H: 'La fin d'une embellie,' in *Les malheurs des temps. Histoire des fléaux et des calamités en France*. Sous la direction de Jean Delumeu et Yves Lequin. Paris: Larousse, 1987.
Franz, Adolph: *Die Messe im deutschen Mittelalter. Beiträge zur Geschichte der Liturgie uns des religiösen Volklebens*. Freiburg im Breslau, 1902.
–. *Die kirchlichen Benediktionen im Mittelalter*, 2 vols. Freiburg im Breslau, 1909.
Funkenstein, Amos: *Theology and Scientific Imagination from the Middle Ages to the Seventeenth Century*, Princeton, 1986.
Galpern, A.N: *The Religions of the People in Sixteenth-Century Champagne*. Harvard Historical Studies 92. Cambridge, Massachusetts, 1976.
Ginzburg, Carlo: *The Night Battles. Witchcraft and Agrarian Cults in the Sixteenth and Seventeenth Centuries*. Baltimore: John Hopkins University Press, 1992.
Goodich, Michael E.: *Violence and Miracle in the Fourteenth Century: Private Grief and Public Salvation*. Chicago: University of Chicago Press, 1995.
Grauss, František: *Pest-Geißler-Judenmorde. Das 14. Jahrhundert als Krisenzeit*. Veröffentlichungen des Max-Planck-Instituts für Geschichte 86. Göttingen: Vandenhoeck & Ruprecht, 1988.
Guidoboni, Emanuela: 'Riti di calamite: terremoti a Ferrara nel 1570–1574,' *Quaderni storici* 55 (1984).
–. 'Les conséquences des tremblements de terre sur les villes en Italie,' in *Stadzerstörung und Wiederaufbau. Zerstörungen durch Erdbeben, Feuer und Wasser*. Hrsg. Martin Körner. Bern – Stuttgart – Wien: Haupt, 1999.
Grosses Universallexicon aller Wissenschaften und Künste. Vol. N-Net. Leipzig – Halle, 1970.
Gurevich, Aron: *Medieval Popular Culture. Problems of Belief and Perception*. Cambridge: Cambridge University Press, 1990.
–. *The Origins of European Individualism*. Oxford: Blackwell, 1995.
Guyotjeannin, Oliver: *Salimbene de Adam un chroniquer franciscain*. Brepols, 1995.
Hanska, Jussi: *"And the Rich Man also died; and He was buried in Hell". The Social Ethos in Mendicant Sermons*. Bibliotheca historica 28. Helsinki: Suomen Historiallinen Seura, 1997.

–. 'Cessante causa cessat et effectus. Sin and Natural Disasters in Medieval Sermons', in *Roma, magistra mundi. Itineraria culturae medievalis. Mélanges offerts au Père L.E. Boyle à l'occasion de son 75e anniversaire*. Louvain-La-Neuve, 1998.

–. 'Late Medieval Catastrophe Sermons: Vanishing Tradition or Common Custom?,' *Medieval Sermon Studies* 45 (2001).

Harper, John: *The Forms and Orders of Western Liturgy from the Tenth to the Eighteenth Century. A Historical Introduction and Guide for Students and Musicians*. Oxford: Clarendon Press, 1993.

Heath, Peter: *Church and Realm, 1272–1461*. London, 1988.

Hermann-Mascard, Nicole: *Les reliques des saints. Formation coutumière d'un droit*. Paris: Klincksieck, 1975.

Histoire des Fleaux et des calamités en France. Sous la direction de Jean Delumeau et Yves Lequin. Larousse, 1987.

Horton, Robin: 'African Thought and Western Science,' in *Rationality*. Edited by Bryan R. Wilson. Oxford: Blackwell, 1977.

Hughes, Andrew: *Medieval Manuscripts of Mass and Office. A Guide to their Organization and Terminology*. Toronto 1995.

Härdelin, Alf: 'Admonitions and Reprimands to Parochial Clergy. A "Pastoral Letter" from Vadstena,' in *Master Golyas and Sweden. The Transformation of a Clerical Satire*. Edited by Olle Ferm and Bridget Morris. Stockholm, 1997.

Iozzelli, Fortunato: *Odo da Châteauroux. Politica e religione nei sermoni inediti*. Deputazione abruzzese di storia di patria. Studi e testi, fasc. 14. Padova, 1994.

Jansen, Katherine L: 'Mary Magdalen and the Mendicants: The Preaching of Penance in the Late Middle Ages,' *Journal of Medieval History* 21 (1995).

Jansen, Philippe: 'Literature hagiographique et catastrophes aux XIIIe–XIVe siècles: Les raisons d'une réalité absente,' in *Sources travaux historiques* no. 33 (1993). Histoire des catastrophes naturelles. Paysages-enviroment.

Jarvie, I.C.: *Rationality and Relativism. In Search of a Philosophy and History of Anthropology*. London: Routledge & Kegan Paul, 1984.

Jarvie, C. & Agassi, Joseph: 'The Problem of Rationality and Magic,' in *Rationality*. Edited by Bryan R. Wilson. Oxford: Blackwell, 1977.

Jordan, William Chester: *The Great Famine: Northern Europe in the Early Fourteenth Century*. Princeton N.J.: Princeton University Press, 1996.

Jung, C.G: 'Psychoanalysis and the Cure of Souls,' in *Psychology and Religion: West and East*. The Collected Works of C.G. Jung, vol. 11. London: Routledge & Kegan Paul, 1969.

–. 'Psychotherapists or the Clergy,' in *Psychology and Religion: West and East*. The Collected Works of C.G. Jung, vol. 11. London: Routledge & Kegan Paul, 1969.

Kaeppeli, Thomas: *Scriptores ordinis praedicatorum medii aevi*. 4 volumes. Roma: Istituto Storico Domenicano, 1970–1993.

Kendrick, T.D: *The Lisbon Earhtquake*. London: Methuen, 1956.

Kershaw, Ian: 'The Great Famine and Agrarian Crisis in England 1315–1322,' *Past and Present* 59 (1973).

Kieckhefer, Richard: *European Witch Trials. Their Foundations in Popular and Learned Culture, 1300–1500*. London: Routledge & Kegan Paul, 1976.

Krötzl, Christian: *Mirakel und Alltag. Formen des Verhaltens im skandinavischen Mittelalter*. Studia Historica 46. Tampere: Finnish Historical Society, 1994.

Ladero Quesada, Miguel-Angel: 'Earthquakes in the Cities of Andalusia at the Beginning of the Modern Era,' in *Stadtzerstörung und Wiederaufbau*. Band 1. *Zerstörung durch Erdbeben, Feuer und Wasser*. Hrsg. Martin Körner. Bern – Stuttgart – Wien, 1999.

Lauwers, M: '«Religion populaire», culture folklorique, mentalités. Notes pour une anthropologie culturelle du moyen âge,' *Revue d'histoire ecclesiastique* 82/2 (1987).

Le Goff, Jacques: 'Culture cléricale et traditions folkloriques dans la civilization mérovingienne,' in J. Le Goff, *Pour un autre Moyen Age*. Paris: Gallimard, 1977.

–. *Time, Work, & Culture in the Middle Ages*. Chicago: University of Chicago Press, 1980.

–. *Medieval Civilization 400–1500*. Oxford: Blackwell, 1988.

–. *The Birth of Purgatory*. Aldershot: Scolar Press, 1990.

Lerner, Robert E.: 'The Black Death and Western European Eschatological Mentalities,' *American Historical Review* 3/1981.

Logan, Richard D: 'A Conception of the Self in the Later Middle Ages,' *Journal of Medieval History* 12 (1986).
Maier, Christoph T.: *Preaching the Crusades. Mendicant Friars and the Cross in the Thirteenth Century*. Cambridge: Cambridge University Press, 1994.
Les malheurs des temps. Histoire des fléaux et des calamités en France. Sous la direction de Jean Delumeu et Yves Lequin. Paris: Larousse, 1987.
Malinowski, Bronislaw: *Magic, Science and Religion and Other Essays*. Westport, Connecticut: Greenwood Press, 1984.
Manselli, Raoul: *Il sopranaturale e la religione popolare del medioevo*. Roma: Edizioni studium, 1986.
Martimort, A.G.: 'Processions, pélerinages, jubilés,' in A.G. Martimort, *L'Église en prière. Introduction à la liturgie*. Paris – Tournai – Rome – New York, 1961.
Martin, Herve: *Le métier de prédicateur à la fin du Moyen Age 1350–1520*. Paris: Cerf, 1988.
Matz, Jean-Michel: 'Le développement tardif d'une religion civique dans une ville épiscopale. Les processions à Angers (v. 1450–v. 1550)', in *La religion civique à l'époque médiévale et moderne (Chrétienté et islam)*. Sous la direction d'André Vauchez. Collection de l'École Francaise de Rome 213. Roma, 1995.
McGaughey B.G., Hoffman, Kenneth J. & Lewellyn, Graig H.: 'The Human Experience of Earthquakes,' in *Individual and Community Responses to Trauma and Disaster. The Structure of Human Chaos*. Edited by Robert J. Ursano, Brian G. McGaughey and Carol S. Fullerton. Cambridge: Cambridge University Press, 1995.
McHardy, Alison K.: 'Liturgy and Propaganda in the Diocese of Lincoln during the Hundred Years War,' *Studies in Church History*, 18 (1982).
Meyers Enzyklopädisches Lexikon. Band 16 Mei-Nat. Mannheim, 1976.
Moeller, Dom Edmond: *Perspectives de recherche*. In Corpus benedictionum pontificalium. CCSL 162 B. Turnhout, 1973.
Morburgo, Piero: 'La peste: dinamiche di interpretazione storiografica', in *The Regulation of Evil. Social and Cultural Attitudes to Epidemics in the Late Middle Ages*. Edited by Agostino Paravicini Bagliani and Francesco Santi. Micrologus' Library 2. Firenze, 1998.
Morris, Colin: *The Discovery of the Individual 1050–1200*. London, 1972.
Morris, R.J.: *Cholera 1832. The Social Response to an Epidemic*. London: Croom Helm, 1976.
Moulinier, Laurence e Odile Redon: '"Pareano aperte le cataratte del cielo": le ipotesi di Giovanni Villani sull'inondazione del 1333 a Firenze,' in *Miracoli. Dai segni alla storia*. A cura di Sofia Boesch Gajano e Marilena Modica. Roma, 2000.
Murray, Alexander: *Reason and Society in the Middle Ages*. Oxford: Clarendon Press, 1991.
Ostrow, Steven S.: *Art and Spirituality in Counter-Reformation Rome. The Sistine and Pauline Chapels in S. Maria Maggiore*. Cambridge, 1995.
Ovitt, George Jr.: *The Restoration of the Perfection. Labor and Technology in Medieval Culture*. New Brunswick: Rutgers University Press, 1987.
Peterson, William et alii.: *Reason and Religious Belief. An Introduction to the Philosophy of Religion*. New York – Oxford: Oxford University Press, 1991.
Platt, Colin: *King Death. The Black Death and its Aftermath in Late-Medieval England*. London: UCL 1996.
Razi, Zvi: *Life, Marriage and Death in Medieval Parish: Economy, Society and Demography in Halesowen 1270–1400*. Cambridge: Cambridge University Press 1980.
Reeves, Marjorie: *The Influence of Prophecy in the Later Middle Ages. A Study in Joachimism*. Notre Dame: University of Notre Dame Press, 1993.
The Regulation of Evil. Social and Cultural Attitudes to Epidemics in the Late Middle Ages. Edited by Agostino Paravicini Bagliani and Francesco Santi. Micrologus' Library 2. Firenze, 1998.
La religion civique à l'époque médiévale et moderne (Chrétienté et islam). Sous la direction d'André Vauchez. Collection de l'École Francaise de Rome 213. Roma, 1995.
Roest, Bert: *Reading the Book of History. Intellectual Contexts and Educational Functions of Franciscan Historiography 1226–ca. 1350*. Groningen, 1996.
Rosenberg, Charles E.: *The Cholera Years. The United States in 1832, 1849 and 1866*. Chicago: University of Chicago Press, 1962.
Rouillard, Philippe: 'Procession,' in *Catholisme hier, aujourd'hui, demain*. Vol. 53 Primauté-Propres. Paris, 1988.

Runciman, Stephen: *The Sicilian Vespers. A History of the Mediterranean World in the Later Thirteenth Century*. Cambridge, 1992.

Ruotsala, Antti: *Europeans and Mongols in the Middle of the Thirteenth Century: Encountering the Other*. Annales Academiae Scientiarum Fennicae, ser. Humaniora 314. Helsinki, 2001.

Salonen, Kirsi: *The Penitentiary as a Well of Grace in the Late Middle Ages. The Example of the Province of Uppsala 1448–1527*. Annales Academiae Scientiarum Fennicae 313. Saarijärvi, 2001.

Salvadori, Patrizia: 'La peste e la lebbra in Medioevo Latino. Un prospetto biblio-geografico', in *The Regulation of Evil. Social and Cultural Attitudes to Epidemics in the Late Middle Ages*. Edited by Agostino Paravicini Bagliani and Francesco Santi. Micrologus' Library 2. Firenze, 1998.

Schmitt, Jean-Claude: *Le saint Lévrier. Guinefort guérisseur d'enfants depuis le XIIIe siècle*. Paris: Flammarion, 1979.

–. 'Religione e guarigione nell'Occidente medievale,' in J.-C. Schmitt, *Religione, folklore e Società*. Bari: Laterza, 1988.

–. *Religione, folklore e Società*. Bari: Laterza, 1988.

–. *Medioevo «Superstizioso»*. Bari: Laterza, 1992.

Schmugge, Ludwig, Hersberger, Patrick & Wiggenhauser, Beatrice: *Die Supplikenregister der päpstlichen Pönitentiarie aus der Zeit Pius' II. (1458–1464)*. Tübingen: Max Niemeyer Verlag, 1996.

Schneyer, Johan Baptist: *Repertorium der lateinischen Sermones des Mittelalters für die Zeit von 1150–1350*, 11 vols. Münster: Aschendorffsche Verlagsbuchhandlung, 1969–1990.

Segal, Pierre-André: *L'homme et le miracle dans la France médiévale (XIe–XIIe siècle)*. Paris: Cerf, 1985.

Siberry, Elisabeth: *Criticism of Crusading 1095–1274*. Oxford: Clarendon Press, 1985.

Slack, Paul: *The Impact of Plague in Tudor and Stuart England*. Oxford: Clarendon Press, 1990.

Stadtzerstörung und Wiederaufbau. Band 1. Zerstörung durch Erdbeben, Feuer und Wasser. Hrsg. Martin Körner. Bern – Stuttgart – Wien, 1999.

Sutherland, Steward: 'Evil and Theology,' in *Companion Encyclopedia of Theology*. Edited by Peter Byrne and Leslie Houlden. London: Routledge & Kegan Paul, 1995.

Taylor, Gabriele: *Pride, Shame, and Guilt. Emotions of Self-Assesment*. Oxford: Clarendon Press, 1985.

Taylor, Larissa: *Soldiers of Christ. Preaching in Late Medieval and Reformation France*. Oxford: Oxford University Press, 1992.

Tentler, Thomas N.: 'The Summa for Confessors as an Instrument of Social Control,' in *The Pursuit of Holiness in Late Medieval and Renaissance Religion*. Edited by Charles Trinkaus and Heiko A. Oberman. Leiden: Brill, 1974.

Thomas, Keith: *Religion and Decline of Magic*. New York: Scribners, 1971.

Toussaert, Jacques: *Le sentiment religieux, la vie et la pratique religieuse des laïcs en Flandre Maritime et au "West-Hoeck" de langue flamande aux XIVe, XVe et debut du XVIe siècle*. Paris, 1963.

Tubach, Frederic C.: *Index exemplorum. A Handbook of Medieval Religious Tales*. FF Communications no. 204. Helsinki: Academia Scientiarum Fennica, 1981.

Van Engen, John: 'The Christian Middle Ages as an Historiographical Problem,' *AHR* 3/1996.

Vauchez, André: *La sainteté en Occident aux derniers siècles du Moyen Age: d'apres les procès de canonisation et les documents hagiographiques*. Rome: Ecole Française de Rome, 1988.

–. *The Laity in the Middle Ages. Religious Beliefs and Devotional Practices*. Notre Dame, 1993.

–. 'Lay Belief around 1200: Religious Mentalities of the Feodal World,' in André Vauchez, *The Laity in the Middle Ages. Religious Beliefs and Devotional Practices*. Edited and introduced by Daniel E. Bornstein. Notre Dame, Indiana, 1993.

–. 'Liturgy and Folk Culture in the Golden Legend,' in André Vauchez, *The Laity in the Middle Ages. Religious Beliefs and Devotional Practices*. Notre Dame, 1993.

–. 'Medieval Penitents,' in André Vauchez, *The Laity in the Middle Ages. Religious Beliefs and Devotional Practices*. Edited and Introduced by Daniel E. Bornstein. Notre Dame, Indiana, 1993.

Vaughan, Richard: *Chronicles of Matthew Paris. Monastic Life in the Thirteenth Century.* Gloucester, 1986.

Webb, Diana: *Patrons and Defenders. The Saints in Italian City-States.* London & New York, 1996.

Weinstein, Donald & Bell, Rudolph M.: *Saints & Society. Christendom, 1000–1700.* Chicago: University of Chicago Press, 1982.

Verger, Jacques: 'Nouveaux fléaux, nouveaux recours,' in *Les malheurs des temps. Histoire des fléaux et des calamités en France.* Sous la direction de Jean Delumeu et Yves Lequin. Paris: Larousse, 1987.

Vermij, Rienk: 'Natuurgeweld geduid,' *Feit & fictie* 3 (1996).

Veyssière, Gérard: 'Miracles et merveilles en Provence,' in *Miracles, prodiges et merveilles au Moyen Age.* XXVe congrès de la SHMES. Paris: SHMES, 1995.

Viard, Jules: 'La messe pour la peste,' *Bibliothèque de l'École des Chartes* 61 (1890).

Wilson, Stephen: 'Introduction,' in *Saints and their Cults. Studies in Religious Sociology, Folklore and History.* Edited by Stephen Wilson. Cambridge: Cambridge University Press, 1983.

Vincent, Bernard: 'Les tremblements de terre dans la province d'Almeria,' *AÉSC* 1974/3.

Vogel, Cyrille: *Medieval Liturgy. An Introduction to the Sources.* Translated and revised by William Storey and Niels Rasmussen. Washington, 1986.

Index nominum et locorum

Adam 33
Aegidius de Lessines OP 105, 107
Alcuin 82
Aldobrandino da Toscanella OP 74, 121
Almeria 90
Andalusia 91n, 115
Andrea della Robbia 43
Angerinna de Rectoris (laywoman from the diocese of Milan) 98–99
Angers 60
Antichrist 112–113, 174
Antioch 96
Aragon
Arezzo 43
Aristotle 107, 108n, 109–110, 131, 155, 165, 173–174
Arnold Royard OFM 185
Assisi 15
Augustine of Hippo 32–33, 118, 133, 135, 142
Austria 123
Avignon 18, 114

Bamberg 84
  diocese 159
Barcelona 92, 125
Bartholomeus Anglicus OFM 173
Bernardino (cardinal of Porto) 104
Bernardino da Busti OFM 61–62, 67, 110–112, 125–126, 131, 138–142, 187
Bernardino da Siena OFM 26, 40, 93–94, 126
Bernardino Tomitano da Feltre OFM 40, 76–77, 110, 136–137, 187
Bertrand de Tour OFM 69–71, 75, 138–140
Birger Gregersson (archbishop of Uppsala) 186
Birmingham 20
Bologna 40, 89, 104, 106, 186
Boniface VIII (pope 1295–1303) 89
Brescia (diocese) 97–98
British Isles 17 *see also* England, Scotland
Broc 156
Burchard of Worms 37
Bury St Edmunds (Benedictine monastery) 21
Bury St Edmunds (town) 88

Cardano, Girolamo 165
Carinthia 115
Carlo Borromeo (archbishop of Milan) 36n, 96, 153, 159
Cecil, William 162
Cervera 125
Chalautre–la–Grande 153–154
Champagne 153–154
Charlemagne 82
Charles of Anjou 104
Clement VI (pope 1342–1352) 20, 83
Clement VII (pope 1523–1534) 98
Clement XI (pope 1700–1721) 144–145, 158
Courlon–sur–Yonne 154, 156
Cromwell, Thomas 162–163

Darwin, Charles 167
David (king of Israel) 139
Defoe, Daniel 146
Descartes 166
Detmar OFM 90
Durance 18
Durkheim, Emil 145–146

Eastern Europe 38, 113
Eden 32
Edington (bishop of Winchester) 55
Elbe 162
England 16, 18, 39, 51–52, 54–55, 64–65, 84, 104, 107, 113, 155, 160–162, 165–168
Étienne de Bourbon OP 31, 40, 103–104, 119–121
Eudes de Cambrai (archbishop) 82
Eudes de Châteauroux (cardinal) 51, 67, 80–81, 92, 109, 114, 117–118, 120n, 128–130, 137, 175, 180–182, 189–201
Eugenius IV (pope 1431–1447) 187

Federico Pisano Visconti (archbishop of Pisa) 44, 48–49, 62–63, 71, 80, 121
Ferrara 102, 106, 155
Finland 152, 163, 167
Flanders 18
Florence 15, 55, 89–90, 100, 105–106, 119, 124, 128, 174, 187
France 17, 19, 28, 30–31, 49, 56–57, 64–65, 67, 87, 114, 179, 181, 184
Francesco Pipino da Bologna OP, 89, 96, 120
Frederic II (emperor) 103
Freud, Sigmund 147

Gabriel Barletta OP 187
Genoa 89
Georg Bernhard Petri te Zaandam 165
Germany 17, 22, 36–37, 39–40, 84, 87
Ghent 50
Giovanni Boccaccio 55
Giovanni Bono (blessed) 96
Giovanni Regina da Napoli OP 72–75, 81, 185
Giovanni da Parma 92
Giovanni Villani 89, 105–107, 119, 124, 127–128, 173–174
Givry–en–Bourgogne (parish) 19
Granier (mountain) 108, 120–121
Gratian 131
Gregory the Great (pope 590–604) 34–37, 49–51, 53, 57, 61, 70–71, 153
Gregory VII (pope 1073–1085) 120n
Gregory IX (pope 1227–1241) 103
Gregory of Tours 118–119
Grindal, Edmund (bishop of London) 162
Guibert de Tournai OFM 135
Guido Pisanus 88
Guillaume Durand 35n, 55–58
Guillelmus de Sequavilla 72, 186
Guy de Chauliac (doctor of Pope Clement VI) 20
Guy d'Evreaux OP 182

Halesowen (manor in Worcestershire) 17, 20
Hamburg 168
Harlburn 104
Henry V (holy Roman emperor) 88n
Hermannus 96–97

Herod 138
Holland 21, 104, 165 *see also* Netherlands
Honorius Augustodunensis 36
Hubert Meurier (canon of Reims) 156
Hugues de Saint–Cher OP 139
Hungary 84
Huxley, Thomas 167

Innocent III (pope 1198–1216) 132
Ippolito de Roberti 155
Irenaeus 133
Isidore of Seville 107, 173
Italy 29–30, 33, 43–44, 51, 67, 88, 96, 98, 102, 104, 106, 112–113, 115, 126, 144, 154, 160, 180, 185

Jacopo da Varazze OP 85, 88
Jacopo da Venezia (blessed) 96
Jacopo Lodovico da Gambara (layman from the diocese of Brescia) 97–99
Jacques Benevais (priest in Savoy) 121
Jacques de Lausanne OP 72, 121, 123, 136, 184
Jacques de Touraine OFM 66
Jacques de Vitry 120
Jean Rigaud OFM 70, 76
Jesus Christ 42, 49, 56–57, 59n, 72, 75, 79, 92n, 97, 112, 117, 129, 137, 157, 170
Joachim of Fiore 112–114, 174
Job 138–140, 143, 175
Johannes Beleth 35n, 71n
Johannes Herolt OFM 70–71, 76
Johannes von Freiburg OP 41n, 143
Johannes von Werden OP 39, 40n, 57, 62–63, 72, 125
Johannes Winterthur OFM 115
Johann von Viktring (cistercian abbot) 123
John Chrysostom 34
John Wycliff 151
Jordan 51
Jung, C.G. 147–149

Kent 143
Konrad Holtnicker OFM 68–70

Latino Malabranca (cardinal) 88
Laurentius Olavi de Vaxald 183
Leibniz, Gottfried Wilhelm 133
Leipzig 10
Leo III (pope 795–816) 36
Leonardo da Utino OP 186–187
Liberius (pope 352–366) 56
Lincoln (diocese) 65, 104
Linköping (diocese in Sweden) 54
Lisbon 67, 91, 158
Lombardy 85
London 52, 88, 107, 146, 161
Lucantonio Choras 158
Lucifer 127
Lucio Maggio 155–156
Lübeck 84, 90
Luther, Martin 89, 163–164

Magnus Eriksson (king of Sweden) 54, 59–60
Mamertus (bishop of Vienne) 34–36, 49, 70–71, 153, 170
Marcello Bonito 29n, 107, 157–158
Marches of Ancona 88, 96
Marseille 61
Marshal, William 162–163
Mary Magdalen 59
Mary, mother of Jesus 42–43, 52, 61–62, 66, 81, 92n, 96–97, 99, 125, 157, 159, 170, 181
   iconographic presentations of 51, 53, 154
Mary, sister of Moses 138
Matteo Villani 105
Matthew Paris OSB 27, 51–52, 60, 104, 107–108, 113, 121, 155
Maurianne 108
Meffreth OFM 71
Melancthon, Philip 164
Messina 159
Michael Agricola 163
Milan 36n, 42, 96, 98, 125–126, 153, 159
Montpellier 92

Naples 29n, 154, 157–159, 185
Nero (Roman emperor) 44
Netherlands 87 *see also* Holland
Nicolas de Gorran OP 72–74, 78–79, 130, 134, 183–184
Nicolaus V (pope 1447–1455) 84
Nicolaus de Aquaevilla OFM 75–76
Nicolaus de Lyra OFM 111
Nogent–sur–Seine 153
Northern Sea 104
Norway 20, 152
Notre–Dame de Paris (church) 50–51, 60, 66, 80

Orderic Vitalis 120n
Orvieto 12, 23, 28

Padua 40, 110
Paris 50–51, 60, 62–63, 66, 78, 105, 172, 180–185
Parker (archbishop of Canterbury) 162
Parma 106
Paschal II (pope 1099–1118) 88n
Passau 157
Paulus Diaconus 85, 118–119
Paul Wann OFM 142
Pavia 77, 85, 188
Pelagius II (pope 579–590) 35, 61
Pelbartus of Themeswar OFM 74–76
Perugia 57, 61
Peter III (king of Aragon) 104
Petit–Pont (bridge in Paris) 51
Petrus Comestor 132
Petrus Lombardus 125
Pierre de la Palud OP 134
Pierre de Saint Benoît OFM 76n
Pisa 44–45, 71, 103
Pius II (pope 1458–1464) 97n, 99
Pius V (pope 1566–1572) 82
Pius XI (pope 1922–1939) 150n
Placido Samperi SJ 159
Po 150

Poland 113
Provence 94
Provins 153

Raniero Fasani (*frate della penanza*) 61
Reims 154, 156
Rhône 18
Rieti 89
Roberto da Reggio (bishop of Brescia) 99
Rossetti (bishop of Ferrara) 155
Rome 35–36, 50–51, 53, 57, 61, 70–71, 85, 114, 153, 158–159, 161, 170
Rouen 186

Saint Agatha 43
Saint Alban
Saint Albans (Benedictine abbey) 52, 60
Saint Ansanus 51
Saint Ayoul 154
Saint Barbara 84
Saint Blaise 84
Saint Bridget 186
Saint Christopher 84
Saint Denis 84
Saint Étienne (church in Paris) 60, 78
Saint Geneviève 50–51, 60, 80, 172, 181
Saint George 84, 155
  abbey 50–51, 60
Saint Giles 84
Saint John the evangelist 72
Saint Katherine 84
Saint Louis (king of France) 181
Saint Luke the evangelist 51, 72
Saint Margaret 84
Saint Martha (sister of Lazarus) 84
Saint Mary (parish church in Saint Albans) 52
Saint Maurelio 155
Saint–Médard (abbey) 50, 60
Saint Nizier–de–Lyon (parish) 19
Saint Oswin 52
Saint Paul the Apostle 138–139
Saint Peter (church in Antioch) 96–97
Saint Peter the Apostle 35, 44–45, 63
Saint Roch 83, 86–87, 153, 156
Saint Sebastian 83, 85–87
  church in Milan 153
  iconographic presentations of 85
Saint Thomas of Cantilupe 95
Salerno 185
Salimbene de Adam OFM 25, 27, 65, 88, 99, 103–104
Salisbury 58n, 59, 80
Salomon 122
San Carlo ai Cattinari (church in Rome) 159
San Francesco (basilica in Assisi) 15
San Piero a Grado (parish church in Pisa) 44, 49
santa Maria in Gradi (church in Arezzo)
Santa Maria Maggiore (church in Rome) 51, 53
Sarlat 185
Savoy 40, 107–108, 120–121
Scandinavia 17, 38, 84, 94, 160, 163

215

Scotland 17, 20, 166
Seine 50–51
Sicardus Cremonensis 35n, 55–58, 71n
Sicily 43, 102, 107, 155, 159
  kingdom of 104
Siena 40, 51, 93–94
Sigtuna 183
Soissons 50, 60
Spain 90–91, 102
Strasbourg 147
Sweden 52–54, 60, 67, 79–80, 84, 131, 152, 180, 183, 186
Switzerland 180

Thames 107
Tiber 35
Thomas Aquinas OP 41, 106–107, 110–112, 155, 174
Thomas de Cantimpre OP 108–109, 173
Tobias 138
Tortosa 125
Toulouse 75, 86, 94, 180, 185
Tours 154
Troyes 153
Turku 84, 163, 167
Tuscany 96
Tusculum (Frascati) 180
Tyre 104, 119–120

Udalric (bishop of Passau) 157
Umbria 96, 144, 158
United States 166
Uppsala 183
Utino 186

Vadstena (Bridgettine monastery) 61, 79, 186
Vallambrosa abbey 127–128
Venantius Fortunatus 139–140
Venice 33, 104
Vera 91
Verona 88
Vesuvius 154, 159
Vienne 34–35, 70–71
Villach 91
Vincent de Beauvais OP 107, 112, 127, 173
Vincent Ferrer OP 40, 92–93, 100, 109–110, 127–128
Viterbo 92, 109, 114, 118, 182, 194
Westminster Abbey (Benedictine monastery) 26
Winchester 104
Windsor 161
Wittenberg 162
Worchestershire 20
Würzburg 159 (diocese)

Yonne 154

Index rerum

acts of canonization processes 45, 94–96
agriculture 15–16, 18, 114, 125 *see also* crop failure
almsgiving 50, 54, 80, 91, 124, 171
amulets 39–40, 45, 100, 171
  Agnus Dei symbol 40
anthropology 32, 116
apocalypticism 112–116, 158, 174
astrology 105–106, 110, 112, 125, 173–174
atheism 133, 152

Black Death 9–10, 12–13, 15, 17–23, 27–29, 33, 54–55, 60, 83–85, 87, 90, 100, 103, 105, 110, 112, 114–116, 169–170, 174
blasphemy 125, 127
cattle, mortality of 26, 82, 123
charity: *see* almsgiving
cholera 22, 166–168, 178
Christian middle ages, problem of 37–38, 41
chronicles 18, 21, 25–28, 50–51, 65–67, 87–90, 92, 96–97, 99–100, 104–105, 114, 118, 120, 123–124, 155, 173
church bells, use of against the demons 40, 89–90
churches, seeking protection in 91, 173
collective memory 21
comets 101, 105
confession: *see* penance
conjunctions of planets 101, 105–106, 111, 173
control over nature 9, 33, 42, 46, 109, 170
Council of Trent 153
Counter Reformation 153, 157
crop failure 10, 16–18, 22, 114

demons 12, 39–41, 56, 89, 93–94, 100, 126–128, 174, 178
devil 12, 56–57
Divine wrath 28, 42, 52, 54, 61, 78, 91, 100, 104, 108–109, 116–129, 132, 134, 141, 147, 155, 159, 162, 165–166
doctors 20, 132, 134, 147–148, 168
drought 10–11, 16, 18, 23, 26, 37, 48, 50, 59, 71, 73, 111, 121, 123, 153, 163, 169, 171, 175

earthquake 9–12, 15–16, 26, 29–30, 35, 43, 48, 64, 67, 71, 81, 88–92, 96–99, 102–105, 107–109, 113–115, 117–118, 120, 125, 128–130, 140, 144–146, 154–159, 165, 169, 171–172, 174, 181–182, 192–201
eclipse of sun 106
elements (earth, water, air, fire) 105, 130
Enlightenment philosophy 41, 151
epidemic disease 10, 16–18, 23, 33, 40, 42, 44, 50, 71–72, 85, 87, 94, 103–104, 111–113, 115, 121–124, 129, 131, 137, 161–163, 169, 176 *see also* Black Death, cholera, plague
excommunication 104, 156
exemplum 31, 37, 88, 114, 120, 127–128, 143

Fall of man 10, 32, 133
famine 10, 18, 26, 28, 44, 48, 51–52, 56, 72, 103, 112–115, 118, 121, 123–124, 129, 134, 154, 169
  in England and Northern Europe between 1315–1317; 16–17, 22, 29
  distribution of food during 17, 52
fasting 35, 50, 52, 54, 56, 99, 162, 165–167, 171, 177

fear and panic 88–90, 149, 155, 157, 166
fire 10, 30, 51, 143
flagellants 10, 57, 61, 63, 78, 113, 117, 144, 174
flood 9–12, 15–16, 18, 23, 26, 30, 35, 44, 48, 50–51, 58, 60, 63, 66–67, 71, 73, 79–80, 89, 96–97, 100, 104–106, 108–109, 118–119, 121–122, 124, 127, 129–131, 134–135, 162–163, 169, 171, 173–174, 181–182
  Noah's flood 47, 109, 118–119, 130–131, 177, 189
fourteen holy helpers 83–85
IV Lateran Council 69, 132, 148, 186

God 12, 32, 35–36, 39, 42, 46–49, 53–55, 62–63, 68–71, 73, 75, 80–81, 83, 89, 91, 92n, 95, 97, 99, 102, 104–106, 109–112, 116, 119, 121–122, 125–131, 133, 135–139, 143–144, 146, 153–155, 158, 166–168, 170–172, 177–178
  omnipotence of 106, 110, 112, 133, 155–156, 164–165, 174–175
Greek mythology 116
guilt 143–145, 149, 158, 176

Heretics 41, 45, 102, 111, 151, 168, 176
holy water 39–40
host 156–157, 159, 171

individualism 24, 100
indulgences 60, 83, 144–145, 158

Jesus, name of (IHS) as a protective sign 40, 93
Jews 102–103, 114, 176, 178
Joachimism 112–113

laws of nature 105, 110, 112, 124, 130, 165, 167, 174, 177
lightning 51, 88–89, 105, 109, 118, 130
litanies 34–36, 39, 49, 55–58, 70–71, 77, 80, 92–93, 127, 161–163, 170–171, 173, 177 *see also* processions
locusts 42, 61
Lollards 151

magic 12–13, 33–34, 37, 39, 45–46, 102, 116, 154, 156, 161, 170
  Christian prayers and items used as 39–41, 93, 151, 156, 159–160, 164, 171
malnutrition 16
mendicant orders 61, 65, 73, 106, 143–144, 153, 155, 179
miracles 28, 41, 49–51, 94–97, 99, 106, 159–160, 166, 173
Missale romanum 82–83
Mongols 113–114
  seen as the armies of Gog and Magog 113
Muslims 102, 120n

natural disasters:
  and political propaganda 103–104
  definitions 10–12
  historiography of 29–31
natural philosophy 101, 108, 112, 125, 152–153, 155–156, 165, 173
nouvelle histoire 30, 37–38, 169

patience 134–135, 138–140, 143
penance 26, 35–36, 48, 50, 52, 54, 56–61, 64–65, 73, 75, 78, 80, 83, 101, 113, 117, 122, 124–125, 129, 134–135, 137, 142, 144–149, 154–156, 158–162, 166, 170–172, 175–177
  contrition 26, 58–59, 61, 65, 69–70, 145, 157, 172
  confession 54, 59, 68–70, 74, 91, 95, 144–149, 172, 177
  satisfaction 54, 59, 69–70, 91, 117, 145, 172
penitentials 33, 37

Penitenzieria Apostolica 97–99, 173
pilgrimage 94–95, 153, 160
plague 9–10, 16–17, 22, 33–36, 40, 42–44, 46, 50–52, 55–58, 61, 64–65, 70–71, 77, 79, 83–87, 89, 96, 98–99, 100, 102–103, 110–111, 114, 116, 125–126, 141, 153–154, 158, 161, 163, 165–166, 186 *see also* Black Death
prayers 35, 39, 44–46, 48, 54, 56, 63–64, 68–75, 79–81, 91–94, 96, 100, 109, 122, 124, 127, 129, 139, 149, 151, 160–161, 166–167, 173, 177
  three obstacles of 75–76
  votive 28, 50, 55, 58, 65, 77, 82, 85, 87, 153–154, 157, 162–163
processions 25–26, 34–37, 41, 44–46, 48–64, 66, 70, 77–81, 83, 87, 91–92, 100, 122–123, 125, 127, 149–150, 153–156, 159–162, 170–172, 177, 181, 185, 189
  as a means of strengthening the community's identity 58
  lay participation 49, 56, 62–63, 125, 154–155, 158
  marching order 55
  role of bishops in organising 60
  station churches 44, 49, 58, 80, 171–172
pseudo–Joachite writings 112–113
purgatory 175

rain 11, 16, 18, 21, 25–26, 34, 50, 52, 59–60, 71, 73–75, 77, 79, 82, 96, 105, 111, 119, 121–122, 134, 153, 169, 180–181, 184–185
Reformation 151–152, 160–164
relics 25, 41, 44, 50–51, 56, 60, 80, 91, 100, 125, 150–151, 153–155, 164, 172, 181
religious revivals 41, 57, 77–78, 144, 165–166 *see also* flagellants
Renaissance 151, 155, 177
reportationes 26, 93
robigalia feast 35, 36n, 170
Rogation days 35–37, 41, 45, 48–50, 56–58, 62–63, 68, 70–78, 80, 82, 109, 121, 125, 127, 138, 161, 163, 170–172

Sacra Congregazione dei Riti 97
saints 13, 25, 28, 35, 42–45, 48, 51–52, 57–58, 59n, 71, 77, 80–81, 83, 85, 91, 92n, 94, 96–97, 99–100, 125, 153, 157, 159–161, 163–164, 170–171, 173, 177, 181
scapegoats 101–104, 176
science 9, 12, 32–33, 46–47, 101, 105–112, 151–155, 157–159, 161, 164, 167, 173, 176–178
sermons 13, 25–28, 31, 48–51, 53, 60–81, 92–93, 109–110, 114, 117, 121–123, 125–130, 132, 134–144, 146–147, 149, 154, 158, 165, 171–172, 175–176, 179–201
  reception 66, 77, 93–94
  survival of 66–67
seven penitential psalms 25, 58, 123, 132, 171
shipwreck 95, 124
sin 47, 51–52, 59, 61, 69–70, 72–76, 78, 80–81, 83, 87, 99, 101–102, 109, 116–118, 120–126, 128–138, 140–146, 155, 158–160, 162, 165, 168, 175
  against the Ten Commandments 69, 148
  Original 32
  Seven Capital 69, 118–119, 148
Sodom and Gomorrah 118–119
sodomy 120, 126
storm 18, 21, 26, 35–37, 39–40, 42, 44, 71, 82, 87–88, 93, 95–97, 115, 118, 125, 127–128, 130, 136, 156–157, 159, 163, 169
superstition 41, 83, 93, 100, 102, 111, 156–157, 161–163, 171, 177–178

technology 12, 32–33, 90, 151
theodicy, problem of 133–134, 141, 175
tribulationes 10, 47, 72, 77, 82, 110, 121, 133–143, 175, 185, 187
Turks 114, 163

Vatican archives 173
vetulae 103

votive gifts 94–95
votive masses 28, 36–37, 39, 48–49, 53–54, 77, 79, 81–85, 91, 160, 162, 164, 171–172
  Missa recordare contra pestem 83–84
votum 98–99, 173
volcanic eruption 11, 97, 154, 159, 169
war 10, 12, 16, 18, 44, 56, 65, 71–72, 81, 105, 113–114, 118, 121–122, 124, 126
'Wettercreuze' 39–40
winter, extremely cold 18
witches 102, 176

www.ingramcontent.com/pod-product-compliance
Lightning Source LLC
Chambersburg PA
CBHW080804300426
44114CB00020B/2829